# The New Wealth of Nations

# By the Same Author

The American Conservative Revolution, 1985.

*La Solution libérale,* 1984.

*L'Etat minimum,* 1985.

Les vrais penseurs de notre temps, 1989
(an English translation was published in India as
*Freedom on Bail,* 1990).

# The New Wealth of Nations

## Guy Sorman

Hoover Institution Press

Stanford University                    Stanford, California

The Hoover Institution on War, Revolution and Peace, founded at Stanford University in 1919 by President Herbert Hoover, is an interdisciplinary research center for advanced study on domestic and international affairs in the twentieth century. The views expressed in its publications are entirely those of the authors and do not necessarily reflect the views of the staff, officers, or Board of Overseers of the Hoover Institution.

Hoover Press Publication 391

First printing, 1990
96  95  94  93  92  91  90    9  8  7  6  5  4  3  2  1
Simultaneous first paperback printing, 1990
96  95  94  93  92  91  90    9  8  7  6  5  4  3  2  1

Manufactured in the United States of America
Printed on acid-free paper

Library of Congress Cataloging-in-Publication Data
Sorman, Guy.
    [Nouvelle richesse des nations.  English]
    The new wealth of nations / Guy Sorman.
        p.      cm. — (Hoover Press publication ; 391)
    Translation of: La nouvelle richesse des nations.
    Includes bibliographical references.
    ISBN 0–8179–8911–0 (alk. paper)
    ISBN 0–8179–8912–9 (pbk.: alk. paper)
    1. Developing countries—Economic conditions.   2. Developing
countries—Politics and government.   I. Title.
HC59.7.S58913   1990                              89–29285
330.9172′4—dc20                                   CIP

*The major concern of a government ought to be to teach the people to gradually do without it.*

Alexis de Tocqueville
*Carnets de voyage*, 1831

# Contents

# Acknowledgments

*The New Wealth of Nations,* a study carried out in eighteen countries between 1984 and 1987, would not have happened had it not been for the cooperation of those who were good enough to receive me and answer my questions. This work, however, is not a mere transcription of my meetings, but a personal interpretation of that information. Several of my interlocutors might prefer not to identify with the pen portraits, which they will undoubtedly deem unfaithful; my sole desire was to contribute to the development of their nations. I therefore extend thanks to the following:

## From Argentina

Alessandro Achaval, Institute for the Development of Executives in Argentina (IDEA); Ingrid Adam, University of Belgrano; Tomas de Anchorena, ambassador of Argentina; Luis Balcarce, University of Belgrano; Luis Berisso Esteban, farmer; Dario Bignoli, University of Belgrano; Natalio Botana, sociologist; Adolfo Brodersohn, secretary of state for economics; Domingo Cavallo, Institute of Economic Studies of Argentina; Enrique Cerda Omiste, Foundation Carlos Pelligrini; Horacio Domingorena, president of Aerolinas Argentinas; Hugo Alberto Filippini, La Serenissima; Martin Giesenov, Cargill; Jose Javier Goni, Commercial Stock Exchange of Buenos Aires; J. L. Federico Korraquin, Ipako (Petrochemical Industries of Argentina); Margot de Kumec, journalist; M. Italo Luder, Justicalist party; Jose Luis de Imas, sociologist; Albert Lynch Benegas, Jr., director of the Eseade School; Bartolome Mitre, director of La Nacion; Juan Terencio Moche, Compagnie de produits animaux; Juan Pedro Munro, IDEA; Vincente Olguin Baca, Commercial Stock Exchange of Buenos Aires; Carlos Ortiz de Rozas, ambassador of the Republic of Argentina in France; Juan Miguel Parodi, chairman of Hewlett-Packard Argentina; Avelino Porto, rector of the university of Belgrano; Jacques Ramondu, vice-president of Renault Argentina; Etchebarne Schwab, economist; Juan Jose Tacoone, former secretary general of the Sindicato de Luz y Fuerza; Jean Pierre Thibaud, industrialist

## From Bolivia

Victor Paz Estenssoro, president of the Republic of Bolivia; Gaston Araoz, ambassador of Bolivia in France; Guilherimo Bedregal, minister of foreign affairs; M. Costa de Rels, director of protocol, Ministry of External Affairs; Phillipe Desjeux, director of the Bolivian Institute of Altitudinal Biology; Jacobo Liberman, adviser to the president of the republic; Pierre Mutter, ambassador of France in Bolivia; Agustin Weise Saavedra, former minister of foreign affairs; Jaime Villalos, minister of mines

## From Brazil

Jose Sarney, president of the republic; Guilherme Afif Dominguo, president of the Commercial Association of São Paulo; Jorge Amado, writer; Roberto Appy, *Jornal da Tarde;* Emanuel Araujo, sculptor; Salvador Arena, chairman and managing director, president of Industria Termo Mecanica; Lise Aron, interpreter; Marco Brandao, minister of economic affairs; Dom Helder Camara, bishop of Recife; Roberto Campos, senator of Mato Grosso; Roberto Castro Neves, IBM Brazil; Gilberto Freyre, sociologist; Celso Furtado, minister of culture; Dilson Furnaro, minister of finance; Antonio de Regodil, president of S.I.D. Informatica; Pr. Jose Goldemberg, rector of the University of São Paulo; Alexander Guasti, Instituto Liberal; Gervasio Tadashi Inoue, Agricultural Cooperative of Cotia; Francisco Ivern, director of the Centre Jean XXIII of Social Studies and Action; Helio Jaguaribe, Institute of Political Studies of Rio; Dr. Pedro Kassab, Brazilian Medical Center; Roberto Kouder Bornhausen, president of Unibanco; Dom Lucianl, bishop of Belém; Henry Maksoud, director of the magazine *Visao;* Jao Carlo Merielles, president of the Society of Breeders; Rui Mesquita, president of the *Jornal da Tarde;* Jean-Marie Monteil, chairman of the Franco-Brazilian Chambers of Commerce; Delfim Neto, senator; M. Odebrecht, entrepreneur; Luis Paulo

Rosemburg, economic adviser to President Sarney; Napoleon Saboia, *Jornal da Tarde;* Carlos Sant'anna, director general of Petrobas; Joaquim dos Santos Andrade, president of the Metallurgical Workers' Union; Luis Ignacio da Silva, also known as Lula, Workers' Party; General Ivan de Souza, president's office; Donald Stewart, Instituto Liberal; Flavio Telles de Menez, president of the Rural Society; Amaury Temporal, president of the Conference of Chambers of Commerce; Dom Timoteo, Benedictine priest from Salvador de Bahia

## From Chile

Hernan Buchi, minister for economic affairs; Sergio de la Cuadra, director of the Economic Institute; Oscar Godoy Ardcaya, director of the Institute of Political Science; Norberto Gonzalez, secretary general for the Economic Commission for Latin America; Victor Manuel Odeja, director of the newspaper *Gestion;* Jose Pinera, former labor minister; Lucia Santa Cruz, *El mercurio*

## From China

Michel Combal, ambassador of France to China; Chen Deyan, Institute of Economic Growth; Dong Furen, director of the Economic Institute of Beijing; Fenz Zhongamao, Iron and Steel Works of Beijing; Hu Yaobang, first secretary of the Chinese Communist Party; Jiang Yiwei, Institute of Industrial Economics, Beijing; Li Poxi, Centre of Research for Social Development; Liu Guoguang, vice-president of the Academy of Social Sciences; Liu Jinhua, Academy of Social Sciences of China; Ma Hong, Council of State Affairs; Ma Jiaju, Economic Institute of Beijing; Wang Hua, China Zhenxing Economy and Trading Co.; Wang Zhiguo, Academy of Social Sciences of Sichuan; Wu Lingmai, Academy of Social Sciences of China; Xu Bo, Institute of International Studies; Yu Zhuyao, Institute of Economics; Yu Gaungyuan, Academy of Social Sciences of China; Zhang Kaiming, Institute of Sociology and Population Studies in Shanghai; Zhang Shuaguang, Economic Institute; Zhao Renvei, Academy of Social Sciences of China; Zheng Suxiang, chief of Tuanjie village; Zhou Xialong, Planning Commission of Shanghai

# From Cuba

G. Regino Boti, Corporacion Cimex; Leyla Carillo, cultural counselor, embassy of Cuba in France; Dominique D'ollone, cultural counselor, embassy of France in Cuba; Hermes Errera, vice-minister of culture; Ricardo Pampin Garcia, *Editorial de ciencias sociales;* Miguel Llanera, Institute of the Book; Jean-Louis Marfaing, French ambassador to Havana; Victoria Penelaver, ministry of culture; Julio Pejaz Perez, vice-minister of health; Antonio Rodriguez, vice-minister of education

# From Korea

Ahn Seung Chul, Korean Institute for Development; Chang Joon Shik, minister of labor; Choo Hakchung, Korean Institute of Development; Choo Soon Ho, minister of education; Chung Hyungsoo, Office of International Information; Chung Joo Young, chairman of Hyundai; Hwa Soo Chung, Ilhae Foundation; Il Sakung, president's office; Jin Nyum, planning commission; Jung Kang Hong, Korean Overseas Information Service; Kang Ae Ryan, interpreter; Kim Cae One, Institute of Social Sciences, University of Seoul; Kim Dae Jung, leader of the opposition; Kim Duck Chong, Daewoo; Kim Jin Jyun, director of the newspaper *Dong A;* Kim Ki Duk, minister of labor; Kim Kihwan, president of the Ilhae Foundation; Kim Man Je, vice–prime minister; Kim Oksin, vice-minister of general affairs; Kim Woo Chung, president of the Daewoo Corp.; Kim Yong Wook, Democratic Justice party; Kim Young Shik, chairman of the Korean Institute for the Development of Education; Ko Kwang Cho, Lucky Gold Star; Lee Hwan San, Democratic Justice Party; Paik Nam June, sculptor; Park Chongha, president of the Sung Kyun Kwan Buddhist Order; Shin Kook Hwan, minister of commerce and industry; Shin Se Ho, Korean Institute for the Development of Education; Yu Taewan, Office of International Information

# From the Ivory Coast

M. Amethier, Société Africaine de plantation d' hévéas; Claude Angelini, director, Institute des savanes; M. Berger, commercial counselor, French embassy; Aka Bogui Timothee, minister of industry; Denis Bra Kanon, minister of agriculture; Alain Doat, Société Africaine de plantation d'hé-véas; Bernard Ehui Koutoua, minister of industry; Lamine Fadiga, president of the Chamber of Commerce of Abidjan; Kakou Kassi, ministry of industry; Auguste Miremont, *Fraternité Matin;* Francois Pointereau, Center for International Cooperation in Agricultural Research; Abdoulaye Sawadogo, former minister of agriculture, professor of geography

# From Egypt

Sabri Abdalla, former minister of planning; Amin Fakhry Abdelnour, European Union Bank; Hazem el Beblawi, president of the Export Development Bank; Boris Catoire, economic counselor, embassy of France; Pierre Comte, French Cultural Center of Cairo; M. Dewidar, minister of health; Mohamed I. Farid, vice-president of the World Development Bank; Hazem Foda, press counselor, embassy of Egypt in Paris; Yahia Hakky, writer; Pierre Hunt, ambassador of France in Egypt; Ali Loutfi, former prime minister, speaker of the senate; Youri Moustafa, minister of economic affairs and foreign trade; Ali N. Negm, Arab International Bank; Wahib Rafaat, Wafd party; Ismael Sabri, chairman of the Franco-Egyptian Society for Agro-Based Industry; Mohamad Zahwi, minister for planning and cooperation

# From India

Montek Singh Ahluwalia, adviser to the prime minister; Amya Bagchi, Center for Social Science Research, Calcutta; Jyosi Basu, chief minister of Bengal; Jerome Bonnafont, embassy of France; Sukhumoy Chakra-varti, economic adviser to the prime minister; de Barun, Centre for Social Science Research, Calcutta; Abid Hussein, planning commission; L. K. Jha, chairman of the productivity council; Prem Shankar Jha, director, *Hindustan Times;* Rajni Kothari, Centre for the Study of Developing Societies; T. N. Madan, Institute for Economic Growth; M. D. Marathe, Voltas Limited, Bombay; J. C. Marize, council, deputy council, Calcutta; Jean Bernard Merimee, ambassador of France in India; Inder Mohan; B. C. Mukherjee, Jessop Industries; Ashis Nandy, Centre for the Study of Developing Societies; R. E. Pendse, Tata Industries, Bombay; Dr. Ramanaan, Atomic Energy Commission, Bombay; S. Rajgopal, Atomic Energy Commission, Bombay; C. Hanumantha Rao, Institute of

Economic Growth; M. V. Rao, minister of agriculture; Narasimha Rao, minister of human resource development; Moonis Raza, vice-chancellor, University of Delhi; Priya Sen; Ashwini Seih, Centre of Agro-Economic Research; Mrs. Sharma, cultural counselor, Embassy of India, Paris; Lalit Sharma, sociologist; Manmohan Singh, planning commission; Khushwant Singh, writer; Dr. Singh, Institute of Agricultural Research; Manveer Singh, Ministry of External Affairs; G. P. Talwar, director, National Institute of Immunology; Romesh Thapar, editor of the journal *Seminar;* A. H. Tobaccowala, Voltas International; Kapila Vatsyayan, Ministry of Development of Human Resources; Francis Wagziarg

# From Mexico

Victor Hinojosa Barragan, chairman of the Franco-Mexico Chamber of Commerce; Norman Borlaug, agronomist, Nobel Peace Prize, 1970; Jorge Bustamente, managing director, Cefnomex; Francisco Calderon, entrepreneur counselor; Fernando Canales, National Action party (PAN), Monterrey; M. Condreau, PAN; Jose Cordoba, Ministry of Planning; Juan Manuel Duran, Technologico de Monterrey; Mario Garza Gonzalez, Société Vitro; Angel Gurria Trevino, Ministry of Finance; Alejandro Junco, director of the newspaper *El Norte;* Javier Livas, PAN; Cassio Luisseli, Mission Economica para America Latina; Jaime Matus, Centre of Agricultural Economics, Chapin College; Fernado Munoz, undersecretary for labor; Sergio Reyes Osorio, Ministry of Agriculture; Octavio Paz, writer; Luis Pazos de la Torre, Free Enterprise Research Center; Ivan Restrepo, director of the Centre de Ecodesarrollo; Fernando Salas Vargas, president's secretariat; Tran Van Kha, commercial counselor, embassy of France; Gregorio Martin Valdes, Cimmyt; M. Santos, legislator, Party of Institutionalized Revolution, Monterrey; Pr. Solir, economic adviser to the president; Guillermo Velazco, chairman, Coparmex (Mexican employers' association); Luis Enrique Wah Ruiz, managing director of the Association of State Industries of Mexico; Jaime Zabludowsky, president's secretariat

# From Pakistan

Dr. Meekal Aziz Ahmad, planning commission; Bashir Ahmad, Bank of Pakistan; M. Beaussou, first secretary, embassy of France; Mirza Qamar

Beg, embassy of Pakistan, Paris; Roger Duzer, ambassador of France, Pakistan; Ijaz Gilani, Institute of Public Opinion; A. G. N. Kazi, planning commission; Farok Lehari, Progressive People's party; Norman Majid, National Development Finance Co.; M. W. Memom, Industrial Development Bank; K. M. Nagra, Industrial Development Bank; Syed N. H. Naqvi, Pakistan Institute of Economic Development; Maqbool Qureshi, Banker's Equity Ltd.

## From South Africa

Gatsha Buthelezi, prime minister of Kwazulu, president of Inkatha; Desmond Colborne, South Africa Foundation, Paris; F. Khashane, director of Pace; James Leatt, University of Cape Town; A. Le Grange, The Development Bank; L. Mvubelo, Garment Workers' Union; J. F. Plessis, South Africa Foundation; Michael Spicer, Anglo American Corp.; J. Suzman, University of Wittswatersrand; Pr. S. Terreblanche, University of Stellenbosch; G. Vandern Viljoen, Ministry of Education; Ike Van der Watt, Metal Workers' Union; P. J. Ullmann, French foreign trade adviser

## From Senegal

Abdou Diouf, president of the republic; Doudou Diop, consul general, Paris; Serigne Lamine Diop, minister of industrial development and handicrafts; Pr. Kasse, University of Dakar; Omar Ngala Ndoye, deputy director of the president's cabinet; Amadou Niang, chairman of Sonaca-Sonabanque; Leopold Sedar Senghor, former president of the republic; Moustapha Sourang, dean of the law faculty, University of Dakar; Iba Der Thiam, minister of national education; M. Versieres, head of the Cooperation Mission, embassy of France

## From Singapore

Chan Heng Chee, University of Singapore; Goh Keng Swee, president of the Central Bank; Richard Hu, minister of finance of Singapore; Lee Hsien Loong, minister of commerce and industry; David Marshall, ambassador of the Republic of Singapore, Paris; M. Pillay, Central Bank;

K. S. Sandhu, Institute for Southeast Asian Studies; Ngiam Tong Dow, minister of commerce and industry; Philip Yeo, Commission for Singapore's Economic Development

# From Taiwan

Paul K. Chang, government information office; Charles Chao-Hsi Chen, director, information office; Li Fou Chen, philosopher; Philip Chen, Asia and World Institute; Tein Chen Chou, professor of economics, University of Taipeh; In Lu Chu, president of Cannotex; Alcko H.W. Hsiung, Kuomintang party; Annie Lan, Asia and World Institute; K. T. Lee, economist; T. S. Lin, Tatung Company; Ying Jeou Ma, deputy secretary general of the Kuomintang; Kelley Tang, television producer; Chen Chou Tein, University of Taiwan; Shoh Chieh Tsiang, economist; Charles C. Wu, University of Taiwan; Chia Kan Yen, former president of the republic; Diane Ying, editor of the journal *Commonwealth*

# From Tanzania

M. Holela, secretary general of the Cooperatives Union; Owen Hugues, Food and Agriculture Organization of the United Nations; Roland Hureaux, first secretary, embassy of France; K. A. Malima, minister of education; Julius K. Nyerere, president of the Revolution party, former president of the republic; Roland Oquist, Swedish Institute for Development and Agriculture; Georges-Emile Vinson, ambassador of France

# From International Organizations and Research Centers

Bela Balassa, World Bank, Washington; G. Dana Dalrymple, U.S. Aid, Washington; Milton Friedman, Nobel Prize for economics, Hoover Institution, Stanford, California; Marc Gentilini, head of the department of tropical medicine, Pitié-Salpêtriére Hospital; Jacques de Larosiere, International Monetary Fund; Arthur Lewis, Nobel Prize for economics, Princeton University; Nathan Rosenberg, Stanford University, California; Edward Schultz, World Bank, Washington; Theodore Schultz, Nobel Prize for economics, University of Chicago; Guy Vallaeys, president of Cimmyt

This study would not have been possible had not Air France carried me safely across the seven seas and the five continents. I would like to thank in particular the captains, navigators, stewards, and air hostesses who allowed me to journey in comfort and surety.

   I would also like to express my gratitude to the following: Steven Kaplan for his encouragement and advice; Michelle Gaillard, who drew up my itinerary; France de Malval, who went through the various drafts; Guy Rossi-Landi, who helped in preparing the final version; and Asha Puri, who translated the manuscript from French to English.

# Prologue

His brown stetson pulled down low, wearing dark Rayban glasses and a well-cut, well-pressed military shirt, William Doelittle, a lieutenant in the U.S. Border Patrol, stands guard at the Mexican border. In front of him the brightly colored pink and purple shacks of Tijuana mark the boundary between the two Americas. To the north lies the prosperity of the Anglo world; to the south, the poverty of Latin America. Nowhere else does such an arbitrary frontier—three thousand kilometers defined by the fortunes of war and the vicissitudes of history—separate the wealthy from the Third World in such stark contrast.

In 1967, Doelittle was fighting in Vietnam. Today, although the Colt pistol on his belt is just a deterrent, in his eyes, the mission is the same: to protect the free world, white civilization, material prosperity against . . . what exactly?

On the Mexican side about a thousand men are wandering on the narrow strip of ground that separates the edge of Tijuana from U.S. territory waiting for the U.S. lieutenant to get back in his car and check on some other illegal border crossing. Knowing this, Doelittle calls for backup and, with four vehicles and six men, forms a thin line. The two groups watch each other: one thousand to six. Overseeing the operation a border patrol helicopter flies back and forth along the line, up to the Pacific coast and back again, noisy and useless. This game will last until nightfall, which in these latitudes comes abruptly. Night, however, facilitates the observations of the border patrol, which is equipped with infrared binoculars. The Mexicans don't know this. Convinced that darkness protects them, they suddenly start running straight toward the

United States. Doelittle and his men shout at the invaders to stop. Curiously, they all stop, seeming to obey some unwritten rule of the game or perhaps simply panicing, a reflex action of the Mexican peasant confronted by *officiales*.

That night, fifteen hundred illegal immigrants will fail in the attempt and be taken to the border patrol station at Chula Vista, but two or three times that number will succeed, swelling the human sea rising and overflowing the border between Tijuana and the Rio Grande. This invasion, not by an enemy, but by poverty, hunger, and the determination to break through obsesses and frightens the North Americans. According to various estimates, between two and four million Mexicans live illegally in the United States. In addition, a million seasonal migrants come for six months, return to their homes, and come again the following year.

Those who crowd the doors of the industrialized world are not young. Most of them, 40- or 50-year-old heads of families, have left wives and children behind. But beyond their apparently common fate, each has his own story. I will tell the one of José Zaragoza, who ashamed of appearing before *officiales* of the United States in such clothes, muddied and dirtied by his journey, insisted on showing me that underneath he wore a clean shirt and trousers to meet an eventual employer and under that a third set of clothes for Sunday mass. Zaragoza had nothing more than his three superimposed costumes; an unscrupulous recruiter had gone to his village, in Ahueanetzingo in the state of Morelos, and relieved him of his life's savings, one thousand dollars, in exchange for the imaginary address of a U.S. employer, a farmer in New York! Zaragoza, who spoke not a word of English, merely repeated over and over, "*Nueva York, Nueva-York.*" A border patrol agent tried to explain that New York was still another five thousand kilometers from Tijuana and that, in any case, no land was available.

Those Mexicans refused entry spend a few hours at the station being separated from the other Latin Americans. Guatemalans, Hondurans, Salvadoreans, and Colombians can choose to which country they will be expelled, but the Mexicans are legally required to state a name, any name, before climbing aboard a vehicle with screened windows to be driven back to Tijuana. Most of these people have already tried many times to cross the border. Often they succeed, work in the United States for a time, return to their families, and then decided to try their luck again. They all know that the imaginary line and Doelittle's patrol can't stop them forever; not a one doubts, his or her eventual success. The game is practically without danger, for there is no violence, no abuse on the part of the U.S. authorities. Doelittle did nothing more than lecture them, in his poor Spanish, on the legal basis of their expulsion to Mexico. By contrast, as soon as they get off the bus in Tiajuana, the Mexican police harass them and strip them of money and valuables. Doelittle's agents advise novices undergoing their first deportation to hide some money in the hope of avoiding a clean sweep.

In the border station waiting room before climbing aboard the bus, the Mexicans protest not against the United States, but against their own government: "It is because the politicians have fattened that the people are so poor!" Doelittle's colieutenant Dick Cisneros, a Chicano born in California, suggests to his compatriots that they should remake the revolution and follow a new Zapata, the mythical hero of Mexico's landless peasants. And to each, Cisneros wishes better luck the next time around.

William Doelittle remains silent, for he knows not much can be done about the thousands of illegals who mingle with the crowds in San Ysidro. A thousand times he has seen Mexicans run at top speed for the red streetcar to San Diego and melt into the sea of passengers; the law of the United States does not permit him to get on the streetcar and arrest them. Neither can Doelittle stop the invisible immigration of Mexican capital to U.S. banks. He can't stop drugs (50 percent of the marijuana sold in the United States comes from Mexico) nor stem the Mexican *fuga de cerebros,* "brain drain." One hundred and forty years after the Mexican-American War, we see a veritable Hispanic reconquest slowly working its way north from the border. (Since May of 1987, U.S. employers have been subject to legal sanctions if they hire illegal aliens. This new rule should slow clandestine immigration of the United States, but it also risks aggravating social problems in Mexico, as well as causing problems for North American employers suddenly cut off from their supply of cheap labor.)

Doelittle claims that he no longer recognizes his white America, that everything in southern California now evokes Latin American culture— the architecture, the faces, the colors, the sounds. Nevertheless, the lieutenant does not anticipate quitting the border patrol. For twenty thousand dollars a year, he will continue to wage this absurd guerrilla war, unable to stem the global tide of northward migration. For the men and women of the south reject not only poverty, but the yoke of monstrous police forces, raving dictatorships, crushing bureaucracies. They are inclined toward a world that is both wealthier and more respecting of the human person.

We rub shoulders with these people of the Third World every day in our streets and in their own countries. But most of the time we don't see them because we're just passing through or because we project on them our own analyses, our good or bad conscience. For their development we conceive of solutions that reflect our values and viewpoints, not necessarily theirs. In Tijuana, I decided to leave Doelittle and cross the line myself, but in the other direction. For three years, I traveled from north to south, and often I felt as though I were going through the looking glass.

## BASIC ECONOMIC DATA OF THE COUNTRIES VISITED COMPARED WITH FRANCE

| | Area in 1,000 km² | Gross national product (thousands $) | 1984 per capita income ($) | Annual average growth |
|---|---|---|---|---|
| **South Africa** | | | | |
| *pop.* 32.7 *million* | 1,221 | 74.0 | 2,260 | 2.8 |
| **Argentina** | | | | |
| *pop.* 30.1 *million* | 2,767 | 67.0 | 2,230 | −0.2 |
| **Bolivia** | | | | |
| *pop.* 6.2 *million* | 1,099 | 2.5 | 410 | 0.3 |
| **Brazil** | | | | |
| *pop.* 132.5 *million* | 8,512 | 227.0 | 1,710 | 4.4 |
| **Chile** | | | | |
| *pop.* 11.9 *million* | 757 | 20.3 | 1,710 | 2.2 |
| **China** | | | | |
| *pop.* 1,030.0 *million* | 9,561 | 318.3 | 310 | 6.1 (?) |
| **South Korea** | | | | |
| *pop.* 40.5 *million* | 98 | 84.8 | 2,090 | 7.0 |
| **Ivory Coast** | | | | |
| *pop.* 9.9 *million* | 322 | 6.0 | 610 | 4.5 |
| **Cuba** | | | | |
| *pop.* 9.8 *million* | 121 | 8.0 (?) | 820 | n.c. |
| **Egypt** | | | | |
| *pop.* 46.2 *million* | 1,001 | 33.3 | 720 | −0.2 |
| **Hong Kong** | | | | |
| *pop.* 5.5 *million* | 1 | 30.6 | 6,330 | 9.1 |
| **India** | | | | |
| *pop.* 750.0 *million* | 3,288 | 197.2 | 260 | 4.2 |
| **Mexico** | | | | |
| *pop.* 77.0 *million* | 1,973 | 158.3 | 2,060 | 5.0 |
| **Pakistan** | | | | |
| *pop.* 92.4 *million* | 804 | 35.4 | 380 | 6.2 |
| **Senegal** | | | | |
| *pop.* 6.4 *million* | 196 | 2.4 | 380 | 2.4 |
| **Singapore** | | | | |
| *pop.* 2.5 *million* | 1 | 18.2 | 7,260 | 8.2 |
| **Taiwan** | | | | |
| *pop.* 19.1 *million* | 36 | 52.0 | 2,740 | 7.0 |
| **Tanzania** | | | | |
| *pop.* 21.5 *million* | 945 | 4.4 | 210 | 2.6 |
| **France** | | | | |
| *pop.* 55.0 *million* | 547 | 490.0 | 9,760 | 2.3 |

SOURCE: World Bank according to figures sent by respective governments

ONE

# When the Peons Awaken

AT SIESTA TIME IN AHUEANETZINGO IN THE NARROW SHADE OF THE church, an old man, wearing a large sombrero, leaning on his cane, gazes intently at the stranger who would like to hear his story (the villagers already know it). The man, Elijio Martinez Cuevas, met Emiliano Zapata in nearby Ayala in 1910 and heard him demand the restitution of peasant lands. Zapata returned afterward with his comrades in arms as far as Ahueanetzingo where he may have spent an hour; Martinez was there also. Whether the story is true is unimportant because all Mexican peasants of Martinez's generation saw, or believe they saw, Zapata, sometimes even after his assassination. Zapata, "who died," wrote Octavio Paz, "as he had lived, embracing the land," is the melancholy hero of the campesinos.

Ahueanetzingo with its dusty deserted roads, hard light, whitewashed walls and low houses with tightly closed wooden shutters looks like everyone's idea of Mexico. At this hour the tequila sellers doze behind their bar counters. A television station broadcasts an educational program to empty chairs. (Because the village has no teacher, the pupils are supposed to attend class unsupervised in front of the TV screen.) The baroque church, built by the Spaniards on the ruins of an ancient Aztec temple, has been closed since 1940, when the Catholic clergy tried to mobilize the people against the revolution, as detailed in Graham Greene's novel *The Power and the Glory*. The House of the People, however, is open, and a young secretary from the Party of Institutionalized Revolution (PRI)—which has been in power since 1929—is in charge. He is a bureaucrat from Cuernavaca, the capital of Morelos, with a lighter complexion than that of the local population. He represents the absolute power of the state over people as well as over land.

Three-quarters of a century after he heard Zapata's proclamation, Elijio Martinez still awaits a true restitution of land to the peasants of Mexico. Of course, the immense haciendas of Morelos were expropriated in 1936, and the landlords who had exploited the peasants were either executed or fled to the United States. But for all that, Martinez did not become a landowner because private property was declared contrary to Mexican tradition!

By a prodigious historical sleight of hand, the PRI government of General Cardenas resuscitated an ancient Aztec institution called *ejido*, whereby land is held in common by the community, but worked on an individual basis. Each family was given by the Aztec Empire—today by the PRI—the precarious right to cultivate a parcel of land. The ejido may be neither sold nor rented, but only worked by its holder. This occupancy right is heritable only by the widow or the eldest son. The *ejidatario* thus lives in a permanent climate of legal insecurity and dependence vis-à-vis the state, which remains the owner of the land. Situations where the ejidatario works his parcel without legal title, along with boundary disputes, are innumerable. Fifty years after the reform, the government still had not delimited the boundaries of plots, a deliberate slowness that allows it to remain the arbiter of the ejido. Common in the Mexican countryside are peasant processions to the seat of local government and sometimes to the capital to acquire formal legal title to the ejido from the bureaucrats and politicians. Thus, under the cover of Aztec tradition, the progressive PRI ensures the docility of the campesinos. "But the peasants don't seek private property," the PRI secretary assured me. The proof? The National Action party (PAN), the conservative opposition, is for private property but loses all the elections. Therefore, the peasants are against private property!

Agrarian reform has transformed this part of Mexico into a patchwork of tiny plots. The area of the ejidos in Ahueanetzingo is rarely greater than an acre; consolidation is forbidden, and increases in productivity are impossible. In the very place where corn was first domesticated by man, the yields from these thin scattered stalks on parched land are among the world's lowest. Mexico must import at high cost one-third of its consumption. But if the peasants don't apply modern agricultural techniques, it is not out of ignorance or conservatism; caught in the squeeze between their scanty allotment of land and the low prices at which the government buys the surplus, they have no incentive to invest or to produce more than they consume. The peasants of Ahueanetzingo are, in their own right, perfectly logical and don't overwork. They prefer to watch television or emigrate to the United States.

Of 1,200 inhabitants of the village, 80 adults have left, supporting their families who stayed behind with their remittances. The numerous parabolic antennae on the roofs of Ahueanetzingo permit reception of North American programs, which testifies to the arriving dollars and to the real center of interest of these peasants.

Squashed by a totalitarian bureaucracy, mystified by political propaganda, dispossessed of his rightful history, alienated to a foreign culture, locked into poverty by an absurd economic system, the Mexican peon carries on his back the entire weight of the Third World. He may well, says Octavio Paz, be its symbol.

## The State of the Third World

Octavio Paz, a poet and the national oracle, is resoundingly hailed in Mexico and Latin America. For a long time he was one of the regime's dignitaries, until the day, October 12, 1968, the government ordered its agents to fire on a student demonstration in the Plaza of Three Cultures in Tlatelolco, a suburb of Mexico City.[1] Paz then publicly dissociated himself from the PRI, became a dissident intellectual, and holed up in his apartment on the Avenida de los Insurgentes, in the center of the capital, surrounded by books, pre-Columbian objets d'art, and statues brought back from India, where he was ambassador. The cracks on the ceiling recall the earthquake of 1985, which just barely spared his building, but razed all of the surrounding skyscrapers too hastily built during the oil boom. This man with the heavy features of an enigmatic *cacique,* (an Indian chief) is one of the continent's most influential thinkers, an implacable opponent of his government's policies; only his notoriety protects him. He is in the forefront of all antitotalitarian struggles, the enemy of Augusto Pinochet, as well as of Fidel Castro.

No people, Paz tells me, belong more to the Third World than the Mexican people because none has been or remains more dominated; crushed by the Aztecs, the Spanish conquistadors, the Catholic missionaries, the village leaders, and the revolutionary caudillos, Mexicans today live under the boot heel of the bureaucratic totalitarianism of the PRI.

Paz sees the PRI as the archetypal state apparatus, whether dominant or one party, that oppresses the poor. It is a sort of Bolshevik party, he says, that has succeeded—by respecting the appearances of democracy and pluralism—in winning all of the presidential elections for 60 years. Furthermore, this bureaucracy is hereditary: ministers are sons of ministers, presidents descendants of party notables.[2] This absolute domination of the Mexican people by the PRI, explains Paz, derives not only from the usual methods of totalitarianism—violence, corruption, intimidation—but from the way they manipulate the naive peons. The PRI has adapted its rites of power from the ancient Aztecs. Thus the president of Mexico exercises a secret and personal authority, unequaled in the world; at the end of his nonrenewable six-year term of office, however, he becomes, at the hands of his designated successor, the object of extreme criticism. This ritual sacrifice allows the regime to perpetuate itself: popular discontent spends itself while the power of the party is eternal and better assured than in any other dictatorship.

According to Paz, this explains why Mexican governments have promoted a veritable cult of the Aztec and celebrated it to excess in museums, murals, statues, and speeches. Yet the Aztecs, invaders from the north, brought little more than their bloody rituals; their culture was mediocre, their art gross and inferior to that of the ancient Mexican Mayans and Toltecs whom they overwhelmed. But, Paz tells me, the Aztecs were for Mexico the inventors of the central state; celebrating the Aztecs is to legitimize historically the perpetuation of such a state. Thus, by a combination of the cult of the past and a modernist discourse, the dynasties that have controlled the PRI since the revolution have succeeded in joining absolute power to the legitimacy of an apparent progressive democracy.

In any case, bemoans Paz, we never see Western intellectuals mobilized against the dictatorship in Mexico in the same way that they assailed Pinochet. Is this not, for all Third World despots, the incontrovertible mark of success? I was waiting for Paz to give me a few clues to or at least a definition of the Third World. Or was it absurd to lump together such a vast array of diverse situations?

For Paz, the Third World does indeed exist, for the people in it identify with it and see it as a live reality. But the unity of the Third World does not seem to him, contrary to popular opinion, an economic one; it is not per capita income, technological backwardness, the skewed distribution of wealth, the nature of relations with the wealthy countries, colonization or imperialism that define the Third World. Membership of a nation in the Third World is, above all, connected with its political system. The Third World is dominated by authoritarian or totalitarian forces and by political castes that manipulate words and institutions. The Third World is not only mass poverty but—to varying degrees—the permanent victory of the strong over the weak and the reign of delirious ideologies;

the priority of politics over economics, hierarchy over talent, ignorance over human rights; the absence of legality; the rejection of pluralism; the forbidding of criticism; and the distrust of the individual.

Paz adds another criterion that, according to him, determines immediately whether a nation belongs to the Third World: political corruption. He believes that where the representatives of the state—bureaucrats or politicians, from top to bottom of the hierarchy—are corrupt or where the practice of corruption is quasi official, we are in the Third World. At the other end of the hierarchy, the president himself embezzled several million dollars before retiring from public life. Another side of corruption is denunciation: each new chief of state attacks the turpitude of his predecessors and sets out to rid the country of this plague. But we must, Paz specifies, judge corruption neither superficially nor from an alarmist standpoint. Westerners are too often tempted to see it as a deplorable habit, a characteristic of local culture, or a consequence of poverty, but this is wrong! In Mexico, as a general rule, corruption is an institution basic to the proper functioning of political authority. By virtue of the personalized distribution of those positions most favorable to illicit gain, the party assures itself of the servility of the bureaucracy.

Most profoundly, corruption reveals an absence of law. In most Third World countries the law is not a set of rules imposed equally and impartially on all; power relationships are always personalized. The covert remuneration of numerous intermediaries is the only way for citizens to access the administration to obtain protection from power. In Mexico this corruption starts at the lowest level with the *mordida,* or bribe to the police officer.

The English economist Peter Bauer calls this type of political system a *kleptocracy.* The state is not equivalent to the state in Europe but is private property. Concludes Paz, this misappropriation of the state by cliques constitutes the common denominator in the Third World.

## Octavio Paz's Reversal

Octavio Paz putting the state on trial was scarcely what I had expected. I had come to Mexico to meet the surrealist poet, the companion of André Breton, the veteran of the Spanish Civil War, the leftist intellectual. I was misinformed. Paz has become a liberal in the economic and historical sense, a man who now believes that the development of his country must be achieved through democracy and free enterprise.

This is not the easy or the most comfortable way, on this continent where liberalism has a bad reputation. The term itself is ambiguous and does not mean the same in every country. The rhetorical abuse of the term by the military dictatorships of Brazil, Argentina, and Chile led to an identification of market economy with political authoritarianism. In Mexico liberalism is synonymous with anticlericalism and also has a North American connotation, which south of the Rio Grande is an abomination. Finally, here as elsewhere, *liberalism* is considered the ideology of the bosses against the workers, of the haves against the have-nots, of the rich nations against the Third World.

Paz knows all these caricatures but believes that tortured liberalism is no different from other global interpretations of history and that it has been betrayed by those who would lay claim to it. Has not Christianity often been betrayed by the church? Is not Marxism perpetually betrayed by the communist parties? By the same token, liberalism is often the victim of the bourgeoisie, which appropriates it, and the politicians, who debate it. It is both the burden and the greatness of the liberal intellectual, according to Paz, to take on all of these contradictions and enlighten liberal society while criticizing it.

To be liberal is to believe that there is no Mexican road to development but that universal principles apply equally to Mexico. The Mexican, observes Paz, who in his country conforms to the cliche of the passive, lazy peasant, suddenly becomes hardworking and enterprising when he crosses the U.S. border.[3] Is this not proof that poverty and servility are products of the Mexican political system rather than deriving from historical or natural causes? Liberalism lies in the realization that people are naturally neither good nor bad, efficient or inefficient, progressive or backward but adapt their behavior to institutions that can indeed be good or bad.

This is a crucial analysis. In every country I explored, development theorists always divide into two camps. On the one hand, it is held that only a nationalist, statist, or socialist strategy can solve the problem of poverty; this approach, with few exceptions, has been dominant in the Third World since World War II. On the other hand, it is claimed that the spirit of enterprise, free trade, and democracy are universal principles that are perfectly applicable to all cultures. The passage of Octavio Paz from the former to the latter camp surpasses Mexico in symbolic value. Here is a man whose life story is that of the century and who has been a participant in all of its struggles. That, at the end of a life of reflection, he calls on Latin America to choose the liberal path because it seems to him to be universal may be taken as the sign of a profound reversal.

## The Relevance of Adam Smith

My encounter with Octavio Paz proved decisive for this work. Starting with the goal of elucidating a few general principles on development, I worried, at the beginning of my journey, that this pretence of transporting an analytic framework from country to country, from culture to culture, might result in a total European ethnocentrism. That one of the great spokespersons for the Third World confirmed the validity of a universalistic approach encouraged me to pursue this inquiry and to meet many other people who, in their own ways, in their own languages, and in their own cultures, would also deem this a realizable goal. Again, we must be clear on the meanings of words. The opposite of dogma, liberal thought is not a recipe or incantation taken from some work of revelation to be applied under all circumstances and in all latitudes. What we are proposing here and in the following pages, is above all an attitude, a way of observing human beings and interpreting facts with an open mind, sensitive to place as well as to time.

I visited eighteen[4] countries to write this book, which means that I missed some hundred others. I particularly avoided countries at war, like Ethiopia or Iran, considering that in these cases the economy was totally reorganized on a war footing, which rendered development policy irrelevant. Of course, this exclusion is debatable because foreign and civil wars are an important aspect of the Third World. My choices were arbitrary, not random. I tried to select situations representative of a hope for the future in preference to disasters and failures; I examined fewer facts than perspectives. The literature on the Third World is a pessimistic tradition and, to my mind, poorly represents the efforts of these energetic peoples, for the Third World moves, works, innovates. It is in no way the inert and hopeless mass we often think we perceive in the West. I sanction the notion of development even though it undermines traditional equilibriums, engulfs venerable cultures in its industrial storm, and does not necessarily make people happy. I don't pretend that development is under all circumstances a higher value than ancient civilization, but I claim that it corresponds to what the Third World itself wants, to the quest of the migrants we saw flooding northward. Right or wrong, the general aspiration of these people is for a material life similar to that lived in the West and for a less exotic world.

Finally, the title of this book, *The New Wealth of Nations*, was borrowed from the Scottish economist Adam Smith, whose *An Inquiry on the Nature and Causes of the Wealth of Nations*, which appeared in 1776, is often considered the origin and foundation of economic liberalism. He put forward a method for simultaneously developing prosperity and advancing equality in the distribution of wealth; a defense of economic freedoms that ran counter to all of the perceived notions of his time. Adam Smith wrote in a Europe that in many ways resembled the Third World of today: the intertwining of great wealth and great poverty, traditional cultures shaken by modernization, conflict between despotism and democracy, intense intellectual ferment. But my ambition, much more modest than Adam Smith's, is to impart that which I often saw too quickly and to share my impressions. The borrowing of this magnificent title implies both payment of the debt that I owe it and my personal commitment to a school of thought that, for two centuries, has tried to promote freedom and rights against arbitrariness and research against the pretense of knowing all.

These observations convinced me that the poverty of nations is not inevitable but is the consequence of bad policies based on a false idea. This false idea, under various guises, is the notion that political leaders and everything that legitimizes them—powerful state, single party, military, public sector enterprises—constitutes progress. Inversely, everything private—the individual, dissidence, the critical spirit—is always backward. Nevertheless, as we shall discover, all along our journey, through changing continents, histories, and cultures, the Third World's experience since the 1960s proves exactly the opposite. However, false ideas don't arise in a vacuum. The essence of economic thought in Latin America comes out of an unexpected and unique laboratory: Santiago de Chile.

# Santiago and Its Two Masters

WHY SANTIAGO OF ALL PLACES? BECAUSE IN THE 1960S IT WAS IN THIS city that Raoul Prebich, an economist of Argentinean origin, devised a theoretical model for growth based on industrialization and protectionism. This model was to inspire leaders not only of Latin America but of Asia and Africa as well. Prebich was to Third World economics what Keynes was to the industrial world. Prebich died in 1985, but the Economic Commission for Latin America (ECLA) lives on in Santiago and remains an international center of national industrialism. With its provincial ways, it is hard to believe that Santiago could be the capital of any place other than Chile. Indeed, it was chosen capital at a time when world opinion had it that Chile was the most reasonable democracy on the South American continent. Chile and Uruguay were together called the Switzerland of Latin America. Today the only thing that comes close to being Swiss is the snowy panorama of the Andes, which encircles this miniscule and remote territory of the United Nations and enshrouds it in an atmosphere of political hostility.

What is paradoxical is that Santiago is in the midst of experiment diametrically opposed to the ECLA school of thought, namely, the "liberalism" of the Pinochet government, which it claims is influenced by the American Chicago School, particularly Milton Friedman. Between Prebich and Friedman, this small town at the end of the world can stake a claim as the ideological capital of Latin America, a continent with a passion for ideology.

This called for a visit to Santiago, but I undertook the journey with a certain amount of trepidation. As we approached the Andes, it suddenly occurred to me that perhaps I would share the same fate as Mermoz (a French pilot who crashed in the Andes; despite terrible conditions he managed to survive). Fortunately I proved wrong on that score. The Air France 747 soared effortlessly over the parallel range of mountain peaks in less than a quarter of an hour with not so much as a shudder. Looking down from my window, I could see Argentina behind me and Chile ahead. I was rather nervous as we landed, for I feared my first encounter with the dictator's regime stemming from my inability to hold in check a spontaneous aggressiveness that surfaces every time I come face to face with power. Imagine my surprise when at this modest airport the only person I met from Pinochet's hordes was a policeman standing with a German shepherd to detect narcotics! The plane from Paris being chock-full, I could hardly claim to be the adventurous traveler. To enter or leave Chile at will, all you need is a journalist accreditation card. In September 1986, Santiago was no longer under a state of emergency. That one could openly protest against the regime was proof enough; in the initial stages of Pinochet's government such dissent was unheard of.

The contrast between what I had imagined and reality was further accentuated during a lecture on liberalism I was invited to give at the Catholic University of Santiago. I took the opportunity to explain that economic freedom without democracy is both a practical and theoretical aberration. The students and teachers who crammed the hall seemed to have already accepted this contention, and we discussed it freely without any kind of constraint. The next day, the *Mercurio,* a leading conservative newspaper, faithfully reproduced the hostile remarks I had made about Pinochet's government and his liberal collaborators; the article was entitled: "A Critical Vision of Chile." Although Chile can't be called a democracy, it is certainly not the unlivable hell it is made out to be; Pinochet's regime is authoritarian, not totalitarian, and is somewhat similar to the last years of Franco's rule in Spain. What is unfathomable is why the Chicago Boys claim that market economy and political authoritarianism make for a good marriage, thereby giving the Third World a very distorted image of liberalism.

## A Minister both Liberal and Satisfied

Hernan Buchi, Pinochet's finance minister, is perfectly aware that his country does not enjoy a good reputation abroad, being considered an outcast in the same way as South Africa and Taiwan. The forty-year-old minister, like his compatriots, commutes on a crowded bus to his office facing the Moneda presidential palace. He climbs the ten flights of stairs to his office to keep fit and wears his hair long, sporting the Beatles look of the 1960s. This hirsute man bounding with energy is certainly a far cry from what one visualizes as an associate of Latin America's toughest dictator.

According to Buchi the image of Chile that has gained ground internationally is the result of communist propaganda. Legend has it that the good guy, Salvador Allende, after having been democratically elected to power, was overthrown because of a wicked U.S. plot hatched to safeguard the interests of U.S. companies threatened by nationalization. Buchi reminds us that things were not quite so simple: Allende had only managed to secure one-third of the total number of votes and owed his presidentship to a divided opposition. His management of the economy with the help of his communist ministers led to the highest rate of inflation and greatest disorder ever known in the history of Chile; when all is said and done, the uprising of the middle class played an even more significant role in Pinochet's coup d'état than the CIA. The legend continues that Washington saddled Pinochet with a group of technocrats, trained at the University of Chicago by Milton Friedman, who fanatically swore by capitalism and the market economy. Buchi, who was educated at the Massachusetts Institute of Technology in Boston, informs us that the Chicago Boys were not parceled to Santiago through the diplomatic bag from Washington for the simple reason that they had been around for ages. Apparently, it is customary for all economics students of the Catholic University of Santiago to complete their training in Chicago under an exchange program supervised not by Milton Friedman but by Arnold Hardberger. Hardberger belongs to the intransigent school of thought influenced by the Austrian economist Ludwig von Mises, who systematically advocated the cause of laissez-faire. When Pinochet came to power, he knew little about economics, but these youngsters were at hand, brilliant and teeming with new ideas. The dictator placed them in positions of great responsibility in the Central Bank and Ministry of Finance. The despot was giving the Chicago Boys a chance to apply in real life what they had learned from textbooks. Chile became their experimenting ground. In the words of Buchi, they are "only the technicians of the economy. The Chicago Boys have not taken any political decisions, even if they were conscious of the implications of their participation in the Pinochet Government."

The minister of finance thus proposed to give us a strictly technical account of the Chilean attempt to return to a market economy. Indeed some results are worth looking at: in 1973, when Allende fell, the country depended on copper for 90 percent of its exports; now copper represents no more than 45 percent of the total volume of exports thanks to a remarkable diversification of small and medium industry in the agricultural and industrial sectors. Such a switchover in the nature of the components of foreign trade is essential, as it proves that Third World countries can overcome the handicap of excessive dependence on foreign markets for the sale of a single raw material whose price keeps fluctuating.

Buchi pointed out that all Chile has done is apply a basic precept of the liberal doctrine, that is, let comparative advantage take its course. The country therefore virtually turned its back on the protectionism recommended by the ECLA, brought down duty to 10 percent, did away with quotas, devalued its currency, and unfroze wages and prices on the domestic market. Such measures resulted in a basic reclassification of economic activity. Industries that could only prosper if sheltered from foreign competition were swept away, and new ones emerged and prospered, taking full advantage of cheap, available labor and natural resources. That is how fruit, wood, and light industrial goods came to overtake copper on the export market. During the same period, income and employment were given a jolt, partially as a result of such policies but more so because of the world economic crisis. Buchi and most Chilean economists feel that on the whole their country fared much better than any other Latin American country in those difficult years; the number of jobs went up in Chile whereas it fell in both Bolivia and Argentina. Growth rates, which were stagnating or even declining in most of its neighboring countries, seemed to be moving upward in Chile.

## The Chicago Boys—Enlightened Despots

All the Chicago Boys are not as modest as Buchi, and it would be wrong to assume that they are willing to confine themselves solely to economic management. Pressured by public opinion both at home and abroad to restore democracy, they claim to be preparing its advent. José Pinera, former labour minister, is of the view that a return to democracy in Latin America will remain an illusion as long as social organization continues to be centralized and confers on the state—democracy or no democracy—excessive power over the civilian population. The return of democracy in both Brazil and Argentina has, according to Pinera, done nothing more than give legitimacy through universal suffrage—honestly exercised for the most part—to institutions that by their very nature are

totalitarian. Viewed in this light, he seems to be taking a stance close to
the theoretical positions of Hayek, Friedman, or even Tocqueville, positions that stipulate decentralization of institutions and liberalization of
society as necessary preconditions for the process of democratization to
set in: this is exactly what Chile claims to be doing.

As part of this effort, Pinera cites the example of the privatization of
pension funds (it is the only one to date). Previously pension funds had
been managed by the state in Chile, thereby giving the government,
whatever its political colors, considerable financial resources and the
means to pressure the people. Since 1985 pension funds have been privatized, and all wage earners have the right to choose from among some
twenty-odd private organizations offering competitive subscriptions and
services. (This freedom of choice had been denied under the previous so-
called democratic regimes.)

Just as they do not mince words about democracy, the Chicago Boys
have not tried to dodge the question of social justice. According to the
major economists of the Institute of Economic Studies, who belong to the
liberal school, especially Sergio de la Cuadra, former finance minister,
the new Chilean growth is beneficial to all strata of society, thanks to the
progress in agriculture and export-oriented small-scale industry. Here is
an illustration of the famous trickle-down effect, so popular in Reagan's
America and the main plank of liberal orthodoxy; it demonstrates,
though not yet conclusively, that the capitalist system is the most efficient
and that it guarantees greater equity than socialism. Later we shall deal
with South Korea and Taiwan, where the trickle-down effect has undoubtedly been at work since the 1960s. In the case of Chile, it is not so
obvious. De la Cuadra says the infant mortality rate is steadily declining
and suggests that this is the best index for measuring real progress and
social justice. He adds that by handing the responsibility of economic development to the private sector, the government can now concentrate
public effort on serving the poorest. Once again we have a theoretically
sound proposition, but the contrast between the living quarters of the
poor and the posh residential areas of the bourgeoisie and the *officiales*
remains just as striking.

In all likelihood, the wealth distribution pattern has hardly varied
over the last thirteen years, the Chicago Boys faring no better than any
other Latin American government in redistributing the fruits of development. For those economists who claim to be champions of the free market system and assure us that it is both efficient and just, the Chilean case
must be somewhat awkward. If the benefits of development have trickled
down, the process is so slow that it is almost imperceptible. This is all the
more true in the case of an authoritarian government, suspected a priori

of being unjust. Impressive statistics on infant mortality notwithstanding, public perception remains negative. That Chile has a smaller percentage of poor than any other Latin American country—it is traditionally a country of the middle class—makes this kind of injustice even more unpalatable. In all probability, the Chilean people, with their heightened political awareness, will not have the patience to wait for the beneficial effects of the Chicago Boys' manned economy to trickle down. Herein lies its basic flaw, and it is certainly not the only one. The Chicago Boys committed the cardinal error of assuming that the government had given them carte blanche to conduct their experiment, an experiment distorted from the outset, for Pinochet allowed the Chicago Boys to operate only in those fields where his authority could not be questioned, namely, free price movement, free exchange rates, and private pension funds. The public sector is very much intact: the ministry of finance's authority over the Central Bank is as strong as ever, though the liberals have been clamoring for an ease-up on this stranglehold; banking, iron and steel, energy, telecommunications, transport, and television are still under direct control of the government. When all is said and done, the economic sway of the Pinochet government is as dominant as that of Allende's; it has even increased in some industrial sectors as the government stepped in to take over private companies unable to stand up to its liberal policies and the crisis. The naïveté of the Chicago Boys was to have imagined otherwise and to think that a military dictatorship would willingly let go of its power. They repeated the error of the eighteenth-century liberals who believed that, through an association with enlightened despots, they could contribute to the welfare of the people. The moral of our story for the moment is that although liberal solutions do lead to economic progress, they also result in a technical and political impasse when they are used within the framework of what public opinion considers to be an illegitimate regime.

Now we shall take a look at the other Santiago model, the national industrialism model, which confers legitimacy to the governments applying it even if the end result is an economic failure.

## Raul Prebich's Heritage

Raul Prebich was undoubtedly an exceptional being with a brilliant mind, but his reasoning was faulty. He spent his entire life lording over the ECLA, and it was only with his successor and disciple Norberto Gonzales that I was able to discuss the life and work of this master of Santiago.

According to Gonzales, Prebich was no more a socialist in the strict sense of the term than Keynes. Perhaps, but both strove toward the socialization of nations and idealized governments that were quick to take up their suggestions. Prebich was nonetheless an avowed antiliberal, hostile to the market economy and firmly convinced that the Third World was a victim of the affluent nations' imperialism. According to his theory, the Third World could not develop because the industrialized world kept it deliberately in a position of dependence or in a "center-periphery"–type relationship. It was Prebich who systematized the notion of historical deterioration of the terms of trade—the constant and inevitable decline in the value of raw materials exported by poor countries in comparison to the rising value of industrial goods sold by the rich countries. Difficult to prove, given the different periods referred to, this deterioration is one of the most persistent Third World myths, but it is accepted with great alacrity as it affords the rulers of poor countries the opportunity to blame the affluent nations for their woes.

Thus Julius Nyerere, president of Tanzania, pointed out at the 1981 Cancun conference that whereas his country could buy a tractor for four tons of coffee in 1965, fifteen years later 20 tons were required. This apparently foolproof argument fails to mention that though the coffee is of the same quality, the same is not true of the tractor. Although Tanzania, or for that matter any other country functioning on similar lines, continues to supply the same product on the market without bothering about diversification or quality control, the producers of industrial goods have never ceased to invest and innovate. If, for the sake of argument, we assume that the industrialized countries are selling the same tractor they did twenty years ago, it is likely that its relative price would be much lower. Thus to make the deterioration of the terms of trade the cause for underdevelopment is tantamount to reversing the order of the factors of production. Such deterioration is more often than not the result of erroneous developmental policies.

The newly industrialized countries of Asia have overcome the so-called inevitable deterioration of terms of trade by consistently varying the products they have to offer on the world market. Prebich was well aware of this, for he offered a solution to arrest this deterioration in the terms of trade: import substitution. The underlying principle is simple enough. The Third World should seal its borders to industrial goods and develop indigenous production as a substitute; protectionism ought, of its own accord, set in motion a substitute industrialization process that should in turn enable the poor countries to attain both material prosperity and political independence. Such a strategy calls for decisive governmental action to protect domestic markets from foreign competition and to channelize savings toward the investment required for import substitution. One basic premise of this model was the infant industry theory. Governments were required to mollycoddle, through various forms of aid and border protection, industrial activity in its infancy stage when it could not face international competition. Prebich thus provided a justification to those who used this model with moderation if not with a heavy conscience. Henceforth, governments were able not only extensively to adopt such practices but also to provide a theoretical alibi, even if, as Milton Friedman said in jest, the major problem with industries in their infancy is that they never grow up.

## A Contagious Theory

The influence and the role played by the ECLA group are now widely acknowledged in Latin America, and the Prebich model is held largely responsible for the widespread inefficiency of protected industries. "We have really had to pay the price for ECLA," says Professor Leopoldo Solis, economic adviser to former Mexican president Miguel de la Madrid. Solis adds with rare candor, "The Mexican crisis cannot be attributed solely to the fall in oil prices; its deeper origins lie in the type of economic model Mexico chose to adopt, based as it is on protectionism and import substitution."

Such are the political gains of this model that, despite its numerous flaws, it has caught the imagination of the powers that be, prompting some governments to experiment with it in new areas. Thus in the case of microcomputers, the Brazilian government launched an extremely ambitious import substitution drive, the first of its kind in the world, when, in 1982, all imports were banned to ensure 100 percent Brazilian production. From then on, national enterprises, both public and private, have been making computers that look like IBMs, are compatible with IBMs but are not IBMs. These machines, sold under the name of Cobra or Scopus, are assembled by Brazilians using imported components, imitation parts, indigenous imagination, and a great deal of counterfeit.

The Brazilian computer experience illustrates the ambiguity of the import substitution model. The policy of market reservation in the field of computers is seemingly very attractive: 250,000 jobs, a generation of young engineers to design programs and hardware adapted to local conditions, national independence, no dues to foreign companies. The drawbacks, though not quite so obvious, are nonetheless considerable: Brazilian computers cost twice as much as their international counterparts, they do not work half as well, and they are technically outdated. It is ultimately the Brazilian user who suffers the most from such indigenousness, and the growth of Brazilian firms is often held up for want of reasonably priced, efficient machines. Even so, the government is persevering in its efforts as the new computer wallahs form a powerful lobby with links to the bureaucracy and the army, where new jobs for young engineers are being created all the time; the users, deprived and dispersed, can hardly make their voices heard. Finally, any opposition to the program is considered unpatriotic in Brazil; in the Third World, the appetite for blast furnaces has given way to a burning desire for computers, the newfound symbol of independence.

The Prebich model is not restricted to Latin America but extends all over the Third World due to the quest for power of the new elite of the decolonization era. Thus A. G. N. Kazi, chairman and one of the main architects of Pakistan's development with which he has been associated for the past 30 years, acknowledges that until recently he had been deeply influenced by the ECLA school of thought. According to Kazi, its success can be attributed not so much to economic factors as to the strength it derives from its anticolonial stand; the popularity it enjoys stems not from any development rationale but from a simple desire for revenge. The same pattern of industrialization was adopted, but this time it was directed against the colonizer. Kazi believes the appeal of the Prebich model also explains why countries as far apart as Brazil and Pakistan neglected the basic needs of the people such as water, health, and education that were to have been satisfied, according to Prebich's theory, in the second phase, when the effects of industrialization had been felt. The notion of human resources, which seems so vital for development today, did not figure in the thinking of the 1960s. For Kazi, the neglect of health and education, typical of newly decolonized countries, cannot be explained away by the feudalism of the ruling classes. On the contrary, in most cases the traditional feudal classes were swept aside at the time of independence, leaving power in the hands of a new elite—political bureaucrats and the intelligentsia, products of decolonization. This new elite, fascinated by the Prebich model, which served to reinforce their newly acquired authority, decided to sacrifice human resources at the altar of industrialization. Moreover, international organizations actively supported Third World governments in this action. For instance, as Kazi recalls, Pakistan only selected projects for which financial aid was forthcoming from these institutions. It was impossible to escape this model, just as it was impossible to go against the spirit of the times.

Norberto Gonzales assures me that this is not what Prebich wanted; that his theories were far more sophisticated than their practical application would have us believe. Prebich did not deny the existence of the market, of entrepreneurs, or of foreign trade. Gonzales adds that a strict socialist state—controlled orthodoxy had no meaning for Prebich, as the Third World required both a strong state and a robust private sector.

The work of the Santiago master has undoubtedly been distorted, but Prebich's fate brings out the key role played by the economist. As Keynes himself enunciated in the conclusion of his general theory: politicians the world over do nothing more than apply, generally without even knowing it, methods defined by economists dead and gone whose names have long been forgotten. Prebich and his school of thought ought thus to be held responsible for the strategies developed in their name as well as for the ensuing consequences.

The Third World has become a vast laboratory where painful experiments are conducted with national economies serving as guinea pigs. Such strategies are largely responsible for the chronic poverty of these nations. Argentina bears this out better than any other country. It was at one time prosperous; it is no longer so. The people and culture are much the same, only the policies have changed. This turn in the course of their history has put them on the road to underdevelopment.

# THREE

# The Nostalgia of the Gauchos

BUENOS AIRES IS AN ASSEMBLAGE OF SPLENDID RELICS, NOSTALGICALLY reminiscent of the old continent, with a charming mélange of Spanish and Russian cafes crammed with snooker or card players at all hours, elegant Parisian boulevards right out of the early 1920s, and Neapolitan alleys and streets. The city is crowded with monuments to its glorious past: any bourgeois general or hero in a riding coat who could claim a victory in battle, however insignificant, against the disintegrating Spanish army around 1810 had the right to the grandiose title of *Liberador* and an equestrian statue. Buenos Aires was once one of the world's most affluent capitals; the Colon Theatre and the private mansions on the Avenida Alvear testify to this.

In the 1930s, if you were wealthy, you were "rich as an Argentinean"; the image of the *estanciero*, or owner of vast tracts of the pampas, was much the same as that of today's oil sheikhs. Much of what was written about Argentina sounded like a description of the great American dream, as in 1929 when Ortega y Gasset wrote, "The Argentinian people are not content at being just one among many, they have set their sights much higher." Given its favorable climate, natural resources, and essentially European population, Argentina should have, in the rightful order of things, become the Latin American counterpart of the North American giant. Indeed, until the Second World War, Argentinean incomes were comparable to those of Australia and Canada. But in 1945 fate took a strange twist, and Argentina won the dubious distinction of being the only country with a European population to slide gradually toward the Third World.

## Que Nos Pasa?

Argentineans are not yet impoverished; they are still one of the most privileged peoples of Latin America. But compared with other nations of European stock, those who claim to constitute the sole white population of both the Americas[1] seem to be the poorest of the lot. In terms of per capita income Argentina is at the same level as Algeria and Yugoslavia. This tragedy makes any kind of frivolous comment impossible in Buenos Aires; the only topic of discussion is the fate of the nation. Seminars, conventions, symposiums, and editorials take up all the intellectual space available. I know of no other nation that devotes so much time to self-analysis, added to which is a lot of grandiloquence in Castilian, a language particularly well suited for such rhetoric, especially when spoken with an Italian accent: ¿Que nos pasa? (What's happening to us?). This is the major obsession of most Argentineans as their standards of living fall, bringing them closer to their immediate neighbors, who are steadily crossing over into the country—the Chileans from the south and the Bolivians from the north. A wave of Indian and colored immigrants is slowly transforming the character of the nation. But the most worrying part of this decay has nothing to do with either economics or race. The morale of the people is down, and most Argentineans no longer want to stay in their own country. According to an opinion poll published by a major Buenos Aires liberal daily, La Nacion, in 1986, half the population wished to emigrate, preferably to Spain, thus completing a strange cycle of colonial history.

An inherent sense of fatality characteristic of the colonial psyche and Spanish temperament is often used to explain Argentina's enigmatic downhill slide. Once agriculture ceases to be profitable, Argentineans readily turn their backs on the spent soil! But this kind of historical interpretation cannot explain why a great, prosperous country was suddenly no longer so. Moreover, trying to understand contemporary Argentina by constantly referring to its origins, only seeing it as a projection of seventeenth-century Spain, would be doing injustice to the Italian, German, and Russian immigrants who have mingled over the ages with the first settlers. We shall see that Argentina is victim of neither its history nor its people; if anything, it is a victim of faulty economic policy. A visit to the pampas—the main source of national prosperity—is enough to understand firsthand the effects of a veritable strategy of degeneration.

## Crime on the Pampas

Toward the west, beyond Buenos Aires, lies the *pampa humeda,* the most fertile soil in the world, with more than three yards of humus, a moderate climate, and rain year-round. A single-propeller plane, not very reassuring but capable of landing anywhere, is the sole means of transport to this hinterland. The pilot follows the Rio de la Plata to find his way. More than an estuary, the old trail leading to the heart of southern America is a kind of shallow lagoon, turned yellow by the alluvium deposits. Small steamers, often carrying contraband, sail upward to Paraguay. Flying no more than three hundred meters above the earth, looking through clouds that seemingly graze the ground and a layer of mist, you can see an infinite expanse of fields dotted with clumps of trees, huge grain silos, and windmills that attract herds of prosperous-looking cattle. The average size of an *estancia* (property) in the province of Buenos Aires is between two and three thousand acres. When visibility becomes zero, our pilot lands wherever he can, waiting for a break in the clouds to continue. During one such forced halt in Colón, at the fringes of the Santa Fe province, we killed time eating empanadas, small bread rolls stuffed with meat and spices. After four hours of adventurous cloud hopping, our plane finally came to a stop at the gate of Albert Duncan's *estancia,* La Paquita.

I am met by a group of gauchos mounted on Creole long-maned horses with sheepskin saddles. With their pointed boots resting firmly on the stirrups, two knives—one short, one long—stuck in their canvas belts that separate their flared trousers from their short jackets, these taciturn men look more menacing than picturesque. The gaucho, in contrast to his American counterpart the cowboy, is depicted by Argentinean folklore and literature as an antihero. According to José Luis Borges, he is the "fugitive deserter who loves a fight." Immortalized by José Hernandez in his epic poem "Martin Fierro," a poem every Argentinean knows by heart, the gaucho is neither good nor fair; he is dishonest, as the following stanza illustrates:

> Cruz and Fierro took
> the horses from an estancia
> Pushed them in the pampas

As expert gauchos would,
crossed without their being seen
way beyond the border.

Adolfo Bioy Casares, a writer and Borges's literary companion, feels that the gaucho's shifty character comes from his uncertain race; a gaucho is an Indian of mixed blood hiding his origins in an Argentina that claims to be wholly European but is actually not.

The gauchos of La Paquita cook whole oxen on huge wood fires, and, to keep it warm, the carved meat is brought in wheelbarrows loaded with live charcoal. Beef to the Argentineans is what rice is to the Chinese and tortillas to the Mexicans. The per capita consumption of beef is a record 80 kilos a year! Nothing could be cheaper than meat in Argentina; the real cost of production is half that of America or Europe. Thanks to Argentina's climate and abundant pastures, an animal reaches a weight of five-hundred kilos in only two years, whereas in Brazil it would take four years. The soil of the pampas is an inexhaustible reservoir, and all the Argentina breeder has to do to regenerate the earth is alternate pastures with cereals. To run an estancia, you don't have to invest a penny, just use the earth and the space available. Running costs are at a minimum on the pampas: hardly any labor, no fertilizers, no additional fodder, little equipment, and a modicum of finance. But despite these natural advantages, meat production has fallen drastically at La Paquita, as it has all over Argentina.

Argentina, at one time the first and foremost meat supplier to Europe and America, is now consuming 90 percent of what it produces, and its exports have hit an all-time low. The reason is clear: Alberto Duncan cut down his production because it is no longer a profitable business. His behavior is rational in the light of patently absurd policies. Given what he is expected to pay in taxes, Alberto Duncan gets from his meat and cereal half the international price and a zero profit margin. The European farmer, in contrast, receives a better price than the prevailing one in the international market, thanks to European Economic Community (EEC) subsidies. As if this were not enough, galloping inflation, repeated devaluations, price controls, export taxation, and high public transport costs have made the domestic price structure in Argentina absolutely unpredictable. Successive governments in Buenos Aires have ruled out any possibility of planning for the future. Duncan can only subsist by minimizing his risks and by never making long-term commitments. He cannot invest because it would be impossible for him to recover his investment. He has to watch for the slightest fluctuation on the world markets, and depending on their prices, he keeps rotating his crops so as to minimize his losses.

Another explanation for the setbacks faced by the *estanciero* (land-lord) may be that La Paquita is more a victim of the international market than of domestic policy. Wheat and meat prices are fixed on the world market, and any price variation leaves the estanciero very vulnerable. Moreover, cutthroat EEC competition has dislodged Argentina from its traditional markets through a series of subsidies. Nonetheless, Duncan could face such competition had his own government not weakened his capacity to meet the market challenge. He is not asking for an impossible reform of foreign trade regulations or for an illusory price stability, but he does not mince words when it comes to the national system making it increasingly difficult for its own citizens to stand up to the vagaries of the foreign market. Worse still, Duncan and the other estancieros consider the decline of the pampas to be the result of a deliberately executed policy. The Argentinean state inspired—or foolishly taken in—by wrong theories, deems it necessary to give priority to industrialization over agriculture by using the rents of the estancieros to finance the industrial workers, the consequence being the impoverishment of both.

## Evita's Children

"The state," says Juan José Taccone, "must be at the forefront of development as Argentina does not have a capitalist bourgeoisie: the estancieros behave like rentiers, quick to speculate on world prices and export their profits abroad rather than invest them in their own country." He adds that it therefore becomes necessary to confiscate the estanciero's profits and keep the prices of wheat and meat as low as possible to maintain the Buenos Aires worker and to finance national industries and protect them from foreign competition.

Taccone, one of the General Confederation of Labour bosses, does not belong to the world of the estancieros but to the other Argentina, the world of the common man, Italian immigrants, *descamisados,* the blue shirts so dear to Evita Peron, and feels he has never been a part of white bourgeois, outward-looking Argentina. Taccone, impressively built, perspiring and constantly wiping his face with an enormous checked handkerchief, is not violent by temperament, something rare for a man of his calling. Self-taught, he thinks for himself, chooses each word carefully, weighs his sentences, and does not get carried away by the volubility so typical of Argentineans. Another trait that distinguishes him is that people actually suspect him of being honest!

Taccone loves football and Juan Peron,[2] the dictator who styled himself along the lines of Benito Mussolini. In the 1940s, Peron cut Argentina off from the rest of the world and embarked his country on the path of autarchic development under the control of the state, thus breaking away from the liberal tradition that until then had guided the country. Peron set the example for many Latin American caudillos, and his Third World fascism gained numerous adepts, particularly after Raul Prebich, with his import substitution theory, conferred intellectual legitimacy on it. For Taccone, Peronism is much more than a development strategy: it is a social plan, an original attempt to associate workers with the process of industrialization without a class struggle or any rupture with Catholicism. A reconciliation of traditional values with the modern world, Peronism saved Argentina from the threat of communism! Besides, adds Taccone, this philosophy is so closely linked to the fate of the nation that all governments after Peron have continued with Peronism, Peron or no Peron.

National industrialism, strangely enough, has thrived and prospered in Buenos Aires in its purest form. One wonders why—is it electoral opportunism, the taste of absolute power, or perhaps that the Confederacion General del Trabajo, even in the opposition, is capable of paralyzing the capital with a general strike? In any case, the militia, in power from 1976 to 1983, although paying lip service to the market economy, was carried away by a penchant for large-scale public works and armament plans that owed more to Peron than to Milton Friedman. Raoul Alfonsin, following on its heels, did not prove to be any more coherent. He showed exemplary courage when he sought to defend human rights, and in 1986 he began to open the borders with Brazil. Although he tried to control state expenditure, he left intact the public sector—citadel of Peronism—as well as the entire national industrialist apparatus that gave rise to the very material and moral decadence he wished to fight. Thus behind the thunder and fury of Argentinean politics, all the governments that came to the Pink House (seat of the president of the republic), whether radical or justicialist, civil or military, followed the same policy: penalizing profitable activities such as agriculture and animal husbandry to support unworkable ventures. The administration has spread its tentacles in all directions, and the public sector is bankrupt. The latter is not a profitable venture precisely because it is public, because it is protected from domestic and foreign competition, and because the size of the market does not justify an import substitution strategy. The revenue from taxation cannot cover the deficit, and the government has had to resort to massive deficit financing, leading to runaway inflation and huge debts. Thus an expensive, inefficient state has created around itself the objective conditions for economic decline.

## The Clandestine Economy

In Ezeiza, a suburb of Buenos Aires, Terencio Moche, an estanciero who shifted from breeding to food processing, has established the most modern slaughterhouse in the country. Truckloads of animals arrive in a continuous stream at one end of the factory and leave from the other in the form of frozen and canned meat. Between entry and exit a complex slaughtering process takes place, ensuring that each and every part of the machinery is put to use. The company, the biggest Argentinean exporter of corned beef, sells exclusively to Great Britain via Holland so that the British consumer, traumatized by the Malvinas (Falkland Islands) affair, does not find out its true origins. Here is a model factory for Argentina, an excellent example of intelligent diversification, geared toward the world market. But Moche, who does business on an international scale, is confronted with an unexpected obstacle: though he is only 30 kilometers from Buenos Aires, he's not on the phone! He was willing to pay for a private communication system to overcome this deficiency of the public sector but was refused permission. He thus had to install a radio antenna on his modern factory, which is illegal. This radio enables him to communicate with his office, set up in the capital only so that his company's executives could reach him on the phone!

This is but one of many anecdotes symptomatic of the mixing up of roles in Argentina: on the one hand, the state, which does everything except what it is supposed to do, on the other, the citizens, who must invent makeshift solutions. Every roof in Buenos Aires is fitted with an antenna and uncovered electric wires—for a telephone or electrical connection. It goes without saying that both have been hooked up without asking anyone's permission. These tangled networks, linking the capital's buildings, reveal the hidden face of the Argentinean economy: a vigorous parallel economy that, by resorting to illegal means, allows the people to survive the excessive, even absurd, intervention of the state. According to the economist Alberto Benegas Lynch, Jr., about 40 percent of the country's real production is carried out on the black market. Hermano de Soto, a Peruvian economist, estimates that the informal sector accounts for 70 percent of Lima's economy. De Soto explains that to complete the necessary formalities to set up a small textile factory, he had to employ four people on a full-time basis for a year, and for this alone he had to spend an amount equal to 32 times the minimum wage. A similar experiment could be carried out in Buenos Aires unless one chooses to shorten the delays by lining the pockets of the officials.

Thanks to the means they have to get around the inertia and exactions of the government, people manage, and the economy is not as badly off as official statistics would have us believe. If one were to go by figures alone, with the cumulative effect of 40 years of negative growth, Argentina ought to have ceased to exist. The Argentinean people are nevertheless alive and kicking and constantly setting up new markets, thanks to their entrepreneurial spirit, which the government is doing its best to destroy. Thus when Juan José Taccone tells us there is not enough private initiative, it is not because there is a shortage of entrepreneurial spirit but because as things stand you need to have a temerity bordering on madness to be willing to invest in a domestic environment that is even more confused than the international market.

# The Art of Refusing to Pay Back One's Debt

In a nutshell, Argentina's main weaknesses are inflation and external debt, both of which provide an artificial prop to the public sector. Argentina's debt, often presented as an external hindrance to growth, is in fact a direct result of its domestic policies.

Argentina's debt—like Mexico's, Peru's, or Venezuela's—is the biggest swindle of the century![3] Argentina is unable to repay her debts because the $50 billion lent to that country by Western banks have for the most part been redirected between 1975 and 1983 to private accounts in the United States and Switzerland. The International Monetary Fund estimates that in Argentina's case, 70 percent of the funds have been misappropriated, this being an all-time record, followed by Venezuela (50 percent), Peru (35 percent), and Mexico (33 percent)![4] What makes matters even worse is that the poor of Latin America are being made to pay the debt through a drastic reduction in their standard of living, which does not prevent some Latin American governments from posing as champions of their people and accusing Western creditors of bleeding them while they or their accomplices are investing this money in their own names. None of this is ever denounced, as we are witnessing a typical case of a reversal of guilt, the conscience of the West being somewhat uneasy when it comes to the Third World. The debtors claim to be the injured party and accuse the West of frivolously having lent them too much! Because I have talked about the source and the dubious destinations of these vast sums of money, let me also say that neither Argentina nor for that matter Mexico are in any position to repay their debts. That is why debate usually centers around technicalities, rescheduling, and the like, whereas the main issue—how does one explain this flight of capital from some Latin American countries?—is always carefully skirted.

The flight of capital is nothing new; money has a way of fleeing badly run economies and protecting itself from the follies of politicians. What is unique in the Argentinean case is not that money has flown but that it has never come back. This was not the case at the beginning of the century, when Argentina appeared to be a land of political stability and economic openness. To express indignation on moral grounds is no use: the blame is not so much with the Argentinean elite as it is with a political system that has caused it to behave in a manner harmful to the economic interests of the nation but rationally at the level of the individual. As long as Argentineans are scared of their own government, of its potential violence, of its violations of the law, and of its contempt for savings and property, capital will continue to flee and Argentina continue to drift toward the Third World.

## Tango in the Soul

"I am French, but also part English and have a bit of Scandinavian blood: that makes me an Argentinian," Borges tells me in perfect French, the kind that is still spoken in some circles of Buenos Aires. "We have inherited a bit of everything from all over Europe," he adds.

Not so long ago Jorge Luis Borges (who died a few months after our meeting in Geneva in June 1986) could be found every afternoon at Claridge's bar, a stone's throw from his home. He dictated his work to his companion of the beautiful Japanese profile, Maria Kodama, whom he married before he died. Past 80, the poet still had the smooth, round face of a baby. His eyesight gone, his blank eyes would look around for the person he was talking to, and his expression always appeared to ask, "Where are you?" The clients at Claridge's waved discreetly to the old master, ran down Maria Kodama in low whispers, and then loudly expressed their indignation over the fact that Borges never managed to lay his hands on the Nobel Prize because he was not a leftist and because nobody loves Argentina.

So much excitement over a cup of tea on a rainy day amused Borges no end. He loved to say that, to the limited extent he was concerned with politics, he had always been a conservative, although in the British mold, he was quick to add. Openly hostile to Peron's populist dictatorship as well as to the military juntas, for him this was moral issue. In his own words "being a conservative means above all expressing one's scepticism in the face of stupidity." Borges was fond neither of Argentinean politics nor of the country, both of which he found solemn and humorless. "Few countries have had such a short history as ours, yet I know of no other country where people are so besotted with anniversaries, patriotic festivals and the tombs of their illustrious forefathers," he would say. Then the poet would break off, ask to be left alone to work, and chase away his intruders. Borges represented the cosmopolitan, universal, outward-looking face of Argentina—a country that once looked toward Europe and the United States! That face of Argentina, however, may no longer exist, for the remaining face is the face of Juan José Taccone, fiery, wholesome, and full of passion. Unfortunately, it is also the face of the Malvinas war. "Las Malvinas son Argentinas" schoolchildren chant in the hope that these islands, the last bastion of the British Empire, will eventually return to them. That Argentina is a gigantic, underpopulated country and that the Falklands, a handful of grazing pastures for sheep, are thousands of miles away are ignored. The popular fervor for football is another face of this Argentina; the 1986 World Cup victory caused a night of jubilation in the streets of the capital—unless one was publicly waving the national flag, one stood out from the crowd!

Between these two poles of Argentinean civilization—reason versus ideology, open versus closed, politics versus economics, national strength versus individual prosperity—history seems to dither as Argentina tries against all odds to reconcile its dual nature. Like Carlos Gardel's[5] poignant tangos—full of passion in both words and music, given to excessive gestures, voice, and emotion—so the Argentinean people seem only capable of veering from one extreme to another.

The rest of Latin America enjoys digs at the Argentineans: "They are Italians who speak Spanish, pretend to be English and imagine they are living in Paris." But it is just this diversity that constitutes its wealth, and to replace it with an artificial, elusive unity based on a nationalist ideology can only make it poorer. When the individualist phase of enterprise was ascendant, Argentina prospered. When it slid toward a policy of closed-door nationalization, it fell. What is worse, the narrow-minded ideologies are capable of plunging the country in a civil war. National industrialization appears to be as much to blame for violence in Argentina as economic decline. The first to plant bombs in the streets of Buenos

Aires were leftist supporters of Peron who wanted to purge society. In Peron's time the country got stuck in a cycle of terrorism and repression from which it has never been able to emerge. Peronist rhetoric, although branding the urban crowds Progressive and calling the countryside reactionary, has set two faces of Argentinean tradition against each other—a case of diversity versus unity at all costs. The nationalist economic strategy cannot be dissociated from the social brutality it gave rise to.

Juan José Taccone confesses somewhat bitterly that both his sons were among the 50 percent who preferred leaving the country for good in the *La Nacion* survey. A touching confession, but isn't the ideology Taccone defends directly responsible for his children's desire to leave the country?

# Bandeirantes and Favelas

OLACYR MEDITATES. ON A MAP OF BRAZIL, HIS FINGER TRACES LATIN America's fertile crescent of the future, a vast circular arc stretching more than three thousand kilometers, from Rio de Janeiro to Salvador, and embracing a major portion of the Amazonas. Even today these lands remain for the most part unexplored. Olacyr is the first man to have produced Brazilian soya and maintains that he was the first to introduce this crop to the world. He believes he has inherited the legacy of the Portuguese and Marrano pioneers, the *bandeirantes,* who refused, in the seventeenth century, to accept the pope's arbitration and pushed back the borders of Brazil by going up the river carrying the flag of their new nation. From the window of his private jet, he showed me the river Paraná, which his forefathers crossed, and a little later he pointed to the border with Paraguay. Like his ancestors, he feels that the border is a nuisance and serves no purpose. All he dreams of is forging ahead with his tractors, bulldozers, and insecticide spraying machines.

After 90 minutes of peaceful flying from São Paulo, reverie gives way to reality as the Cessna touches down on the private air strip Olacyr constructed in the midst of the small township set up by his company for the four thousand people he employs. The standard of living is much higher than that of the average Brazilian. A car stands in front of every house, and there is a school and a dispensary. As for himself, Olacyr has a palatial *fazenda* on top of a hill. The luxurious, impersonal, empty rooms, the tennis courts, the swimming pool, and the dining room were designed for several hundred guests. They have been fully used only once, when the president of Brazil and his entourage came to visit. Olacyr rarely stays here; he simply does not have the time as he lives solely for his work.

A truck farmer's son, he began at the age of fifteen delivering home-grown farm produce to the markets of São Paulo. Five years later, he acquired his own truck and started delivering cement. From then on, Olacyr's fate was closely linked to São Paulo's urban explosion as he became one of its leading civil works contractors. But like all Brazilians, he has a passion for the land and reinvested his entire fortune in agriculture. For a paltry sum he purchased a 100,000-hectare property in the state of Mato Grosso on the border of Paraguay. The land, which had been abandoned several years earlier by a British company, was uncultivated, as the previous owners thought it was barren, too acidic. All that was required was enormous quantities of slake lime to set things right. Olacyr thus purchased a limestone quarry situated one hundred kilometers from the farm, using an uninterrupted line of wagons to link the two. He then had to contend with the problems of drought, which he managed by building an irrigation network from the neighboring rivers. Seen from the air, his estate is a vast stretch of red earth where, thanks to irrigation, huge green patches can be seen that stretch over one hundred hectares of soya field. Olacyr is particularly proud of his silos that hold mountains of dried grain just waiting to be delivered to the oil mills. Next year, Olacyr intends to set up his own factory on the farm and is planning to use harvest waste to feed 30,000 head of cattle who will be waiting in their sheds. These sheds, several hundred meters long, will protect the animals from the sun. The mangers have been set up, but the animals have yet to arrive. A strain capable of standing up to the vagaries of the weather and the drought must be selected, probably a cross between imported bulls from the United States and zebus from Brazil.

That's Brazil! the coming together of a spirit of enterprise and extravagance. But Olacyr, for the most part taciturn, sets me right; he is not Brazilian, he belongs to São Paulo, which leads a much faster life than the rest of Brazil. São Paulans do not share the nonchalance of the Cariocas, the dwellers of Rio, but move at the same pace as the dwellers of any other big city of the world. How exciting it is to belong to São Paulo and how superior its natives feel to the rest of the Brazilian population. São Paulo is the real capital of this country (that is in fact a continent) and is the driving force behind Brazil's spectacular development over the last 40 years.

If it's picturesque nostalgia you are looking for, forget São Paulo. This is a city to be discovered in the way you would New York or Tokyo. Nothing reminds one of the past. On the Avenue Paulista, which runs through the heart of this monstrous city, the Moorish hotels of the coffee barons have disappeared, giving way to the glass towers of modern Brazil. The rare mansions that have somehow managed to survive have been taken over by banks or converted into corporate offices. In the space of twenty years, São Paulo's population has gone from two to twelve million inhabitants. This population explosion took place amid utter chaos and has given rise to the most tightly packed, noisy, polluted metropolis in the world. São Paulo's history is the history of Brazil, starting with the plantations of the past and reaching the status of an industrial power in the present, from the time of the Portuguese colonizers to the newfound era of cosmopolitanism, with its mixture of German, Japanese, Jewish, Italian, and Turkish [1] inhabitants. São Paulo is New York in the middle of the African jungle. Extreme wealth co-exists with extreme injustice, a case of Japanese growth combined with the poverty of the Sahel. Half the population of São Paulo lives in the comfort of a developed society, the other half in *favelas* (slums).[2] São Paulo has been split in two by the modern epic of development. It is as if there are two countries, one rich, one poor. Therein lies the riddle of modern Brazil. How is it that a country that is the world's seventh largest industrial power has thrown the majority of its population in a state of abject poverty?

## Children of Slaves

Alaide de Lourdes, who left Bahia to come to São Paulo, lives in a favela in the hollow of a moist valley, in one of a number of shantytowns in the capital. Her shelter is a cardboard and crate wood box, and as you enter through the tiny yard you can see her clothes hanging. Alaide nonetheless flashes a toothless smile, her skin black and wrinkled, as she stands, prematurely aged, full of cheer. She feels that hers is a good favela as it is near her place of work, has an electric bulb, and is near where she can get water from a tap that serves five to six hundred people. An inferior favela would not offer all these amenities and could be at least a two- to three-hour bus journey away from the city. What could be worse than living in a favela? staying in *corticos*, the slums, the name given by the inhabitants of São Paulo to the crumbling apartments in the heart of the town, abandoned by their old owners. They are let out by intermediaries, one family being allotted one room. Comparison favors the favela. Alaide's five children can at least splash about in the mud and run down the alley.

Alaide built her own shack with material she found on construction sites and footpaths. Favelas mushroom anywhere there is an empty space in the city and sometimes even spring up on footpaths. They come up side by side with the business and stylish quarters of the city, offering a perfect contrast: extreme luxury on the one hand and total deprivation on the other. No statistics are available, but it is certain that six of the twelve million inhabitants of São Paulo live in surroundings that the municipal authorities deem precarious. As the favela population remains more or less stable, these temporary constructions acquire permanence. Alaide has been living in a favela for more than fourteen years. As time goes by, the municipal authorities, giving in to the pressure of favela dwellers' organizations, local politicians, or priests, grant water and electricity connections. Little by little, wood is replaced by bricks and the favela becomes a village, though the poverty and unhygienic conditions persist. The favela is not a temporary place for Alaide, a transit camp from which she will eventually move out; this is her lot for good.

In most big cities of the world, for most people, jostled by the pace of industrialization, the future assumes the shape of an apartment in a multistoried building. Not so in Brazil. Here, public money allocated to social housing is invested in buildings intended only for those who are well-off. In Brazil, a country "on the move," Alaide de Lourdes, cleaning lady for the same company for years, earns the equivalent of one hundred dollars a month. She has the right to work but not to decent accommodation.

I know that slums exist the world over, that poverty exists in several forms, and that Alaide de Lourdes is relatively much better off, given the scale of human misery. She has a roof over her head, electricity, and a regular wage. The same contrast of affluence and poverty can be seen elsewhere and is one of the basic characteristics of the Third World. Nevertheless, I have never been so infuriated at the inequity of this perverse system as I was in São Paulo. Because what Alaide de Lourdes is being denied, in what to my mind seems a deliberate manner, is the right to enter the new Brazilian society and become a full-fledged citizen of São Paulo. What is even worse, her children have also been denied this right.

It goes without saying that the adults of the favela are illiterate. But their numerous offspring also go unlettered and are likely to remain that way. The favela has only two schools, a nursery school and a primary school, for more than five thousand children. Fatima, the sole teacher, had to move heaven and earth to get the municipal authorities to allow her to teach in the favela where she was born, rather than go and teach in a town school. She was compelled to break all kinds of rules to divide the children in two groups, each with a different timetable, so that she can teach eighty students at a time. Each child can spend only three hours in school, the stipulated minimum time for school children in Brazil. Despite the ensuing darkness and the heat, Fatima is forced to close the wooden shutters of the only window in the room while she teaches because the school is besieged on all sides by those—and there are hundreds of them—she had refused admission to. With her pittance of a salary—eight hundred curzados (half of what Alaide de Lourdes earns)—teaching for Fatima is more than anything else a labor of love. Her only support is the Catholic church, which has provided her with furniture and books. Of these eighty children who can read and write, only four or five will continue their studies beyond the favela. Parents are discouraged by the long bus journey and the high cost of secondary education, which they will have to bear. Thus the favela population, engulfed in ignorance and eternally dependent, lives like immigrants in their own country.

Perhaps their only fault is that their skin is not sufficiently white. You only have to visit the favelas to realize that all the inhabitants are either black or coloured, never white. Could it be that social inequality is just the reflection of racial discrimination?

## Race or Class?

Jorge Amado asks me, "Do you really think I am 100 percent white?"

Taken by surprise, I look at him more closely. One of the most famous Brazilian writers, Amado has become a national institution. His books sell like hotcakes, and those Brazilians who have not read them watch them in serial form on television. In Salvador de Bahia, the city of his birth, an avenue has been named after him, a monument has been constructed in his honor, and his villa has become a tourist spot. Everyone recognizes him and he is on first name terms with just about everyone (ironically the man whose work derives its inspiration from the Bahia life has to take refuge in Paris for four months of the year so that he may write in peace).

After careful scrutiny, Jorge Amado seems 100 percent white. My mistake! His heavy, handsome face, his ironic gaze are the result of his Indian blood, seasoned with a few drops of black blood. "No one in Brazil is fully white, no one is fully black. Just look at a Brazilian woman walk on the street and you'll know how much we owe Africa!" he says.

From the time of its origin, Brazil has been a melting pot of races. If one were to believe Gilberto Freyre, the founder of Brazilian sociology, the first Portuguese settlers (who had more than a strain of Moorish blood), seized by sexual frenzy, jumped on any woman they could lay their hands on. All this gave rise to a gradation of infinite colors. Aesthetically, women of a mixture of Japanese and mulatto blood (mulattos being a cross between blacks and Indians) are adjudged the best. Such cross-breeding constitutes the basis of Brazilian cordiality,[3] the much-vaunted hugging and kissing, effusiveness, generous sprinkling of terms of endearment in the most ordinary conversations, and calling everyone by first names in both public and private life. Employees call their bosses by their first names, and candidates carry out election campaigns using only their first names. The ideological school of thought founded by the dictator Getulio Vargas goes by the name of Getulism, not Varguism.

Even if we accept both the mixed blood and the cordiality hypothesis, one still does not understand why the rich are whiter than the poor and why the governed are more colored than those who govern. How can one fail to notice that this supposed absence of discrimination does not hold up in the reality of Brazilian society. The president and his ministers are white, the industrialists are white; the lawyers, the journalists, the politicians are white! But the poor of the favelas are black and the peasants are colored, with few exceptions. Is Brazilian society really a melting pot, is the Brazilian really cordial? Or is it just a case of so many myths to justify the pre-eminence of the whites over all other races? If such had been the case, why all this talk of the capacity of a multiracial society to raise itself to the rank of an industrial power? Brazil ought to have gone all out to prove the economic superiority of the whites, of white imperialism. Conversely, if Brazil is what it pretends to be, a heterogeneous multiracial society that has no parallel in the world, this would prove that whites do not have any kind of monopoly over modernization. Trying to determine the nature of Brazil boils down to a general question of race and development. If whites are modern just by virtue of being white, everybody else's fate is sealed. The answer to the Brazilian enigma should hold good for the whole world.

Amado's theory is that racial prejudice is unknown in popular culture but that the elites in power use cordiality to establish their power and forestall social dissent. Amado adds that race is not the natural cause of underdevelopment and poverty, that it cannot explain why some can and others cannot enter modern society, and that it is not responsible for economic backwardness, but is at best a superficial reason. According to him, segregation has nothing to do with race but is class related. The blacks are not poor because they are black but because they are descendants of slaves, and slavery was abolished only toward the end of the nineteenth century. Their children and grandchildren are still prisoners of cultural and family schemes and of educational backwardness that stems from their social origins, not through any fault of their race. A Brazilian black is not poor because he is black but because he is the son of a slave. Besides, in Brazil, a black who succeeds becomes white! Amado relates that a writer from Bahia did not have any readers and put it down to the fact that he was black. But one of his novels was a roaring success. Since then he considers himself white and so do others. The famous bishop of Recife, Dom Helder Camara, also holds the class struggle to be at the root of all social injustice in Brazil.

## The Sin of Capitalism

"Aren't the favelas the very symbol of savage capitalism?," asks Bishop Dom Helder Camara. For the bishop, if blacks and mulattos are poor, it is not because of their origins but because they belong to the proletariat. Brazilian capitalism was able to create a vast industrial power in 25 years only through the exploitation of the masses; the phase Brazil is going through corresponds to a natural phase of development, similar to Europe's during the Industrial Revolution. For Dom Helder all this is amply clear; there is nothing to argue about. The bishop assures me that he is neither taking a political stand nor giving any kind of economic analysis when he says this.

Few men have been able to bring about such a deep transformation in both Brazil and the Catholic world as Dom Helder, who broke the historic links between the Latin American clergy and the conservatives. It was he who inspired the liberation theology, and another Brazilian priest of German origin, Leonardo Boff, gave it shape. Today Dom Helder has lost none of his passion or his desire for sainthood. He has been living at Recife for more than 30 years in the basement of his parish church, a small, damp dwelling with whitewashed walls and a paved floor across which cockroaches run in all directions. A hammock, a few books, a table, and a television set are all the furniture his room boasts of. A lone photograph on the wall shows the mass held in one of the favela quarters of Recife with John Paul II standing in front of a million believers. Most Brazilian priests and bishops live in the same conditions of deprivation. The evening I met him, Dom Helder, who is nearing 80, had just returned from leading a street demonstration against urban violence, held despite an equatorial downpour. He had just enough time to change his wet clothes for a magnificent, white starched cassock.

For the last 30 years, Dom Helder has been doing the rounds of the favelas to create an awareness among the people and form grass roots communities. Such prayer and action groups get together to solve the day-to-day problems of the community. But Dom Helder asks them to pressure the authorities when they are in need of what only the administration can provide: water, electricity, schools. Although the Brazilian rightist elements charge him with trying to whip up people's emotions, he says, "My words are not subversive, it is the subhuman conditions in which half the Brazilian population lives that are subversive." Dom Helder feels he has no choice but to denounce the scandalous injustice of the situation; to keep quiet would be a sin of omission, as "God did not wish to divide Brazil into two peoples." The liberation theology is not a deliberate choice of the Brazilian clergy but has, according to Dom Helder, been imposed on it by virtue of coming into contact with poverty.

It is difficult not to get carried away by the imprecations of this wonderfully inspired orator. No one can deny that half the Brazilian population refuses to see the other half. But how can one agree with him when, from talk of injustice, he swings to an oversimplified analysis cloaked in elementary socialism. The entire church of Brazil, following Dom Helder's example, seems to have moved from the divine toward the temporal and its prophecies turned into semisocialist, semi-Christian plans that have become the bywords not only for the conference of bishops but also for the workers' union and the leftist parties.

Lula, the spokesman and star of this socio-Christian vulgate, is a young, bearded, loquacious metallurgical worker who drinks endless cups of black coffee and puffs away at his brown tobacco cigarettes. Lula is called the Brazilian Walesa; he is charismatic, a word and a quality essential in Latin America! Starting out as a militant unionist, pampered by the priests and leftist intellectuals of São Paulo, he is the symbol of their hope as the chief of the workers' party and the workers' union, the Centrale d'Union des Travailleurs (CUT). After twenty years of military dictatorship, Lula has come to represent all that is positive for the establishment of an authentic Brazilian left wing with ideas of its own. Unfortunately, most of these ideas have been borrowed from the kind of European socialism that is on its last legs; just listen to Lula explaining—it sounds more like reciting—that capitalism in Latin America can only produce wealth for the bourgeoisie through the exploitation of the laboring masses, that the growth of São Paulo is nurtured by the subjugation of the proletariat, that the state is of necessity in the service of the oligarchy, that Brazil's external debt is proof of a multinational conspiracy and that its reimbursement must be submitted to popular referendum, and that the answer to rural poverty lies in the redistribution of rich owners' lands. For the church, land reform has become the instrument for the spiritual conquest of the peasantry. Situated somewhere between the peasant revolutions that haunt Latin America and a romantic brand of socialism, this is the main bone of contention and could be the principal factor of destabilization in Brazil today. In the most sensitive regions, priests incite landless laborers—the church claims there are fourteen million of them—to invade fallow lands. Such initiatives are sometimes the cause of violent clashes with landowners. The Episcopal conference, which maintains a record of all those injured and killed, avers that these martyrs proved more often than not to be union militants of CUT rather than genuine peasants.

To my mind the anticapitalism and land reform advocated by Dom Helder and Lula do not tackle the real issue: the misguided path of development Brazil has chosen to tread. When Lula proposes to raise the level of mass awareness in the first phase so as to socialize the means of production in the second phase, it is evident how such a step could put a brake to Brazil's growth but not how social justice will be furthered. The Brazilian left is mistaken in its analysis and its aims.

Brazil's exceptional growth over the last 25 years as well as its almost equally staggering inequality are in no way the result of capitalism. They are the consequences of a very specific development strategy followed by the state, a sort of state capitalism that owes precious little to the capitalists and everything to the Brazilian government.

## The Fault of the Savage State

Because development has been state directed and not in the hands of private entrepreneurs, the Brazilian growth strategy has aggravated injustice, or so says the provocative hypothesis of Robert Campos and a handful of liberal economists who find themselves quite isolated in Brazil. Since the return to democracy, however, these ideas are gaining ground.

Roberto Campos is a bit of an outsider in Brazil's political setup. With a doctorate in economics from Yale University, the current senator of Mato Grosso and former finance minister of the military government (thereby a branded rightist) is in fact a liberal of the British School, and it is difficult to place him in any partisan category. His appearance would seem totally British—reserved, dignified, flannel, pin-striped three-piece suit—were it not for an enormous gold signet ring with a flashy diamond stud mounted on top. Campos is undoubtedly Brazilian but a rare Brazilian, with incisive irony and an analytic mind.

For Roberto Campos, Alaide de Lourdes in her favela and Brasília are two faces of the same political coin; that is, an erroneous understanding of the role of the state. All public money has been invested in giant projects, whereas the government has neglected its traditional tasks. This scenario of *desenvolvimento,* development à la brézilienne, appeared in the 1930s when Brazil, isolated from the rest of the world due to the crisis, could no longer survive on its traditional exports. The international market was unsteady and Brazilian entrepreneurs scarce. The government, headed by Getulio Vargas, decided to take exclusive charge of industrialization. Thereon, Getulism became for Brazil what Peronism was for Argentina, although Vargas, for historical reasons, was more influenced by the Portuguese fascism of Salazar than that of Mussolini.

For the last 50 years, Vargas or no Vargas, all subsequent political regimes, whether civil or military, leftist or rightist, have never tried to change this basic direction. Getulism has remained the dominant economic philosophy of the Brazilian state. For the rest, ample proof of the irrelevance of partisan labels is the fact that Getulio Vargas, after having headed a fascist dictatorship between 1930 and 1945, returned to power in 1950 as a democratically elected leader with a program that had labor overtones.

Getulism is based on the postulate that the state is the instrument of development and necessarily incarnates economic progress. Desenvolvimento seemingly enjoys partisan neutrality and the merits of progressiveness. What it boils down to, however, is the handing over of all available capital to a new bourgeoisie chosen by the state: army officers, technocrats, businessmen, and politicians. The state bourgeoisie has, over the last 50 years, managed to set up a gigantic industrial complex. All that is big is good for Brazil; thus the country has the largest dams, the first nuclear power plant, the longest highway (across Amazonia), the first arms industry, and now the first computer industry in Latin America. Small industry, which finds no place in this pharaonic scheme of things, is struggling to survive as all available funds are earmarked for large-scale projects. Agriculture, not considered a factor of national strength, has also been neglected. The main social consequence of such centralized capitalistic development is the sidelining of all those workers and peasants who have nothing but their brute force to offer the job market. Three-fourths of the population are thus excluded from the growth process based on massive investment. Contrary to Marxist analysis, which explains development through the exploitation of the masses, the Brazilian masses are not exploited but simply ignored. Such unjust development allows a handful of fake entrepreneurs, who owe their existence to the state, to flourish. This system, more likely to give rise to monopolies than to create real wealth, is expensive, financed as it is by inflation and international debt. All public resources are earmarked for the state, the sole producer, and nothing is left over for housing, education, or health. Alaide de Lourdes in her favela is not so much a victim of her social origins, capitalism, or industrialization as she is of the power play of the Brazilian state. She has been completely excluded from the fruits of the development process.

As I listen to Campos in his Senate office, my eyes wander contemplatively over this bewildering capital city. Brasilía in a nutshell is what the national development ideology is all about. Constructed in just four years, inaugurated in 1960 by President Juscelino Kubitschek, nothing could be more incongruous and out of harmony with its natural environment. The architect, Oscar Niemeyer, has distributed rectangular buildings devoid of any charm or imagination according to their function—banking quarters, hotels—on either side of the central highway. No matter where one is in the city, one cannot escape the noise of the traffic. To take a walk or to stroll around in this city is about as unthinkable as finding a quiet spot or a bit of shade. Brasilía has no interesting street corners, no trees, no refuge. This architectural folly reaches its apogee in the cathedral, where the conical roofing made of glass slabs laid on concrete frames concentrates the tropical sun's rays, turning the building into an unbearable furnace so that holding mass becomes impossible. The odors of Brazilia are just as unnatural. All one can smell is car fuel made from sugar cane, which the dry, still air can never remove. The city's only significance is as a symbol of power. All streets converge toward Parliament House and the presidential palace, and only here does the architecture improve somewhat. That Brasilía has become the reference point for many Third World leaders desirous of building a capital in the wilderness tells us a lot about their megalomania.[4] Brasilía is the concrete dream of an elite—technocrats, military men, and demagogues—on a quest for national power. Brasilía and the favelas are not the two faces of capitalism but the two faces of the same misguided policies.

This development ideology is characteristic not only of Brazil but, like the dominant party or the kleptocracy, an archetype of the Third World. Development is the alibi for all political excesses; everything is allowed in its name. Brazil, like many other Third World countries, is developing at a rapid pace, but only the state, the bourgeoisie, and the bureaucracy are enjoying its fruit—the rest of the population is ignored. Another trait common to Third World countries is that development is not perceived as a better standard of living for its people but rather as the strengthening of national power, which could well explain the strange paradox of those Third World nations where wealth and poverty coexist. Brazil is both strong and poor, not due to her colonial origins, feudal

ways, class struggle, or racism. It is the product of misguided development whereby the modernization of the state comes before the improvement in living conditions. All this may be in the process of changing as
democracy finally comes to Brazil.

## ·The Autumn of the Caudillos

On November 15, 1986, Alaide de Lourdes voted for the first time in her
life. Until then, universal suffrage had never really existed, not even before the time of the military dictatorship. Only the literate population, 12
out of 80 million, had been allowed to exercise their franchise. Alaide's
adventure is not an isolated case, as within three years a democratic
storm blowing from Argentina carried in its wake almost all the authoritarian regimes in Latin America and the Caribbean Islands. The immediate cause of the autumn of the caudillos was the inability of the military
men to deal with the economic crises of the 1980s as well the disenchant-
ment of business circles with army officers who, once installed in power,
proved to be mediocre, anticapitalist managers. But Latin America has
also experienced what Natilio Botana, the Argentinian sociologist closest
to the French economist and philosopher Raymond Aron, has termed a
profound awakening of civilian society as well as a crisis of authoritarianism in all its forms: family, church, army, industry, and state. In all
the countries of the continent, the oligarchy power structures are being
questioned and gradually replaced by the growing middle classes, mod-
ernistic employers, new professionals, executives, experts, and technicians who until now have been kept at an arm's length from the political
decision-making process. The desire of these new classes to participate
finds expression in the profusion of young political parties, associative
movements, and study circles mushrooming all over Latin America.[5]

The Brazilian economist Celso Furtado, minister of culture after a
long exile in Paris, is of the view that besides restoring civil liberties—no
mean achievement in the Third World—this democratic wave will bring
about profound changes in the development strategies that his country
has followed to date. The old model—national industrialism, neglect of
agriculture, absence of public services—could only have been conceived
and made to succeed by keeping the masses at bay. People's intervention
in the economic process was bound to upset the apple cart. It is a thing of
the past, Furtado informs us, that more or less enlightened despots can
juggle with debts and inflation to finance outrageous industrial and arms
projects. Today, should you wish to get elected in Brazil or elsewhere,

you must promise schools and hospitals and sooner or later fulfill your promises. The role of the state will change and public money will be redirected so that the poorest may benefit. Democracy necessarily leads, according to Furtado, to both growth and more egalitarian forms of development.

Furtado's analysis seems wonderful in theory, but its practical results are still awaited. Three years after the process of democratization was set in motion, there is nothing, except rhetoric, to show that a change in orientation has taken place. Inflation and grand projects continue to dominate the Brazilian economic scene.[6] Perhaps democracy is too recent to be judged or perhaps it is a mere illusion. Having witnessed the electoral campaign of 1986, I came away feeling that universal suffrage does not necessarily mean that democracy is at work. To cite one of many comical situations, in the state of Bahia, Waldir,[7] one of the candidates for the post of governor—in true Brazilian tradition he used only his first name throughout his campaign—declared that he was democratic and socialist although his opponent, Josaphat, also claimed to be a democrat and a socialist. Waldir Pires, a minister in President Goulart's cabinet, had lived in exile for twenty years and seemingly belonged to the socialist left wing, whereas Josaphat Marinho was supported by the military. It is impossible, in the Brazil of today, not to be a democrat and a socialist, but in doing so you commit yourself to nothing at all.

Alaide de Lourdes certainly went to vote. One wonders, however, whether she knew whom she was voting for. Until today democracy in Brazil has done nothing more than change the access road to power. But the nature of power remains unchanged. Often the men in office are the same, and the state remains as it was, centralized and omnipresent. To all evidence, universal suffrage is not enough to democratize power. Similarly, democracy on its own is not enough to steer development for the benefit of the masses.

More than Brazil, with its very recent experience of democracy, India bears witness to this. India has been a democracy for the last 40 years, and we shall discover a line of development comparable on all fronts to that of Brazil, including the ensuing social injustice. This dual face of power and poverty, which symbolizes both Brazil and India, seems to confirm that the development strategy chosen by a government is on the whole far more decisive than the reference to socialism or capitalism or, for that matter, the nature of the political regime.

# The Second Death of Mahatma Gandhi

"THE LOVELIEST VIEW OF INDIA IS THAT FROM THE SHIP TAKING ONE back to England." Recalling this old Britishism I, with some relief, spied the tricolor emblem on the 747 that would bring me home from Bombay! From the very first hours of my stay in India, I had experienced only the desire to leave. This country envelops you, sticks to your skin, and becomes physically unbearable to us—fragile Westerners—overwhelmed by too much light, too much color, too many sounds and smells, and finally, just too many people.

It all began two months earlier, when, in front of the Kashmiri Gate, jammed into the back seat of a taxi scooter, I enumerated the obstacles that for hours had kept us from entering Old Delhi: an ox cart, a horse-drawn carriage, five handcarts, ten cycle rickshaws, a camel in harness, an ancient bus packed to the roof, scooters, puttering taxis, motorcycles of assorted vintage, a few thin but sacred cows browsing on old newspapers, and even an elephant with its mahout. Mutilated beggars—some with no limbs, lepers, somber and desiccated women, children with that penetrating stare demanding a rupee by miming the evocative gesture of the hand taking food to the mouth—took advantage of my forced immobilization. They tugged at my clothing, pinched my arms, and shamed me, but I did not give in and neither did they. We all knew that if I gave a rupee to one irresistible child, five hundred others would overwhelm the sector in a flash.

Suddenly a fight broke out. The crowds in Delhi always seemed to be on the verge of rioting whether because of their sheer numbers, the intensity of the too luminous stares clouding my judgment, or the tangible reality of the hatreds arising among the boundless variety of peoples. The army is omnipresent in the streets of Delhi, and brutal policemen with their long *lathis* contain the flood of humanity. Reading the local press, one realizes that every day, in some part of India, communal clashes take dozens of victims.

India surpasses all analysis and understanding. It has neither beginning nor end and is profoundly and infinitely diverse. It is a universe of sensation rather than comprehension. Its impenetrability is such that everything written about India in the West is nothing better than cunning autobiography. For me, India is synonymous with its music, which makes you choose between flight and immersion. It was after hearing Zakir Hussain that I decided to stay.

Hussain, round-faced, long-haired, and wild-eyed, is a celebrated tabla player. At the beginning of his concert, he announced in English and Hindi that the length of his recital would be a function of his relationship with the audience. He tuned his instruments, two drums, by massaging the skins at length with the tips of his fingers and the palm of his hand. At first I believed I was hearing set rhythms, but Hussain was improvising. I was drawn into the music and its rhythms, never-changing yet always different, and phrases, long, short, unpredictable, endlessly echoing, inseparable from the increasingly possessed look on the performer's face. A few hours later, as dawn rose over Delhi, Hussain abruptly stopped, "liberated" his audience, and vanished. During the following weeks, I could not free my mind from the rhythm of the tabla; its musical phrases bounded around in my head at all hours of the day and night.

Conversations with Indians are like this music. They take place in an apparently comprehensible language, Anglo-Indian—English overlaid with an inimitable accent and a more flowery vocabulary than the European original. In it conversation is risky and unpredictable. Intellectuals and entrepreneurs pretend to communicate, to share in our logic and partake in our investigations, but this is illusion. The Westernization of Indians, explains sociologist Ashis Nandy, is only a ruse for dominating Westerners. In reality, like the tabla player, the Indians bombard us with their formidable intellectual agility, play on their sense of superiority, and flit ceaselessly between benevolence and arrogance, excelling in all that renders verbal exchanges scintillating, labyrinthine, and prolonged. Westerners are bent on getting from point A to point B, but the Indian intellectual will lead you from A to A after a series of brilliant and sinuous detours.

But then, aren't we speaking here of the India that is accessible to us, of the elite Indians, the self-styled middle class, the urban, English-speaking minority that, by its dual culture, provides the link between India and the West? This community, estimated at about twenty million, is almost a nation in itself. The other India—some say the real India—six hundred thousand villages; thousands of castes, untouchables, and tribals; hundreds of distinct languages, is even more elusive. We are free to look, but we will understand nothing beyond the pronouncements of the middle class, the findings of anthropologists (who spend five years studying a village without arriving at any conclusions), or the musings of novelists in quest of exotic forms of misery. In that India, each of our habits—looking, questioning, shaking hands, eating, drinking—is inappropriate, or worse, a social or religious transgression. How can one understand a people who, to say yes, wag their heads from right to left wearing a faint smile and seeming, at the same time, to say no?

But how not to write about India? even if, more than any other country in this book, we are reduced to impressions, to hypotheses. Here then, if not the "real" India, is at least an impression.


# Drink Campa-Cola

Advertising in India has no equivalent anywhere and is one of its great curiosities. For instance, Coca-Cola™ is ubiquitous around the globe, from the poorest countries to even the socialist world as far as Peking, but not India. Here consumers must rely on the national substitute, Campa-Cola, whose trademark looks like Coca-Cola's, which tastes like Coca-Cola, but which is not Coca-Cola. This 100 percent Indian soft drink is a symbol of one of the Third World's most unique polities. For if India's ruling elite has an obsession, it is not economic development but national independence. Campa-Cola is symbolic of the Indian road to independence as mapped out by men like L. K. Jha.

L. K. Jha, a survivor of the vicissitudes of India's decolonization, partition, and development, lives today in a superb, white-verandaed villa left in Delhi by the worldly British. Curiously, Jha's villa, like most of these former colonial residences, has a blooming garden and impeccably trimmed lawns maintained with hand clippers by an army of gardeners but a completely unkempt interior. Jha, an elegant and frail old gentleman, belongs to the great generation of Indian high civil servants who, having ably served the British, brought to the new India an exalted conception of the state. During the 1930s, Jha studied at Oxford under

Keynes, whose economics would as greatly influence India as the West. Jha lives surrounded by souvenirs and photographs showing him with Jawaharlal Nehru and Indira and Rajiv[1] Gandhi—the elected dynasty— and with Nixon and Kissinger, when he was ambassador to the United States. In a country that abhors discontinuity, Jha remains a permanent fixture (he is Rajiv Gandhi's economic counselor as he was his mother's and grandfather's before him). He is also one of the authors of the de-regulation (free market) policy inaugurated by Rajiv.

Since independence, according to Jha, the priority has not been eco-nomic development per se but state formation, a brand-new notion for a subcontinent divided from time immemorial into a multitude of king-doms and principalities. "Reflect," Jha says, "that for over five hundred years, Indians, dominated in turn by the Moghuls, the Muslims, and the British, were no longer masters in their own home." The lack of a unify-ing state made India vulnerable to all these invasions. The behavior of the ruling class—a deep distrust of the Pakistanis and the Chinese, to-gether with an even more acute sensitiveness toward the Americans and their multinationals, perennially suspected of all manner of plots and atrocities[2]—can be entirely explained by this fierce will to unity and inde-pendence. Consequently, measuring India's success or failure in terms of income or consumption per capita is largely to miss the point. The In-dian "miracle" is not, for L. K. Jha, economic, like Korea's or Japan's; it is political. For the first time in history, the nation is gifted with a state that is Indian and that works.

# A Prussian State

This centralized state, despite some subsidiary powers that reside in the 24 states of the federation, exercises, for the first time in history, au-thority over nearly all of India's peoples. Independence, however, has had as one consequence three wars in 40 years against real or imagined threats, plus incessant struggles against internal dissension and rebellion. This is why military spending occupies a preponderant place in the na-tional budget and why the entire economy revolves around defense. At least one-quarter of public revenues are earmarked for the one-and-a-half-million-strong, well-equipped professional army. The real figure is higher, probably double, if one adds Soviet arms deliveries and manufac-tures under license. The only truly modern factories are those manufac-turing defense material with technology imported from the West. The entire economic development strategy has been built around this will to independence and national defense.

"India is a Prussian state that cannot get over being independent," remarked Barun De, an eminent Bengali academic. Thus the Indian model is largely an instrument for building national strength, not one for improving the lot of the masses. This model is not pragmatic; it was conceived by intellectuals and economists like Mahalanobis, chief of the first plans (now dead) and L. K. Jha during years of struggle preceding independence.

Even if profoundly Indian, this model is also the synthesis of multiple external influences, a sort of local syncretism of Keynes, Paul Prebich, Soviet planning, and the spirit of caste. From Keynes, and more generally from the British Labourites who supported decolonization, India borrowed the conviction that the state must be the decisive factor in economic progress. To Prebich and Gunnar Myrdal the Indians owe a pessimistic analysis of the world market and a fierce sense of autarchy. India thus disqualified itself from the world market to the benefit of the less well endowed, like Pakistan and Korea. The idea of import substitution was well received in India, especially because it supported a natural inclination toward self-reliance. As in Brazil, this preference for national industrialization led to the neglect of human resources. Education and health were supposed to spontaneously benefit from industrial development, but this was not the case. Finally, from the Soviet Union, admired by Nehru, the Indians retained central planning and a preference for the steel industry. Nehru, followed in this by a number of his Third World emulators, saw in the blast furnace the symbol of national emancipation. Indira Gandhi added food self-sufficiency to shield her country from U.S. administrations that used food as a lever to influence Indian foreign policy.[3]

Without a doubt the Indian elite was attracted to these theories because it found in them a modern, scientific mechanism for perpetuating its traditional power over the lower castes. Politicians and high officials are for the most part recruited among the Brahmans, and even when not, the leaders identify with them. This Brahmanic tradition idealizes humanism as opposed to technical activities and places the scholar-administrator at the summit of the Indian hierarchy. Brahmans do not engage in commerce—that is the province of Muslims and certain specialized castes—and do not create enterprises. The first Indian capitalists were and remain Parsis, not Hindus. It is this alliance of a socialized economy and the Brahmanic tradition that characterizes this highly complex system that has been labeled *orthodox Brahmano-Marxism.*[4]

# The Brahmano-Marxist System

India claims to be socialist but has neither nationalized the big capitalist conglomerates like Tata and Birla nor collectivized agriculture. As Nehru put it, the state "commands the heights" of the economy and the rest is private but under surveillance. The methods of this surveillance constitute the most unique character of the Indian system, with all enterprises subject to an elaborate regime of administrative permits, the licenses. The licensing system goes back to the British, when its goal was to restrict Indian industry from competing with imported British goods. It has since been refined, in principle to channel resources toward heavy industry and to ensure equilibrium between large and small enterprises as well as between regions. The license sets what one may produce, where, in what quantity, and with what technical specifications. Without a license, the Indian entrepreneur can do nothing except operate on the black market, as many do.

To complete the system of licenses, the law prohibits the larger enterprises from producing in excess of a certain quantity to leave a share of the market for the smaller industries, who then have little incentive to grow because it might jeopardize their fiscal advantage. The Indian economy is thus fragmented among millions of small businesses who have no incentive to be efficient, who are not allowed to compete with one another, and who are equally protected from foreign competition (except for contraband, which is voluminous, due to the large number of Indian immigrants in the gulf states). Everything is produced in small batches at high cost, thus depriving India of the large home market that would allow it to realize economies of scale.

The absence of competition and the country's isolation have resulted in a lack of consumer goods, and those available are of mediocre quality, technically backward, and, despite modest wage levels, higher priced than the world market. One of the most glaring examples of this shortage is the Indian automobile industry, which for 30 years has been building the same car—copied from a 1950s British Leyland model—in inadequate (and expensive) quantities. The Indian roads are also examples of obsolete technologies.

The number of licenses, or certificates of "nonobjection," that an enterprise must obtain can easily reach two hundred for a medium-scale operation. To acquire them, the candidate must submit to long and tortuous processing by the relevant bureaucrats, which can last several years even when playing on personal relationships and political connections. For the select and the bureaucrats, the granting of licenses feeds an inexhaustible reservoir of arrogance and corruption vis-à-vis the private sector.

To appreciate the flavor of this bureaucratic labyrinth, it is necessary to understand the nature of the high-level Indian official. Selected by means of difficult exams after university graduation, the Indian bureaucrat is both bright and authoritarian, eloquent and condescending, a type comparable to the British civil servant from whom a great deal has been borrowed. The Indian bureaucrat has an overblown conception of the state, is devoted to the ruling party, which has remained practically the same since independence, and evinces a thorough contempt for the private sector. Inaccessible in every sense of the term, if one tries to reach him, the stock response from the secretaries is that "he is not on his seat." The high official's office is a fortress in the generally malodorous and unhealthy administration building, and he is protected by an army of secretaries and assistants. Mail never reaches him, and if it did, he wouldn't respond; he is just as out of reach by telephone. These communication difficulties, exacerbated by the opacity of the state, reinforce the role of intermediaries with access to the corridors of power.

This stereotype of the bureaucratic pinnacle of authority is, naturally, reproduced at the lower levels. Everyone demonstrates their bit of authority by combining the greatest possible contempt for their clients with a maximum of inefficiency. In the ministries of Delhi, the principal activities of the clerks seem to be keeping clients, who are waving written introductions from their government representatives, waiting interminably, slowly copying forms over several times and being served highly sweetened milk tea by peons lower in rank than they.

One cannot help but compare this minute regulation of the economy, where each is assigned a precise role and forbidden to depart from it, with the caste system. To the hierarchy of thousands of traditional castes, the Indian government has added the administration and its clients. For the Indian people, the result, like that of the caste system, is the coexistence of power and misery.

# Between Cow-Dung and the Atom

On the road from Madras to Chingleput that leads toward the Kalpakkam nuclear power plant, one sees women in brightly colored saris collecting cow and buffalo dung in woven baskets, which they then carry to the village on their heads. There they prepare flat cakes of dung by hand

and apply them to the walls of the houses to dry. These sun-dried cakes serve as fuel for cooking and, in most of the Indian countryside, are the only source of fuel.

Surrounded by this immutable tradition, the Kalpakkam nuclear plant has become the symbol of independence for modern India's leaders, taking the place, in their hearts and minds, of the blast furnace idealized by Nehru. A power plant "100 percent Indian," insists Professor S. Rajgopal, director of the Nuclear Energy Commission. Not much on technology, I am unable to appreciate the magnitude of this achievement, but what is Indian at Kalpakkam seems to have to do with its assembly, the materials and technology having been imported from Canada and the Soviet Union. The operation of the plant is indeed 100 percent Indian, but the plant is running at only 30 percent capacity. Kalpakkam thus symbolizes the difficulty of assessing the Indian model after 40 years of implementation. Must I revel in the nuclear power plant or worry about its low output? Should I marvel that India has produced in a generation engineers competent enough that most are lured away by the United States or ask myself why they emigrate en masse? Must one admire Indian universities, which are capable of training world-class elites, or lament that three-quarters of the population remains illiterate so long after independence? Should one lift up one's gaze toward the tall chimneys of Kalpakkam or incline it toward the peasant women kneading the dung? "Nuclear science is not only for the rich; the poor need it most. India is counting on science to escape its backwardness" is the conclusion of Professor Rajgopal's long speech.

In reality, India, like Brazil, has been split in two by industrial development and for similar reasons. The quest for national strength won out over reducing poverty. Both governments deliberately chose industrial growth based on capital accumulation instead of development based on training and employment. This choice in India was openly posed and symbolized by the clash between two extraordinary individuals, Mahatma Gandhi, the man with the spinning wheel, and Nehru, the man of the blast furnace. The blast furnace triumphed, with the consequences as envisioned by Gandhi: the rich became richer and the poor, poorer.[5]

A concrete example shows how the Indian industrial model does not answer the needs of the vast and most deprived mass of the population. Let us look at the Jessop factory in Dum Dum, a suburb of Calcutta celebrated in history for the bullets made there in the nineteenth century; they were so deadly that an international convention banned their use. The munitions factory still exists, testimony to Bengal's long industrial tradition. Since independence, Dum Dum has become, under state auspices, a center of heavy industry, particularly of the Jessop Industries, the leading manufacturer of railroad materials in the country. Only in factories can one truly grasp the economic life of the country, which is often far removed from official ministerial pronouncements and theoretical models.

B. C. Mukherjee, the head of Jessop, was astonished that I had come so far to visit his mills. He dreams, like all Indian industrialists, of associating himself with Westerners, and I had a hard time persuading him that France, up to the highest levels, has no particular designs on his enterprise. But our misunderstanding opened up doors a press card would certainly have closed.

Jessop manufactures, using the slowest and most archaic methods, heavy and tough railroad cars that are well adapted to the mediocre state of the railroad network. Riveting plates is done with great sledgehammer blows amid showers of sparks. The most surprising thing, however, isn't the technological backwardness, it's the age of the workers; none are young, and the average age is close to 50 because Jessop has done no hiring in twelve years. This public enterprise generates no employment in the midst of the greatest and most underemployed labor pool in the world! Jessop thus illustrates the greatest shortcoming of Indian industry: in all of India—seven hundred million inhabitants—there are 25 million regular wage workers, sixteen million of which are in the administration and the public sector!

The primary cause of this lack of opportunity is the high level of wages (for the country) established by negotiations between the state and the unions without any consideration of their effect. These high wages combined with technological backwardness result in Jessop's products costing twice their world market equivalents. In addition, Jessop has become unmanageable due to the behavior of its only client, the Indian government. Even though there is a plan, orders are unpredictable and often canceled at the last moment, but the factory is to be ready at any moment to fill an unforeseen order. This portrait of Jessop—overstaffed, wages unrelated to productivity, technologically backward, lacking a commercial policy, high prices, inability to export, strong unionization, lack of innovation—according to B. C. Mukherjee, is true of all Indian public sector enterprises. What claim can be made on Jessop's behalf? India's capacity to manufacture its own railroad cars! This is a very poor use of Bengali labor, which for centuries has produced dedicated, conscientious, excellent artisans. Over this fiasco organized by the state reigns a brightly colored Hindu statuette, garlanded with red and white flowers and brandishing in each hand a wrench: the God of the Workers!

# 52  THE NEW WEALTH OF NATIONS

But the case against this regimented and inefficient economy is henceforth made by the government itself. The critique, begun under the regime of Indira Gandhi, has accelerated under her son. For Rajiv Gandhi, joined by L. K. Jha, the solution to India's economic backwardness must be liberal. But Rajiv Gandhi is also the symbol of a new generation; the era of the British-educated Brahman has been succeeded by that of the American-educated technocrat. L. K. Jha is reincarnated, 40 years later, in the colorful, high-tech person of Montek Singh Ahluwalia.

## Montek and the Computer

Montek Singh Ahluwalia, economic counselor to the prime minister, is for the 1980s what L. K. Jha was for the 1960s, the inventor of the new Indian model, which he calls *liberalization*. Jha studied at Oxford, but Montek is a graduate of Harvard. The two computers on his worktable announce the preference of the Rajiv generation: modernity against tradition and, needless to say, the United States against Soviet technology and the frugality of Mahatma Gandhi. As indicated by his name, Montek is a Sikh (all Sikhs have added Singh, meaning lion, to their names). He wears his long hair under a magnificent pastel pink turban, in happy harmony with the three sky-blue telephones on the console; the pink of his turban recalls the color of the sandstone and marble of this half-British, half-Moghul government building.[6] I have a hard time believing that the color of his turban was accidental.

Montek belongs to a new generation of technocrats, often from the World Bank in Washington, who, since the beginning of the 1980s, have come to power in most Third World countries. Modernist and almost always trained in the United States, these men evince an unlimited confidence in technological progress and think that they will be able to manage both state and economic development. This generation has not known the anticolonial struggle or participated in the debate on the comparative virtues of Soviet, Maoist, and Castroite models. They have demythologized American imperialism and don't see the multinationals as ogres thirsting after Third World blood. In all the corridors of power—Delhi, Rio, Buenos Aires, Singapore, Islamabad, Seoul, and Cairo—I met these self-assured, superqualified (which does not mean they will succeed) men who are generally well disposed toward the market economy and international trade. This new generation carries the hopes of the Indian middle class and symbolizes its social aspirations, its desire to consume world-class goods, and its weariness of ideological and material constraints.

Montek Singh Ahluwalia's strategy is simple: liberalization (reliance on the free market), privatization, importing foreign technology, progressive elimination of licenses, and—Reagan-like—lowering income taxes for the managerial class, for Rajiv Gandhi counts on them to "enter the twenty-first century." Montek enumerates the forces supporting him: "liberal professions, administrators, the new middle class, modern technocrats, bankers, financiers, the stock exchange, modernized Indians, expatriates desiring to invest in their native country, foreign enterprise, young scientists, and consumers!" The enemies of liberalization are "bureaucrats, unions, and corporate bosses who have a monopoly in the private or public sector." The forces of change, adds Montek, are dynamic, modern, and on the right side of history.

The nameless masses of the Indian peasantry and urban proletariat are thus remarkably absent from Montek's scenario, just as they were from Jha's. It is not clear, then, that Montek's liberal model is all that different from Jha's socialism. The difference is in style and speech, but the goal is the same: modernizing the state and the instruments of power rather than developing the country. What the Rajiv generation wants is to drink Coca-Cola, not Campa-Cola, and to speed along in powerful cars, not drag around in Ambassador's made in India. In Calcutta, in front of the Bengali house of government, there is a monument to the failure of the Indian model. A gigantic telephone, dubbed "the Dead Telephone," reads on the base, "Oh telephone, the people of India were counting on you for communication, but when we really needed you, you abandoned us!" The Rajiv generation would like to telephone New York or London, even though it is often impossible to get Bombay or Madras from Delhi.

But for Montek, the contradiction between the modernization of the state and the poverty of the masses is a false dilemma; the wealth will trickle down. This aforementioned trickle-down effect is referred to in India as *percolating*. Wealth at the top of the social ladder will bring prosperity to the poorest castes. To percolate or not to percolate? That is the question and not only for India. This free market approach, taken from the world's wealthiest societies, raises the hackles of intellectuals and high officials in Delhi who are still very much attached to Indian socialism and who have mounted a typically (for India) aggressive campaign against the Montek model.

# The Revolt of the Intelligentsia

"Rajiv has betrayed the Mahatma. Anyway, Rajiv Gandhi is not a real Indian, and 'liberalization' is only good for Americans." So goes the unequivocal judgement of Romesh Thapar, a dark-complexioned giant with a sombre look, long silver hair, bushy eyebrows, a sort of thundering Brahma buried in multiple sweaters for protection from the winter cold in his unheated offices at Connaught Place, the busiest center in New Delhi. From there he edits, with his wife Raj, *Seminar,* a dry-seeming monthly that for the last fifteen years has exercised considerable influence among the intelligentsia, the bureaucracy, and the middle class. It contains severe criticisms of liberalization, the egotism of the Indian bourgeoisie, private capitalism, and the temptations of Americanization.

For Thapar, the Rajiv generation is alien to India. It does not see, and most certainly does not want to see, the three hundred and fifty million rural poor who will number five hundred million by the year 2000. It is completely at the service of the middle class and dreams only of consuming and living like Americans. The Rajiv generation does not see that a free market economy will only exacerbate the frustration of the masses. Marginalized, the poor will be confronted by a bourgeois life-style totally alien to traditional Indian frugality. The shock will be amplified by the development of television and the proliferation of scandal-ridden tabloids filled with provocative advertising. All the prerequisites will have been met for an Iranian scenario; India no more than Iran will be able to withstand such rapid and profoundly inegalitarian changes. As in Iran, fundamentalism—a phenomenon without historical precedent in India—has arisen. Brahmans are recruiting private armies to attack the mercantile castes (the Sikhs and the Muslims) because they have surpassed their proper station in society. Thapar observes that, all over India, riots and killings between communities have become a daily occurrence. The government has been reduced to sending the army to repress any manifestation of communalism. The flag march, a military procession with a flag at its head, has become the only way to restore calm in a torn-apart India. In Punjab, according to Thapar, the army has already entered a cycle of revolt and repression, with thousands of young Sikhs beaten, tortured, and imprisoned in camps. The methods of dictatorship are eclipsing those of democracy in this harbinger of a future India threatened by fascism and theocracy.

This "antiliberal" speech by Romesh Thapar treads well-worn paths quite familiar in the East: rhetoric and pamphleteering. But he is seconded by a quite different tradition and one more typically Indian: social activism. The people Thapar works with are strangers to all apparatuses and have broken with all the classical forms of politics. They seek no mandate, and their strength lies in their isolation. Following methods evocative of Mahatma Gandhi or the Catholic priests of Brazil, they live among the poor to learn from them and to help them organize a base.

Among these exceptional beings, Inder Mohan is the most endearing and moving. He is ageless, and although he appears fragile, he can roam for hours without tiring in the slums of Old Delhi. Mohan took part in all of the national struggles, earning the precious title of *freedom fighter* in the independence movement. Son of a high official under the British, he broke with his family in the 1940s to organize labor unions in Lahore, thereby earning his first years in prison. Others would follow, many under Indira Gandhi's State of Emergency. The most decisive moment of Mohan's life as a militant was his break with the Communist Party of India in 1961 and generally with all parties and unions. Mohan believes that the political and union establishment evinces total indifference to India's poor, discovering their existence only when seeking their support and playing on the caste system and religious prejudice to get elected. Development and democracy, says Mohan, have become words devoid of meaning in India. One must start over, from the base, before religious fanaticism, the military, temptation, or the blindness of leaders win out.

Inder Mohan's method consists in mobilizing the poorest whenever the administration attacks their most basic rights: the demolition of a worn but inhabited building, the displacement of a public fountain or a school. Mohan also succeeded in organizing a union of stoneworkers, among the most miserable and exploited laborers in the capital. He has carried out many modest or symbolic gestures to advance the work and hasten the awakening of the people. For the people of India will awaken, Mohan is certain, though not in his lifetime. So says this young oldster with the quick step who, with a remarkable economy of speech and gesture, with a single word or sign, encourages, fortifies, and mobilizes those thronging his path.

# The Second Life of Mahatma Gandhi

The Gandhian model thus survives like a small flame in the imagination and works of a few. Among these neo-Gandhians, Ashis Nandy is certainly the most creative. A self-styled social psychologist, he belongs to the small caste of intellectuals rooted in a particular culture whose thought nevertheless aspires to the universal. Ashis Nandy combines in his person the best of both East and West. He is the author, among other works, of an essay ("The Intimate Enemy") on the colonization of India in which he shows that the *colonizer* was profoundly disturbed by his apparent conquest. Through the works of Rudyard Kipling, the apologist of imperialism, he shows us how the British were led to idealize values—violence, domination, white supremacy—that up to that time were alien to their culture and that shook British civilization to the core.

Ashis Nandy is also known as the director, with his colleague, Rajni Kothary, of the Center for Policy Studies, a highly critical—of the Indian model—think tank funded by the state. Not a wealthy institution, the center occupies a run-down villa in the erstwhile British quarter. As always in Delhi, only the garden is kept up; the offices are in disarray—the furniture broken and scattered, the disorder indescribable, the odors gripping. Ashis Nandy works in a dimly lit grotto stacked with books screening off the clutter surrounding him; nothing apparently disturbs the serenity of the researcher.

"The very existence of the center," observes Ashis Nandy, "is testimony to the democratic character of Indian society; India is a democracy not because we regularly vote, but because dissidents are tolerated and even funded." The level of democracy of a nation, he says, is measured by the price paid for dissidence. In India the price is very low.

Even so, this Indian democracy, which is able to fund its own adversaries, is nothing more than a degenerate shadow of what it once was, according to Ashis Nandy. The true Indian democracy, at the beginning, was an everyday democracy, deeply rooted in each village. Its traditional expression was the village *panchayat*, a committee of five men elected by the whole population, including the lower castes. Thanks to the panchayats, veritable schools of tolerance, Indian civilization was able to survive for millennia despite its unbelievable ethnic and religious diversity. De Tocqueville, Ashis informs me, saw in the panchayat an ideal type,[7] perhaps the only one for a stateless society. He planned to do a study of it comparable to *Democracy in America*, but, overwhelmed by his political duties and in pain, he never managed the trip.

Under the impact of colonization and Western ideas that have dominated India since independence, the panchayat has fallen apart. Those surviving are without resources, powerless, or corrupted by political parties. India renounced the form of democracy that was integral to it in favor of an alien concept, the election of a central government. Since independence all resources have been drained by the central state in contradiction to the diversity of Indian society:

The internal equilibrium of India is today sufficiently threatened, believes Ashis Nandy, to make the formulation of a new development model mandatory. This model must be inspired by both Gandhian austerity and Tocquevillian decentralization. He demands as a prerequisite the recognition that India has always been, and can continue to be, poor. Poverty is not underdevelopment; Indian civilization is based on frugality and the rejection of ostentation. This poverty, combined with a complex and sophisticated culture recognizable in any Indian village, is acceptable. What is not acceptable is misery, a relatively recent phenomenon in Indian history, exacerbated over the past 30 years by the centralized growth model. The role of the state should therefore no longer be to steer development but to reduce misery by allotting all of its resources to education, health, and agriculture.

A return to the panchayat[8] is also necessary to prevent the proliferation of communal violence. Instead of reacting as it does to each local demonstration in Punjab or elsewhere by centralizing and militarizing still a bit more, the Indian government should rigorously pursue the opposite track.

Renouncing the illusions of the modern Western state, as well as economic and military power, returning to village democracy, accepting poverty, and eliminating misery could constitute, according to Ashis Nandy, the outlines of a good state. This model is inscribed in Indian tradition, but its relevance is universal. The majority of Third World nations suffer from misdevelopment and are conflictual assortments of diverse peoples. Many had traditions of grass roots democracy but were destroyed by the desire to build a powerful, centralized Western-style state. The Tocqueville-Gandhian model could be an inspiration to them all.

Ashis Nandy is, of course, a utopian, but it is worth recalling the words of Friedrich von Hayek on political utopias: to paraphrase, we must always have a spare utopia on hand because when disaster strikes, utopia becomes the only viable alternative.

## The Barefoot Manager

Budhram Manji has decided to wait neither for the outcome of the debate among the intellectuals nor for the benefits of percolation. He is one of the five or six hundred million Indians who are not concerned about the great debate concerning liberalization and economic models. His own plan is to survive.

In Pilkana,[9] on this morning of February 21, 1987, Budhram rose at dawn, for 21 is his lucky number. Budhram is a rickshaw driver in Calcutta, and, like most of his fellow pullers, he is a Bihari migrant to Calcutta, having left his family behind. Each month he sends his wife and children the remittance crucial to their survival. Budhram does not eat before setting out, thereby saving a rupee.[10] Food, he believes would weaken his legs. A swig of alcohol and he is ready, bare feet and torso, wearing only a long piece of green-and-white checkered cloth wrapped around his loins and a headband to absorb perspiration. With a decisive and confident gesture—it *is* the 21st—he grabs hold of the rickshaw handles, rubbed smooth by the thousands of pullers preceding him. Trotting along the asphalt, still cool in the early dawn, Budhram embarks on the Howrah Bridge, already crowded with buses, trucks, and a multitude of pedestrians filing slowly toward the centre of Calcutta. Underneath, on the banks of the Hooghli River, cremation pyres burn, enveloping the bridge with the acrid odor of burnt flesh. Budhram has legs of steel, all muscle, and the reflexes necessary to avoid the countless obstacles barring the path of the rickshaw: cows, goats, rickety streetcars, buses, and taxis. In one hour, thinks Budhram, he will reach the best locations, a bit ahead of his competitors. By then the city will be immobilized in traffic until dark, and only the rickshaws will be able to weave a path through the back streets of Calcutta.

Budhram does not own his vehicle because he's never been able to raise the thousand rupees necessary to buy it. No bank would ever lend him such a sum, and the moneylenders want 600 percent interest. In any case, Budhram would not be able to obtain a license allowing him to legally operate. For that, he would have to reach the responsible official in the Calcutta city hall, and he has no contact with intermediaries. Anyway, he would not have the means to pay them for leaping the hurdles put up by bailiffs, orderlies, and secretaries to finally reach the greedy bureaucrat who would affix his signature to the precious document. Budhram, like the other 30,000 or so illegal pullers in Calcutta, has no option but to rent his vehicle for three rupees for half a day from a rickshaw owner. For one rupee more, when, exhausted by the day's work, he does not have the strength to recross the Howrah Bridge, Budhram can keep his vehicle for the night and sleep curled up on the moleskin seat.

Arriving at Lenin Avenue, a commercial street, Budhram pauses at a public fountain, bathes on the sidewalk, and vigorously polishes his teeth with a small piece of bamboo, which he carefully conserves. His ablutions done, he is ready to confront the workday. Suddenly he notices, about three hundred yards away, a foreigner, seemingly lost and trying to find some means of transportation. He hesitates a moment before plunging in, knowing that foreigners dislike using rickshaws. Contemplating the puller during the ride, panting and sweating, muscles straining at the limit of physical endurance, gives Westerners a bad conscience. But there being no taxi in sight and no rickshaw scooter either, Budhram moves in on his prey and flashes an irresistible smile.

I have no choice and, being rushed, give in and climb up on the high seat perched between the wheels. We head toward the Writers' Building, seat of the Bengal government. Calcutta has barely awakened, and already crowds are collecting at movie theaters enveloped in music just like in a Satyajit Ray film and papered over with gigantic posters of violent scenes in garish colours. The 21st is indeed Budhram's lucky day. I failed to bargain over the fare before the ride, and I have to pay him at least five rupees.

"We must eliminate the rickshaws; they are illegal, and they are not modern," I was told by Jyoti Basu, the chief minister of West Bengal, in his Writers' Building office. Basu's ambition is to combine all the legal rickshaw pullers into a single union and to replace the human-powered vehicles with rickshaw scooters, never mind the noise, the population, and the traffic. Calcutta cannot, nevertheless, "enter the twenty-first century" with rickshaw pullers. In 1980, Basu tried simply to ban them but in vain. Budhram and his 30,000 colleagues, along with social activists, intellectuals, students, and union organizers, resisted the move with such vehemence that the rickshaw pullers' strike won out over the "modernization imperative."

Basu belongs to the pantheon of demigods where Indian opinion places its political leaders, and he is certainly one of its most respected. He appears to be a typical London-educated bourgeois, very refined and impeccably attired in a long white tunic of Bengali linen. His ideas would seem ordinary if one was not aware that he is the only communist chief minister of an Indian state. He boasts of being the only democratically elected communist head of government in the world. His aura derives from his integrity, such a rare quality in Indian politics that it confers on him an almost supernatural prestige.

Basu's communism does not owe much to Marx; Basu is first and foremost an Indian and a Bengali. The experiences of the socialist camp hold little interest for him and seem unrelated to the particular needs of his country. Like Montek Ahluwalia and L. K. Jha, Basu is for modernization, for industrialization, and even for privatization of the public sector to improve its efficiency. He proposes no other model of development.

The conflict between Basu and Budhram the rickshaw puller, insignificant though it might seem, is a good economic lesson for the Third World, for Budhram's resistance better meets India's needs than Basu's modernization. Because Budhram's livelihood shocks us or seems archaic—and Indian elites' reactions in this regard are the same as Westerners'—we are tempted to eliminate these menial tasks. But what would become of Budhram without his rickshaw? It is the thousands of small occupations—private and unplanned, without capital investments—that constitute the informal sector by which the Budhrams of India and the Third World survive. Thanks to their resourcefulness and to the countless variety of small jobs, the people of Calcutta, poor though they might be, are not as miserable as is possible in India. By contrast, the immensity of the informal sector renders debates and economic policies, which grasp only the surface manifestations of human activity, somewhat insignificant. Like Alaide de Lourdes in Brazil, Budhram eats little and lives poorly; but he does live and has an occupation that gives him status, a place in the social structure of India. Without his rickshaw he would be reduced to the level of Calcutta's beggars, who, equipped with a steel hook, search for their sustenance among the trash discarded in the streets. Budhram is, in his own way, an entrepreneur, and if his business does not develop, if it does not provide enough to escape from poverty, the reasons are less economic than political. Budhram would need to become the owner of his rickshaw, which would presuppose that credit could be extended to the poor without intermediaries. The mayor of Calcutta would need to give him a license, which would require honest officials. An honest regime, an economy at the service of the poorest, such would be for India an *other* development, precisely that envisioned by Mahatma Gandhi.

The reader who has followed me thus far across Latin America and India will almost certainly be surprised at the emphasis on political choices rather than natural and cultural factors as the causes of poverty and injustice. This was not, at first, a deliberate intention. But in my concrete investigation of these differing nations, public institutions appeared crucial to understanding the Third World.

The risk, of course, lies in systematizing this analysis and in trying to decipher everything through a single grid. In approaching black Africa, I believed, whether prudently or in reaction to certain prejudices, that objective conditions would emerge as the basic cause of mass poverty. I certainly encountered drought, disease, colonialism, and people not motivated to change; but humankind has little power over this immutable order of things. Policies, in contrast, *are* reversible, and there again black Africa seems to be pursuing a politics of poverty. Too often, deliberately or in error, its leaders lock their people into an avoidable state of stagnation.

# The White Elephants of Yamoussoukro

BETWEEN DODOMA AND MOROGORO, THE COUNTRYSIDE IS LIKE A SCENE from *Out of Africa*,[1] yellow savannahs, high wooded mountains, skies laden with clouds drifting towards the Tanzanian coast. Only the rain can bring relief from the stickiness of the heat and the humidity. Our Land Rover travels quickly over the tarred surface that—constructed by a Brazilian firm that will probably never get paid by the Dar es Salaam government—is supposed to be the best road in Tanzania. A tall silhouette draped in a red toga suddenly appears out of the vegetal wilderness and is clearly etched against the side of the road; we have encountered a Masai. The driver automatically slows down on approaching him as we cannot but help staring at him as if he were some strange beast. No encounter in East Africa is more astonishing than a chance meeting with one of these pastoral warriors who walk across the high plateaus of Kenya and Tanzania. The man is alone. Nothing can be seen for miles and miles around. Leaning on his lance, his arms laden with heavy jewelry, his hair plaited with pearls, it's anybody's guess from where he came from and where he will go to. History avers that the toga, sandals, and lance, unique in Africa, are of Roman origin. Caesar, two thousand years before Livingstone,[2] sent a legion to locate the source of the Nile. His army never returned, and from that time onward, the Masai wore the toga and the sandals and carried the lance of the Roman soldiers. The Masai are proud of the fact that they can live without money, that they depend on no one but their herd, and that they feed exclusively on the blood of cows mixed with their milk and a bit of urine.

The Masai look at us with indifference and scorn. They are the last of the Africans, perhaps the last people in the Third World who, after coming into contact with Western civilization, pointedly refused to have any truck with it. For the Masai, European wealth does not exist.

Would the dictates of common sense allow Africa to turn its back on development? It is too late for us to speculate on Africa obeying any other destiny. We must also refrain from idealizing the Masai wisdom. Lions no longer attack their herds, and their meager lances pierce only the wind.

In Africa, the time for adventure is over. At the end of the track, in the village of Mvorero, situated I meet with the permanent delegate of the Chama Cha Mapuiduzi (CCM), which, translated from Swahili, means party of the revolution. The CCM is in charge of the state as well as the public sector. Constitutionally, even the government is subordinated to the party. The CCM has its own ideological training schools for its cadres. It is a one party system, but it certainly does not enhance the class struggle. Tanzanian leadership is also comprised of devout Christians and Muslims, both represented on an equal footing.

However far out the village, one can always find the party quarters, a mud or cement hut immediately recognizable because of the green CCM party flag flying outside with the crossed hoe and the spade. The only revolution here is agrarian.

Nothing escapes the vigilant eye of the party. In each village, in every quarter of Dar es Salaam, in every factory, and even in the army, the representatives of the CCM observe and note down everything they see and hear. In this vast country that contains twenty tribes, ethnic diversity is deliberately used to strengthen social control. Party representatives are systematically posted to tribal zones different from their own. At Mvorero, in the Lugurus region, the CCM's representative comes from Zanaki. Thus all comings and goings, all visits from outsiders, are immediately observed and noted in a book maintained by the representative and included in a report specially drawn up for the party office. The only thing likely to limit the scope of such an inquisition is the oft-encountered scarcity of pencils and papers.

The meticulously devised CCM system, unique in Africa, was the brainchild of Julius Nyerere, founder of the nation and still party chairman after being at the helm of Tanzania's affairs for the past twenty years. Since decolonization, no other country has enjoyed so much admiration as Tanzania in Third World circles and no other leader is as respected as Nyerere, nicknamed "Mwalimu," the teacher. Tanzania is considered a model of African socialism par excellence, a reference that is a must in the history of development. Not many, however, are willing to look at it firsthand; Tanzania is very far and terribly uncomfortable.

## African Socialism

Unless one is an experienced ethnologist, nothing looks more like a Bantu village than another Bantu village. The habitat and clothes are remarkably uniform, with little concern for aesthetics. Deprivation in this part of Africa seems complete. The peasants of Mvorero count a hoe and a spade as their sole possessions. Even the land they cultivate is not their own. The dusty village of Mvorero, its mud huts basking in the shade of palm trees, its yam plantations, its mango and cashew trees, seems to belong to an era long gone by. But fifteen years ago, Mvorero did not even exist. It was established as an artificial creation of the Nyerere regime that goes under the name of the *Ujamaa* village.

In Swahili *Ujamaa* means both family solidarity and socialism. It combines aspects of African culture, progressive Catholicism dispensed by missionaries in Africa, and the British Labour party's brand of socialism. Nyerere explains that the new Tanzania should be an extension of the village community to the national level. The Tanzanian people were asked to rise spontaneously to the call, even though collective enthusiasm was somewhat lacking in response to the Arusha declaration, which in 1967 launched Tanzanian socialism. Ujamaa, however, far from being firmly rooted in African tradition, was an artificial construction that could but lead to one thing: after the rhetoric, the constraints. Mwalimu forced his people to *manu militari*, to group together, ten years before the Ethiopian government did likewise. Between 1974 and 1976 more than ten million peasants were chased out of their huts, which were then burned down to eliminate any possibility of return, and regrouped into eight thousand villages. Very few instances of violence were reported. Only the nomad breeders resisted, the rest of the population passively accepted this program of rural resettlement. The Bantus are peaceful by nature and do not have an acute sense of property. The entire international community applauded this new initiative of Mwalimu, considering it progressive, especially after Nyerere explained how the resettling would enable each and every Tanzanian to get primary education, running water, and health care.

Ten years after the restructuring of villages, what remains of Mvorero in terms of the expectations it gave rise to and given the fact that this is a model village, far better equipped than the average?

It is true that children go to school, first and foremost to learn Swahili (Tanzania is the only African country to have imposed an authentic national language). The dispensary also exists, with a barefoot doctor and a nurse full of goodwill who is very generous in handing out advice on health care but has little time to nurse patients; besides, she has hardly any medicine. Water does come to the village, thanks to pumps donated by Holland. Most equipment in Tanzania has been acquired through European aid, generally from Scandinavian countries.

These handful of amenities, so hard to come by in Africa, cannot, however, hide the tragedy of Mvorero. The village has undergone a slow process of impoverishment over the last ten years, proving that the Tanzanian model—a model in the classical mold, found in several African countries, consisting of confiscating agricultural surplus to build a strong central state and uplift the urban population—is crumbling. The government, thinking that it had improved the financial returns of agriculture, had in fact broken the traditional commercial circuits, thus forcing the peasants to sell their produce to the village committees (the party). In the name of efficiency and morality, the creation of public monopoly enabled Nyerere to destroy Indian and Arab traders as well as those of rival tribes. The difference between the purchasing price in the villages and the price on the international market was to have financed public and party expenditures. This scheme, based on the assumption that world demand would remain constant, is patently absurd, as the market, by its very definition, is in a constant state of flux.

It also assumed that traders were dispensable, which was a costly error, as it was they who financed the sowing operations of the peasants and collected their harvests. What Nyerere seems to have overlooked is that very low prices would cause the peasant only to produce for himself, not for the external market.

Agricultural production has continued to fall since the resettlement. Collective holdings, based in the initial phase of Ujamaa on the Maoist model, have been done away with, some peasants returning spontaneously to individual production, but having neither the courage nor the force to walk back in the boiling sun to the lands they had been separated from through resettlement. Content to grow whatever they can around their huts, they confine themselves to subsistence agriculture and gradually reduce the share intended for the official circuit.[3]

On the face of it, the CCM, with its plethora of youth, women's, sports, and elders' associations to which membership is compulsory, controls Mvorero. In fact, the Tanzanian peasant is passively resisting. It is not his vote but his refusal to produce that is the true expression of his will, which has resulted in a steady fall of export crop cultivation and the problem of having to supply the cities with goods. The only way out is international aid. The Tanzanian model, which is directly responsible for this process of impoverishment, is a typical case of state-organized underdevelopment. We shall deal with the part the West had to play in this process later, but a priori African governments are first and foremost responsible for their decisions.

Julius Nyerere, willing to take only part of the blame, prefers attributing all the ills of Tanzania to imperialism.


## Arusha, Twenty Years Later

Mwalimu is an intellectual of great distinction and culture who has translated Shakespeare's *Julius Caesar* into Swahili. But let's set the record straight. Despite his reputation as the wise man of Africa, the political violence perpetrated by the Nyerere regime is no less than that of other African states. He is perhaps the only African leader to have worked toward the downfall of his colleagues. His army, one of the strongest in Africa, intervened in the Comoros Islands in 1978, in the Seychelles in 1977, and in Uganda in 1979, where it resorted to widespread plundering and massacring of the civilian population. Tanzanian troops are currently stationed in Mozambique to assist the Maputo government against the guerillas, and the country plays host to ANC training camps, the ANC being the liberation army of South Africa. Until 1979, Nyerere detained more political prisoners in his jails than the South African government had ever done. In 1986 he was to grant amnesty to some ten thousand prisoners, a figure that gives us an idea of their total strength.

Mwalimu has never gotten fewer than 99 percent of the total votes at the elections, which speaks volumes for his sense of socialist democracy. Moreover, his denunciation of Western imperialism has not stopped him from receiving more gifts from the West than any other African leader. The Scandinavian countries and Holland are particularly generous to Tanzania because Nyerere's rhetoric of a nonaligned Africa, a socialist Africa complete with austerity and idealism, is music to their ears. Nyerere is the only Tanzanian product that has been successfully sold on the international market in the course of the last twenty years, and thanks to him the country has recovered valuable hard currency. Knowing all this before meeting Mwalimu helps resist being taken in by his immense charm.

Nyerere seems perfectly reasonable. He is full of wit, and flashes of British humor add sparkle to his conversation. His marshal's baton in sculpted wood (in Africa a sign of legitimacy) is always in his hand. But seated as we are, it serves no great purpose. The meeting with Nyerere takes place on a plane at an altitude of 10,000 meters somewhere between Jidda and Dar es Salaam, as this is the only way I can get to meet him.

Nyerere, particularly inaccessible to irksome intruders, stipulates that I am not to ask him any questions, for, he explains, Westerners are either blind or malicious as soon as the issue of Africa is raised, stupidly resorting to the criteria of material appreciation without understanding that Mwalimu is forging a nation where previously only scattered tribes existed. These tribes have for centuries been the victims of Arab slave traders and German and British colonization. The creation of a Tanzanian state has, according to him, nothing to do with a nationalist frenzy but was a vital necessity for those who otherwise would have fallen under the yoke of foreign domination. Or warring tribes could have torn each other apart as happened in the neighboring countries of Uganda, Burundi, and Central Africa since their independence. Tanzania has known neither a massacre nor a civil war, and this is not because the Bantus are more peaceful than other African peoples. They would have been equally ready to slit each other's throats if the political system had not created conditions for peace. Besides, in the island of Zanzibar, before it merged with Tanganyika to form Tanzania, as soon as the British left hadn't the African population killed, in a single night, most of the Arabs? Such madness is not possible in Tanzania because there is a state and a party. The CCM has structured a new society based on the three principles of Arusha: an honest government, equality between rich and poor, and economic independence.

Mwalimu says this with a straight face, even though everyone knows that he heads one of the most corrupt administrations in Africa and that the state survives only thanks to Western aid. How then is it that such a perfect society, the Tanzanian nation, has continued getting poorer?

Nyerere's voice begins to fade, as the roaring engine makes it difficult for me to hear. I lean toward him, perhaps a bit too far, for he screams into my ear, "It's Reagan's fault, Margaret Thatcher caught him and the infection spread even to Mitterand!" What is he talking about? The free market, obviously! Tanzania is not the victim of its own socialism; it has been destroyed by our free market theories, which are constantly lowering the price of its agricultural exports.

"I'll let you into a secret," adds Mwalimu, "every morning, I listen to the BBC to find out the price of Tanzanian coffee and cocoa. The destiny of our peasants is being decided in London!"

I want to answer, but apparently the interview has gone on too long. It is rudely interrupted by Joan Wicken, Mwalimu's surly British secretary. She has not left his side since the time they were students together, some forty years ago in Scotland. It is said that Mwalimu, an ardent Catholic, discovered socialism through her. A socialism far removed from the African context and borrowing heavily from Europe.

That is where our responsibility toward Africa lies, not in the economic field, as most people would have us believe, but in the ideological one. We are not guilty of the ills that have beset Africa as Nyerere understands them. There is no proof that the world market is destroying Africa. Although appraisal of the effects of colonization would be controversial, Africa has undeniably come to depend on our values, our codes, our dominant ideas, all our "isms." We are responsible not so much for exporting ideas to Africa but for overwhelming it with the wrong kind of ideas.

Does the fate of Africa really hinge on a delicate balancing act between violent madness and impoverishment? At least one country seems to offer another way out: the Ivory Coast, perhaps the only country in Black Africa that openly proclaims its liberalist credentials. The results are somewhat better, though not totally convincing.

## Felicité Kouassi's Store

Felix and Felicité Kouassi are poor but not because they are idle, especially not Felicité! Her sixth child, whom she carries on her back, does not stop her from completing all the chores that are a Baoule woman's lot.

She has to tend the yams and the sweet potatoes, pull out weeds from the cotton fields, pound grain, cook, produce and raise a large family, and several times a day sweep the floor of the hut dirtied by the itinerant hens and goats. Felix, her husband, prefers working sporadically and only at the cotton plantation. The rest of his time he spends chatting under the village tree, whose sole function is to provide shade to those desirous of a long chat. So life goes on at Brobo in the Ivory Coast grasslands, and one gets the feeling that time has come to a standstill. Such, however, is not the case. Felix and Felicité Kouassi are among the thousands of peasants who have helped agriculture take off in the Ivory Coast.

Twenty years ago at Brobo, only wild cotton grew; today the Kouassis produce one ton of cotton a year on the one-hectare plot allotted to them by the person responsible for the allocation of land in the village. Since independence the national production of cotton has gone up one hundredfold, cocoa, fourfold; coffee production has tripled and bananas, quintupled. The Ivory Coast is the only non-oil-producing coun-try of Africa to have considerably raised its national income.

This is the outcome of a deliberately chosen strategy of agricultural development, unique in the Third World. Instead of trying to break away with the colonial past, Felix Houphouet Boigny, who has headed the na-tion since 1963, has shown a preference for European methods and used them to suit his own ends. Encouraging former colonizers to cultivate land and export crop cultivation are major national goals, which may be because Houphouet is a cocoa planter and idealizes the individual peas-ant, particularly the Baoule peasant. Forest cutting, clearing vast tracts of land, and cocoa plantations have become symbols of the Ivory Coast's newfound identity.

The government has also taken charge of yet another colonial in-stitution, the Caisse de Stabilisation, which has been functioning like a procurement agency since independence. The state thereby has com-plete monopoly over the purchase of agricultural produce, which it buys at a uniform price regardless of the region it comes from. The Caisse has thus become one of the mainstays of national integration as it unites farmers, small and big, of all ethnic groups. Even ministers are called on to become partners, and wherever manpower is scarce, the country throws open its borders to immigrant workers from West Africa. Training and specialized know-how have come to be the prerogative of the French, whose opinions on efficiency are considered the ultimate. Trade with the Lebanese and the Syrians represents continuity in what francophone Af-rica calls *la traite*. The complete absence of xenophobia and anticolonial diatribe requires a lot of political courage and tolerance, more so in the case of Africa, making this a remarkable strategy carried out by a coura-geous people.

But what have the Kouassis received as recompense for their mag-nificent efforts? In front of each Brobo hut is a turret made of dried mud covered with a detachable straw roof, the traditional African store for protecting the Baoule peasant's meager provisions from rodents and the vagaries of the weather. In it two bags of rice, three enameled metal plates from the market at Bouaké (the neighboring country town), and a grilled leg of agouti, an enormous forest rodent that the Baoules are par-ticularly partial to. That's it! Does the Kouassi family, which is relatively better off than the average, receive so meager a reward for its labor? We are told that items of consumption ought not to be the sole criteria ap-plied to measure reward for agricultural production and that we should consider the infrastructure that has been put at the Kouassis' disposal: a dispensary at Bouaké (though medication is expensive) and a hospital (though patients are required to bring their own needle and thread if they want a wound stitched). The health service effort has been, as else-where in Africa, modest. The regime can't, however, stop boasting of the share it allocated to education: 42 percent of total national budget expenditure, a world record by any standard! Unfortunately, this magic figure, which the leadership never tires of repeating, only highlights expenditure, not the fact that no tangible results have been achieved. Only one-third of the population is literate, and no more than 15 percent of the children manage to go to secondary school. There are few offspring of peasants in the seventh grade because admission is bought either through influence or corruption. Thus the Kouassi children will, in all probability, live the same materially and intellectually deprived lives as their parents.

The Kouassis are also afraid to venture out of their village for fear of being fleeced by the police. On the road from Bouaké to Abidjan, the main national highway, a plethora of customs and police officers stop travelers at will, make them get out of their cars or buses, and extract money from them before allowing them to drive off, this in a country where peace and political stability prevail, considered by all African standards as a country where things function!

Since its independence the Ivory Coast has prospered, but what about the Kouassis? What happened to their share?

## Houphouet's Folly

"The Caisse de Stabilisation's accounts are the most jealously guarded secret in the whole of the Ivory Coast" confides Professor Abdoulaye Sawadogo, who currently teaches at the University of Abidjan and who was Houphouet's minister of agriculture for more than ten years. He categorically denies any knowledge of what happened to the money for which he was supposed to be responsible. Only Houphouet knows. "But there is nothing to stop you from visiting Yamoussoukrou," he adds with a satirical gleam.

Houphouet, the "Old Man," as he is called by his people, dreamed of transforming Yamoussoukrou, his native village, into a model city without a trace of the colonial legacy, a city that would testify to the glory of the new Africa, a sort of Brasilía a l'Africaine!

No price was too high to fulfill this ambition. French construction companies were asked to tar roads across the forest without any consideration for cost. Millions were spent constructing wide avenues that lead nowhere and are lit *a giorno* (a light as bright as if it were daylight). Contrary to the initial plans and the Brasilía experience, no office shifted to Yamoussoukrou; the government had simultaneously embarked on constructing luxurious air-conditioned buildings for its countless officials in Abidjan. All that seems to remain afloat in the humid morass of the president's village are so many concrete monstrosities: the Palais des Congres, the Maison du Parti, the Hotel President, and a gigantic civil engineering institute that helped the French contractor Francois Bouygues make his fortune. Houphouet's palace measures 22 kilometers at the boundary wall, and on the banks of its artificial lakes, peasants grow fruit and vegetables. Although they do not have permission, in this absurd capital city, the only normal human behavior is that of these gardener-squatters. The Catholic basilica of Yamoussoukrou, still under construction, will have a dome twice the size of Saint Peter's in Rome. As the Ivory Coast is at present short of funds to complete the project, President Houphouet announced that he would draw on his private resources to do so. The line between his private funds and public money seems, however, to be rather thin.

Irrational projects of this kind, known in development literature parlance as *white elephants,* are scattered all over Africa. They exist in all shapes and sizes: ghost capitals,[4] senselessly large factories that have been deserted, hospitals without doctors, dams without water, airlines with neither clients nor aircraft, and overequipped armies. At least the Ivory Coast got round this temptation by entrusting its defense to France. These white elephants are of absolutely no use to the people of Africa, yet the poorest of the poor have been made to finance them. Take for example the Old Man's palace. The sweat and toil of the peasants has gone into making it and the miles of tarred road around it. National pride or the need for a national symbol are the reasons tendered for such wasteful products. Keep in mind that if such wild flights of fancy have succeeded, it has been with the assent of the industrialized nations of the world.

I must confess that before I came across this African Brasilía, I thought, like others, that the Ivory Coast could serve as a model for the rest of Africa. Much has been written in praise of Houphouet's achievements; he is the only African leader who has had the guts to openly adopt the mantle of the free market economy, and his management has yielded good results. It seemed as if history was out to prove that Houphouet, the son of the soil, the village planter, had stolen a march over Nyerere, the ideologue, and Senghor, the socialist grammarian, more a friend of Paris than of the Sahel peasants. For the visitor in a hurry, Abidjan gives the impression that all's well, with its tropical Manhattan panorama of skyscrapers against a backdrop of lush greenery and blue lagoons. But all this seems like illusion if you travel beyond the city and the Cocody beaches.

Perhaps my judgment is unduly harsh, based as it is on Western perceptions, but on a relative scale, I imagine that the Ivory Coast is an example for Africa. Nevertheless, how can one condone a political elite that systematically exploits its own peasants or leaders who colonize their own hinterlands far more ruthlessly than the foreign colonizers and with an easy conscience?

President Houphouet knew just how far he could go in exploiting his peasants. Although agricultural prices were fixed at a low level, they were not low enough to discourage the Ivory Coast peasant from working, unlike the rest of Africa. The peasant is undoubtedly fleeced but not burned alive, contrary to what is happening in neighboring socialist countries like Ghana, for example, or Mali, Burkina Faso, or Senegal.

If the Ivory Coast is considered liberal, it is so by default. True, private property has not been abolished, traders have not been thrown out, civil rights have not been brutally cast away, or the economy fallen victim to collectivization; no one could be more reasonable than the managers of the Ivory Coast economy. Yet the miracle has come to an end.

## New Deal for the Third World

The inhabitants of Abidjan call it the "situation"; elsewhere in the Third World they talk of a crisis. In a nutshell the Ivory Coast coffers are empty because raw material prices have again begun to fall. For ten years the country enjoyed the benefit of a dramatic increase in cocoa and coffee prices on the world market. An oil syndrome without oil resulted, and the government embarked on large-scale industrial and real estate ventures, accompanied by an inflated public services component and international debts, until the day supply exceeded world demand. Declining market trends were further highlighted by the fall of the dollar. The green gold of the grasslands turned to lead.

Should the international market and the Western buyers be held responsible for the ills besetting the Ivory Coast? Denis Bra Kanon, the minister of agriculture, is a good sport who confesses to having speculated on an increase by reducing the estimated production of his country. But British and American buyers were smarter, and he lost his gamble. He is nonetheless a partisan of the liberal system provided, of course, one is aware that the market is unjust, is manipulated by monopoly interests, and is more like a game of poker than the perfect adjustment mechanisms of the liberal theory. He adds that if other African leaders want to criticize the world market, they should not exclude themselves from it like Nyerere in Tanzania. That an international agreement on trade will be able to ensure perfect market regulation is an illusion in his eyes. Market and regulation do not go hand in hand. The lesson for the Ivory Coast is not to close its markets to the world but, for Bra Kanon, "to diversify our exports, process our own products and market them directly to the consumer."

Both the liberal Ivory Coast and socialist Tanzania are going through a period of crisis. But what exactly is the crisis and who does it affect?

For the Mvorero peasant and his Brobo counterpart, separated as they are by thousands of kilometres and living in countries where the regimes are diametrically opposed, who in any case subsist in conditions of deprivation, the crisis has no meaning whatsoever. If anybody is affected, it is the government: its employees, ministers, and public servants, its grandiose projects and the city dwellers who live on the crumbs of its bureaucracy. We are talking about the crisis of a system where governments, showing a total lack of moderation, have sucked the blood of the countryside. The current state of affairs hits above all at the Third World ideology that the state is the only instrument of development.

Not only have leaders of the Third World, affected by the crisis, lost the opportunity to invest in development, but their political power is also slipping out of their hands. One clear consequence of the crisis in Africa is the newfound dependence not on the old colonial powers but on the representative of the World Bank. This is the person who will be pulling the strings from now on.

The World Bank representative does not exist as an individual but belongs to a race apart, like the graduate of the French Ecole Nationale d'Administration or the British civil servant. He is of indeterminate nationality. He speaks English with a French accent or vice versa. Today in Abidjan, yesterday in India, and tomorrow in Brazil, he is constantly on the move. The role cast on him obliges him to feign modesty; all he does is "enlighten Third World governments about the options open to them" and hides behind their sovereignty. He claims to be nothing more than a consultant and banker. But how can one ignore his advice when one is fully aware that the bankrupt countries cannot be bailed out without his consent.

Our man in Abidjan today is Jean Michel Boulet, but it could very well be another. I am persuaded that his horn-rimmed spectacles and his Swiss accent are part of the armor characteristic of his predecessor that he will pass on to his successor. After having roamed around for 25 years, he can no longer distinguish between the various countries to which he has been posted, and he comes back with the conviction that it is simply a question of applying general solutions to specific problems. It is to Jean Michel Boulet and his colleagues in international technocracy that Third World governments have been turning since the 1980s, and their new economic credo is that of structural adjustment.

For Third World countries, structural adjustment implies spending less than they receive, trimming down the administration, giving public sector enterprises over to the private sector, re-establishing market economy, investing only in profitable ventures, and repaying their debts. From Abidjan to Karachi, La Paz to Cairo, all that governments talk about these days is privatization, individual initiative, competitive exports, and liberalization. The glorification of the market and the entrepreneur has replaced that of plans and industrialization. It is the Boulets of the World Bank who are behind this new U.S. liberal rhetoric. Liberal it is because it favors individual initiative against state centralization, and American it is because it idealizes the smooth functioning of the market and does not overly concern itself with nationalism and social justice. Herein lies a new revolutionary hope for those who promise a new and brighter tomorrow to the people of the Third World.

# SEVEN

# A Cigar on His Lips

ДОБРО, BIENVENIDO. THE SIGN POSTS, ONE IN RUSSIAN AND THE OTHER in Spanish, leave no room for doubt. We have arrived at Havana airport. The Mexicana Boeing winds its way between two Aeroflot Ilyushins. If you think that Marxism in Cuba is just a superficial transplant, tropicalized by local customs and temperament, then Havana is certainly not the place for you.[1] Expecting Caribbean softness, you get socialist austerity, which hits you in the eyes. Castro certainly has not Cubanized socialism the way Mao gave Marxism a Chinese flavor. This is a luxury Castro can ill-afford because he is vastly dependent on Soviet aid to the tune of four billion dollars a year, a figure that represents half the national income without taking into account the arms aid.

Cuba is a people's democracy in the sun, sadly lacking in plurality and ranking among the most orthodox of the Marxist regimes, along with Albania and Vietnam. No concession has been made to bourgeois practices, and there is no question of tolerating dissidents à la Sakharov or reopening the free market as in Moscow or Peking. The rare peasant markets that survived the 1959 revolution were done away with by Fidel Castro in 1986 during his last campaign for ideological reform. The free markets had become so dynamic that Castro banned them, fearing the emergence of a new bourgeoisie. In the ultimate analysis, this new bourgeoisie could well have served as a stepping-stone to an American military intervention, explains Regino Boiti, the famous Cuban economist. A Cuban left to his own devices is very enterprising, as the Cuban exiles in

Florida have amply proved. But, as Boiti tells me, in a socialist regime one can only grow rich through productive work, not through trade. Socialist morality, you see!

## Castromania

"It Is We Who Are Going to Build Socialism!" This slogan of the regime is plastered all over the island. The slogan's history reveals a great deal about the true nature of the regime, for what we have here is a redemptive type of socialism. In 1957, Fidel Castro was an isolated guerrilla in Sierra Maestra with his brother Raul. There are seven men and only five rifles. Raul is disheartened. Fidel spurs him on: "The hour of our victory is fast approaching!" Raul resumes his struggle until the revolution triumphs. This parable of biblical simplicity has been related to me several times, in exactly the same terms, by high-level Cuban leaders with an enthusiasm that only those who meet the *commandante* daily can profess. (In Cuba everybody is called *compañero*, but only Castro is the commandante.) Cuba is a land of revolution. You start with revolution and you carry on with revolution: the rest—especially the economy—is subject to this essential requirement.

Some in the West have graduated from a phase of romantic revolutionism toward Cuba to complete indifference to modern-day Cuban reality. Thus it is easy to be satirical about the messianic character of socialism and to discredit the Cuban model. Today, in Europe, cartoons depict Castro as a slightly comic Latin American caudillo or as a Soviet mercenary.

But neither the poverty-stricken masses of Mexico nor the left-wing Brazilian intellectuals view Cuba in the same light as we do. For them, it has become an article of faith and so it shall continue to be as long as the Latin American elite continues to practice policies of poverty and injustice. This fellow feeling for Fidel Castro is naturally magnified by anti-Americanism: the David from Havana against the Goliath from Washington.

In Latin America, Fidel Castro is still a very positive myth; Castromania has even hit Brazilian intellectuals, who have been coming in large numbers to Cuba ever since diplomatic relations were restored between the two countries. Twenty years behind Europe, the Brazilian Left is bewitched by the revolutionary purity of Havana, the clean but poor side of Cuban socialism. Frei Betto, a Dominican priest from Brazil, concluded in a series of interviews he recorded with Fidel Castro: "I am filled with the feeling of fraternal admiration for Fidel Castro and a silent prayer of praise to the Holy Father comes from within me." This eulogistic account, which Castro used to try to regain the sympathy of left-wing Christians, has proved to be a great success in Brazil. The fascination of Brazilian intellectuals for Castro's Cuban system is astonishing in that these self-same intellectuals fought for more than twenty years in their own country to restore human rights, the same rights that are being denied in Cuba. Similarly, even a child can see that the Cuban economy is in the doldrums, that the standard of living is lower in 1987 than it was in 1957, that industrial diversification has failed, that, according to the Food and Agriculture Organization of the United Nations, the number of calories available per head has fallen during the last twenty years, and that the island exports only sugar[2] and nickel, with no industry to speak of.

To the traditional problems, particularly external debt, that beset Third World countries, specifically Latin America, Cuba has added one more—the problem of socialism. In December 1986, Fidel Castro publicly acknowledged that for the first time Cuba was not in a position to honor its external debts. But these are mere trifles, as, to Castro, economic considerations are of no consequence!

"The Government and the people of Cuba," confesses Hermes Errera, the vice-minister of culture, "were at one point in time tempted into believing that economic progress could solve all their problems." This cardinal error was rectified toward the end of 1986, and "political and social work" has once again become the top national priority. The achievements put forward by the Cuban government illustrate its priorities—social equality, education, health, and culture—but it is almost impossible to visit an industrial establishment. I could not even visit a cigar factory; not a single one was open because bad weather destroyed the tobacco harvest. Generally speaking, gathering information firsthand is extremely difficult; Cuban leaders prefer lecturing in an office rather than demonstrating their achievements. Perhaps they have fallen short of their ambitious goals unless, of course, rhetoric and reality are one and the same! On this score at least Cuba does not differ from other Latin American cultures.

Conducting any kind of objective study in Cuba is impossible because of the communist tendency to oversimplification—aggravated in this country by an obsession with the U.S. threat—and an irritating tendency to divide the world in two camps: the friends of Cuba and the foes of Cuba. The former does nothing but rejoice; the latter are bourgeois reactionaries. Neutrality is forbidden in a world dominated by class struggle. To write anything other than an apologia for Cuba would mean never being able to set foot in that country again.

# Equality or Almost

Havana is a sleeping beauty. Unlike all other large tropical cities, one is neither assailed by noise nor by smell nor by enthusiastic traders. Although entertainment has been hard to come by since the triumph of the revolution, a few cinema halls screen Soviet and North Korean films; the theaters play only Brecht. What is left are the famous bodegas, bars that open on to the road and popularized in Hemingway's novels. It was at the Bodegita Del Medio that he used to drink his mojitos, and at the Bodega De La Floridita, his daiquiris. In both cases one has to be partial to rum!

Havana has practically no shops, no street merchants, no advertising, and hardly any cars. The vehicles on the road, an absolutely amazing collection of the American monsters of the 1950s—Chevrolets and Cadillacs with heavily chromed bodies—are the only tourist attraction in Cuba. Elsewhere, these cars would be museum pieces, but here they are still on the road and maintained at great cost by their private owners (their license plates are stamped *particular*). The other cars—almost all official—are *Estatals* imported from the socialist bloc. The car is the only apparent sign of discrimination in a society that appears to be extraordinarily homogeneous if one goes only by external signs of wealth.

The key to such social equality in Cuba is the *libretta*, a ration card for all basic necessities. With this card one buys freely available goods at state shops at low regulated prices. Thanks to the libretta, scarcity is equitably distributed and poverty in principle eliminated. Besides the regulated market, Cubans can buy from the parallel market, also managed by the state, but the prices are higher, goods harder to come by, and queues longer. What the official statistics do not take into account, which is true of all socialist countries, are the nonmonetary advantages that only the leaders of the regime enjoy: official accommodations, cars, domestic help, travel. But even in Cuba one has to survive, which has given rise to a third market, a prospering black market, where the dollar is exchanged at seven times the official rate.

# Even the Poor Have Teeth

According to Julio Pejaz Perez, the Cuban minister of health, the most remarkable success that Cuba has achieved since the revolution is that even the poorest manage to keep their teeth intact! This is not absurd; in contrast with the rest of the continent, the regime has succeeded in pro-

viding all its people adequate health services. The health system, however, is not seeking to solve the problems of individuals but wants to
achieve broader objectives.

Thus, during my stay in Havana in January 1987, the official daily,
*Granma*, proudly splashed in the headlines the most recent success story
of Cuban socialism. Infant mortality, which now stands at 12.7 per thousand, is a new record. Each time infant mortality goes down, a victory
bulletin is issued. In Cuba, statistics replace arguments, illustrating the
regime's obsession to measure everything, to be able to plan for everything. Figures also seem scientific and progressive; furthermore, they
cannot be verified because no one has access to Cuban figures. Quantitative analysis also allows one to skirt tricky substantive issues. Thus
when the health minister informs me that Cuba has 20,000 doctors for
ten million inhabitants, I am to rejoice over this performance, which is
ironic because after the revolution, half the medical practitioners fled the
country. Cuba has thus had to rebuild its health system on entirely new
scientific and technical lines.

The country is today covered by a network of polyclinics and every
citizen is required to avail her or himself of these facilities. Medical consultation is always free; only the medicines have to be paid for. What are
these 20,000 doctors worth, however? That they haven't studied North
American techniques has been stressed to me as a positive fact. The patients are not in a position to judge, as they cannot choose their own
doctors. When I remark that the absence of choice does not allow one to
distinguish between good and bad doctors, the minister replies that there
are no bad doctors. The selection, which, according to him, is "based on
the political motivation of the candidate as much as his technical capacity" ensures that such an eventuality will not occur.

Overwhelmed by Marxist dialectics, hypnotized by the pouring
stream of Julio Pejaz Perez's babbling, my attention begins to wander to
the immense photograph of Che Guevara, the only element of decora-
tion in this otherwise austere meeting room. Che, with an air of eternal
adolescence and an untrimmed beard, is smoking a huge cigar. Not even
forty years old, he is the messiah of this revolution and his portrait is
ubiquitous. I even saw one of his khakhi berets in the window of a museum named after him. The minister, irritated, interrupts my reverie to
assure me that even if we were to suppose that a doctor was incompetent,
which is highly improbable, the patients could always display their dis-
contentment "through the intermediary of mass organizations!"

The latest innovation, which the regime is extremely proud of, is the
family doctor. The use of the term would have us believe that bourgeois
medicine had been rediscovered, but this is not the case. At the end of a

six-year stretch at the university, the family doctor is posted to a quarter or a village and made responsible for the health of 120 households (about 600 people). Bureaucratic logic dictates that these doctors be installed in new houses—consultation room on the ground floor, accommodation on the second floor—all built in the same manner for the entire country. While they are practicing in the neighborhood, the family doctors pursue their studies in their field of specialization for three years. Not satisfied with letting their patients come to see them when they are in need, the doctors visit them on a regular basis and are required to maintain detailed records on each patient according to government instructions. I am told that blood pressure is currently the number one priority. I cannot help thinking that the doctor's continual monitoring is more a social check than a routine health call. "Can you name any other country in the world that can boast of having one doctor for 600 people?" the minister asks me, happily confusing a goal that he himself had fixed for the year 1995 with current-day reality. I was not able to meet a single one of these family doctors; they had all gone to a meeting that day!

## Health at a Price!

Bureaucratic aberrations apart, Cubans in both the city and the countryside enjoy health standards found nowhere else in Latin America. How did such a poor country achieve such results? Julio Pejaz Perez's ideological explanation is that Cuba manufactures its own medicine at prices much lower than those of multinationals that exploit the Third World! The proof is that medicines are far cheaper today than before the triumph of the revolution. Also, Cuban industry only manufactures good medicines, which are both useful and of guaranteed quality, as the owner of the factory has nothing to gain by exploiting consumers.

This argument seems rational but has no real substance. First, pharmaceutical production costs account for a small part of the total health budget. Second, the Cuban pharmaceutical industry is confined to copying some of the simplest medicines from international laboratories; the basic inputs are still imported. Thus, the saving, when compared with the international price, is negligible. The case against multinational drug companies—a favorite theme in Latin America—does not take into consideration the research and development these companies finance through profits they earn, whereas Cuban industry has come up with nothing new. The minister agreed, saying it was high time the socialist camp exploited the contradictions of capitalism! The low-price argument has no meaning. In a socialist economy, prices are fixed by the government and do not reflect production costs; the value of a product is determined by the social utility ascribed to it. Cuban drugs are thus sold at prices lower than their actual cost of production by virtue of a high price on some other product. That is why some drugs are cheap, but personal comfort pharmaceutical products such as cough syrups, considered without social utility, are expensive. Public health is a political option open to the government of even the poorest country, especially if it receives, as does Cuba, a significant chunk of foreign aid.

To fully appreciate the Cuban health model and discover whether it could be used on a large scale, one has to look back to the health system as it existed in the country before the revolution triumphed. Health standards then were far higher than those of any poor country. Beginning in 1930, Cuba joined the ranks of Western industrialized nations in terms of demography and health care, with mortality statistics comparable to those of France. (None of this, of course, takes into account the tremendous gap between rich and poor, urban and rural, blacks and whites.) But in 1959, Cuba had the third-highest per capita income in Latin America and, according to the United Nations, the best health and social security schemes.

Julio Pejaz Perez is fully conversant with these arguments and responds, "All the statistics for the period before the revolution triumphed are false!" But even if we admit that no comparison is possible, was it really necessary to force a million Cubans to go into exile, curtail individual liberty, and imprison political opponents by the thousands so that the Cuban people could have good teeth?

This is the kind of false choice in which Castro tries to bury us.

## Creating a New Human Being

In 1961, Fidel Castro launched a literacy campaign whereby each and every Cuban who knew how to read and write was to pass on his knowledge to his illiterate *compañeros*. Within a year, 727,843 Cubans—a figure thrown at me without a moment's hesitation by the director of the Institute of Teaching Sciences, Concepcion Marina Borrego—had become literate. Marina is black and somewhat of a rarity in Cuba, for despite the triumph of the revolution, blacks in responsible positions are hard to come by. There are few in government, in the central committee of the communist party, in the diplomatic corps, or in the army, even though they constitute half the population. Concepcion, who prefers being called

Conchita, avoids mentioning that Cuba in 1959 was the most educated country in Latin America, with 75 percent of the under-fourteens going to school. This educational system, did, however, give rise to a lot of inequality, with women and blacks in particular having little access to learning.

One symbol of the new "education for all" policy is setting up schools in luxurious colonial villas that were abandoned, willingly or unwillingly, by the bourgeoisie, as well as in old barracks like Moncada, which Fidel and Raul Castro tried in vain to take over in 1951. In Cuba the school is part and parcel of the class struggle, of the anti-imperialist war, and of the socialist reconstruction program. It makes no distinction between manual and intellectual work, theory and practice. The school-going child, the adolescent who goes to high school, and the university student are all considered *trabajadores* (workers). Jose Marti, a century ago, expressed the desire that schools be called workshops, and what this precursor of independence, who died in the war against the Spanish in 1895, wrote in the past is just as important as what Fidel has to say today.

On the tourist circuit for foreign visitors is the Che Guevara College, a model for secondary education and the first secondary school in the countryside. The day I went to visit, young girls and boys in blue uniforms were taking their final examinations in an atmosphere of tense discipline under a huge banner that proclaimed in red letters: "We must struggle untiringly for honesty in our studies and against cheating in examinations. Signed: Fidel Castro, 1978." Nine years after this call to loyalty, the new Cuban of school-going age does not seem to have materialized. One needs time, as the director of the institute acknowledges, to inculcate the socialist sense of personal responsibility. These children are also required to work three hours every day in the orange and lemon plantations surrounding the institute. For young Cubans who do not go to school in the countryside, the scholastic year is interrupted by a period of two months in the field, generally at the time of the sugar harvest. Both intellectual and manual work are pursued till the end of one's formal education, with training programs in factories at the university level, added to which are two hours of military practice and theory and two hours of Marxism a week. I asked some of the students about the content and the usefulness of such a discipline, and the students at Che Guevara replied in unison that they had to learn by heart and recite without error the sacred texts. After glancing through the textbooks, it is evident that Marxism has found its way in all disciplines. Economics textbooks are particularly edifying, with their illustrations of French unemployed standing in a welfare line.

As Hermes Errera explains, the aim of teaching economics in Cuba is to show young people how to live in a socialist economy. He adds that in the midst of this class struggle, it is not wise to spread the ideas of the imperialist adversary. Generally speaking, the development of critical faculties is not one of the goals of the Cuban educational system. Criticism, according to Hermes Errera, is fully encouraged by the socialist regime, but it must be made within a system whose principles are sacrosanct, which will continue as long as ideological mobilization, discipline, and selection remain characteristics of the Cuban school. The teaching staff cannot escape either. In the hall of Che Guevara High School, an individual emulation chart gives a complete picture of the entire teaching and administrative staff. Small Cuban flags next to some names represent good marks, which were distributed during the general assembly. The headmaster of the school tells me that, at his request, his own flag for January was removed because he was late for work one morning.

When Cuban children are not in school, they are invited to spend their free time working with youth organizations or in summer camps. I am told that participation is voluntary, but 95 percent of the country's children wear around their necks the red scarf of the pioneers—the boy and girl scouts of Cuban Marxism. The remaining indomitable 5 percent, according to the person in charge of the Jose Marti Holiday Camp, are Jehovah's Witnesses. The same gentleman explains that his role as a teacher consists of "instilling in the children a sense of conviction by making them learn the names of heroes, martyrs, and battles as well as the respect due to great men." The pioneer's training, he adds, should be well rounded. Once the pioneer stage has been completed, weekend voluntary work follows. The rectification campaign, although neglected over the last few years, has been reinstated whereby students work in fields, look after public buildings, and clean streets.

# The Cult of the Book

Among the many virtues the new citizen is required to develop is reading, which the regime has attempted to popularize by selling low-priced books. The impressive sales figures furnished by Cuban publishers have always fascinated visiting intellectuals. All publishing activities are looked after by a single organization—the State Institute of the Book—but there is no way to check on the figures, which in any case do not reflect the quality of the reading material. What one can do is visit the large bookshops of the Avenida Obispo in the heart of Havana, which are one of the rare spots where people can stroll about and browse through local books. It is mostly technical, medical, and mechanical textbooks useful for building a communist society that are for sale. The other shelves are cluttered with the works of Fidel Castro, biographies of Jose Marti and Soviet literature in abundance: Lenin, Marx, Gorbachev as well as second fiddles like the Complete Works of Jikov, the President of Bulgaria. The literature corner which draws the largest crowd is the least well-stocked. Could this be so because very few authors are published? Gabriel Garcia Marquez, the Nobel Prize winner, who has extolled the virtues of the regime, is the most well-read author in Cuba. His books are constantly out of stock. That leaves us with poetry. How can one forget the numerous Western and Latin American intellectuals who have waxed eloquent about poetry in Cuba! But there is not much else to read, and poets seem evidently freer—or are considered less dangerous—than novelists or essayists.

Education, medicine, and books do not have the same meaning in Cuba that they do in the Western world. Thus statistical comparisons between Cuba before and after the triumph of the revolution or between Cuba and its neighbors in the Caribbean region do not have much meaning. Our understanding of the terms *health services, schools,* and *culture* is not the same.

This leads me to a general observation on the human factor in development. It is a too-well-received notion in the Third World that investment in education and health will be catalytic to growth, but the Cuban experiment leads me to the conclusion that what counts is the content of education and the system of production it gives rise to. The contrast is striking in Cuba between the diligent, hardworking schoolchildren, individually motivated by examinations, and the bureaucratic future for which they are intended. In the office, the factory, and the farm, socialist inefficiency adds to tropical nonchalance, individual motivation has disappeared, and for the moment nothing has replaced it!

## Exporting the Revolution

The school, the health services, and the books are intended not only for home consumption but also as show pieces for the rest of the world. These achievements are part of a carefully chosen strategy and seem to find favor in the eyes of the West as well as with the Third World elite. Cuba's special role in the socialist camp, which amply justifies the massive Soviet aid it receives, is to export revolution.

We know about the intervention of the Cuban army in Africa, especially in Angola, but we know less about the conditions in which Cuban guerrillas operate in Latin America, particularly in the north of Chile. Cuba also engages in subtle revolutionary combats through the education it offers African youth. South of Havana, in the Isle of Youth—previously Pinewood Island, where Fidel Castro was imprisoned from 1951 to 1956—30,000 African children are recruited from the homelands at the age of eight, to be trained in Cuban schools. Most will return after six years of study. The best will go on to study at the University of Havana and become the executives of progressive Africa, particularly in countries like Benin, Burkina Faso, Mali, Congo, and Guinea-Bissau. Teaching is, for the most part, conducted in the language of the expatriates, but the students are indoctrinated in Spanish by Cuban professors in scientific subjects and Marxism. As is the case of schools on the large island, theory is linked to practice—African children also help out with the grapefruit harvest. This massive education camp for the Cuban state constitutes, even with Soviet aid, a considerable drain on its financial resources.

It is difficult to appreciate the revolutionary efficiency of the system. Optimists believe that some of these children, who have been stolen from their families and exiled for six to eight years, will return home full of hatred for Cuba and Marxism. The pessimists, however, fear that these future elites will return to Africa fully indoctrinated with the Marxist vulgate and be slaves to their intellectual ties with Cuban leaders.

This is what is most astonishing about Cuba. How did reasonably intelligent, educated men and women allow themselves to be drawn into this revolutionary dialectic? To this question, which I asked frankly, I have only received a partial answer, always the same: a revolutionary people can only be led by revolutionary leaders. But the people, even if they have not chosen the path of exile, seem much less revolutionary than the elite. If the Cubans were truly revolutionaries, it would not be necessary to keep them under tight control to educate them, to give them health care, to recruit them for committees for the defense of the revolution, or to serve two years of compulsory social service, followed by three years of military service. The Cuban people have even forged a new, untranslatable word—*Teque*—to describe their rejection of the political system. Teque is the refuge of the citizen. His manner of not looking at posters which scream at him all the time "The Motherland or Death," "The Solitary Star of Our National Flag Enlightens the World," "It is Now that We Are Going to Build Socialism," and so on. Teque is escaping from a conversation when it assumes partisan overtones. Teque denotes the paradoxical depoliticization of a supposedly revolutionary people.

Thus the behavior of the elite, not that of the people, baffles me. Can it be explained by conviction, corruption, historical insouciance, social conformism, or a thirst for power? The explanation is perhaps religious. The Communist Party of Cuba seems to be the clergy of a new conquering theocracy and Marxism for Latin America what Muslim fundamentalism has become for the Middle East. In the Third World, shaken as it has been by the West and destabilized by modernization, totalitarian ideologies are invading the space left by the crumbling traditional civilization. Herein lies the attraction of the Cuban model.

The other model is the Chinese one, which still claims to provide universal solutions to the problems of poverty and injustice.

# EIGHT

# The Half-Open Cage

AT SIX O'CLOCK IN THE MORNING BEIJING IS THE MOST PEACEFUL CITY IN the world, still close to its rural origins. Its configuration in a series of squares is a replica of the old checked pattern of fields, and the roads which previously linked one watering place to another have become lanes, or *hutongs*. Some hutongs follow picturesque paths with quaint names. The Ear Hole Hutong is tiny. Soyabean Hutong is a winding street. Turnip Hutong is swollen in the middle and narrows down at the ends. The hutongs have survived dynasties and tempests. Even the Cultural Revolution, which started a great names game, had little or no impact. Only a few streets here and there—Emancipation of the Peasants Hutong, Wisdom of the Masses Hutong—are signs of those feverish years. But the spade and bulldozer, so active in Beijing, will sooner or later get the better of them. May the names remain even if they just mark the entry into a fifteen-story building or the entrance of a metro station.[1]

At six o'clock in the morning the peasants that live on the outskirts of Beijing enter the city, pushing and pulling handcarts filled with an infinite variety of vegetables to the markets of the capital. The biggest one is situated alongside the Temple of Heaven, where the inhabitants of Beijing come to practice ta'i chi chuan, a form of slow-motion gymnastics whose controlled movements require mastery over breath and gestures that will re-establish harmony between the body, the soul, and the universe.

Liu Guogang insisted on accompanying me to this market to prepare me for the shock of reform. I can't believe my eyes! Prices of vegetables on the streets of Beijing are no longer controlled! Liu, an economist of the Social Sciences Academy announced the good news and provided me with concrete evidence: an open air market that could exist anywhere in the world. Having known China before and after reform, the change is unbelievable. Life, which seemed to stand still under Mao, has started moving once again. Instead of the loudspeakers belching out slogans and patriotic marches, one now hears the animation of trade circles, the new background music of Beijing. The whole city seems to have awakened from a long period of torpor. Business is basically in food products, but clothes, shoes, handicrafts, peasant-made furniture, woven wicker, bamboo in all its forms, and roots of rare flowers, which the Chinese adore, are also being bought and sold, as well as several other items of curiosity, including a ready-to-cook tortoise, jujubes, longevity roots, and horse-shoe scales, which when macerated in water, are an excellent fertilizer for potted flowers. The city dwellers feel each fruit, sniff at each fish, confer, and discuss. The market with furious bargaining, the market as a place, and the market as an economic system merge together here, just as markets did in Europe at the dawn of the Industrial Revolution. For the Chinese, who for 30 years have dealt with scarcity at fixed prices at the state shops, being able to find fresh produce on the streets of Beijing and being able to bargain to buy it is a new revolution; it is said that the old people find it difficult to break their habits. Such is the mystique of China for the Western observer that everything takes on a magnificent hue, even the most ordinary occurrences. Thus we must keep our critical faculties intact and not overestimate the degree of change. The China of 1987 is on the move, but it is also just as unchangeable.

## Prisoners of Mao

Above the gate of the Forbidden City, a portrait of Mao, regularly re-painted, contemplates his own tomb. In Tienanmen Square children fly kites shaped like butterflies and dragonflies. Under the willow trees planted along the side of the red walls of the Imperial Palace, shy young couples sit for hours on end without so much as touching hands. The Beijing crowds are still blue, especially in winter, when they don heavy quilted coats and caps or fur bonnets that cover their ears. Ringing the bells on their heavy black bicycles, thousands cut a tortuous path through the various traffic jams caused by undisciplined pedestrians. Women, no different from the time of the Ming dynasty, cover their face with muslin veils to protect their faces from the dust-laden north wind. Mothers stroll with children in bamboo prams or ride them in small wooden sidecars fixed to their bicycles. Long black limousines, which look more like hearses and are made in China under the brand name Red Flag, at a snail's pace transfer officials behind drawn curtains. A few peasants use head straps to pull huge carts laden with cabbage that they unload in big heaps on the pavement. Sometimes the vegetables get mixed with the coal that is piled up on the narrow lanes. Just as in the time of the Manchu empire, potted flowers and dwarf trees at the windows of the low gray-painted houses present a striking contrast to the deprivation of the over-inhabited dwellings. The Chinese civilization, known for its delicacy and frugality, always seeks protection behind the small things.

I have been going to China every year since 1976, and I always come away with the feeling that the country is not changing as fast as the West imagines it is. Since Mao's death, Sinologists explain to us, the country has opened its doors to capitalism. However, the reaction to the student demonstrations of 1986 and 1989 was enough to cause these same Sinologists to explain that China was veering back toward communist orthodoxy.

My guess is that the Central Committee of the Chinese Communist Party has since 1979 put the country on the slow and narrow path of what it calls *gai ge,* a term that could be translated as evolution or rectification, terms more modest and cautious than reform. Reform was never intended to take China off the path of socialism. On the contrary, the country aims to make socialism work.

I also think that reform, since its inception, has not been linked to the relationship of force existing within the party and that the reformers depend, above all, on public opinion. Public opinion exists though not in the same channels as in the West, and prevents the conservative elements from taking the country backward. Finally, the new campaign against bourgeois liberalism, initiated in January 1987 and accelerated after the Tiananmen Square events in June 1989, does not imply that reform is being abandoned, but, to my mind, reinforces it by making a clear-cut distinction between economics and politics. Economic innovations are not bourgeois as long as they are not detrimental to the political authority of the communist party. Reform should be strong enough to outlive the current Chinese leaders and be imposed on their successors. It is, for all time to come, the new Chinese way.

After being held prisoners by Mao, the Chinese have not become free overnight under Deng Xiaoping. The Chinese people are like the nightingales that the old gentlemen in Beijing take about in round cages hooked onto their fingers. The cages are darkened by velvet covers that the owners remove when they want the birds to sing. Deng Xiaoping has raised the velvet curtain, and the nightingales are singing.

## Yan Hansheng, A Model Peasant

I met Yan Hansheng for the first time in 1976, when he belonged to the Red Orient Brigade in the People's Commune of Tuanjie in Sichuan Province. Gathering rice to the beat of the revolutionary tunes that the loudspeakers blared in the midst of the collective fields, his day was divided between the rice field and the Party school of Tuanjie. Yan spent all his free time listening to discourses on Mao Tse-tung's thoughts by students from the neighboring University of Chengdu, and the maxims of the Great Helmsman could also be heard continuously from loudspeakers in the village. The only source of entertainment for Yan, a model member of the brigade, was when he was designated to show foreign visitors how a communist peasant lived, which is how I got to know him.

His tumbledown cottage was poor but clean. The whitewashed wall was decorated with large portraits of Mao, Marx, and Engels and some red flags Yan had received as a reward for his excellent collective spirit. Every morning before going to the rice field, Yan prostrated himself quickly in front of these posters. His work was remunerated by "points," or coupons, distributed by the chief of the brigade. These points could be used only in the people's commune cooperative, where supplies and stocks were quite scarce. The entire brigade's rice crop was sold to the state shop, but Yan never had to bother about his food; like everyone else, he took his meals at the cooperative canteen. His wife supplemented this with some turnips planted on a narrow stretch of land that ran along the front of their cottage. This kind of private cultivation, although tolerated, was not viewed favorably. When Yan Hansheng raised a brood of ducks, he was branded a capitalist by the chief of the brigade and the ducklings were killed.

Yan's rhetoric of 1976 and his violent tirades against the consumer society were most interesting to Western visitors. Yan and his wife owned only a watch and a radio, enough to make them happy, he told us with pride. China at that time, preoccupied with making the new citizen, refused to lose itself in materialist debauchery.

I was happy to meet Yan Hansheng again, eleven years later, in May 1987 in the same village of Tuanjie. His face is still unwrinkled and just as before, on hot days he rolls up his trousers and pulls his shirt up to his armpits. He now belongs to the community of mature peasants and smokes a pipe with a long copper tube, in the bowl of which he places a few leaves of rolled tobacco. His family has become larger: his mother, now a widow, has joined him, and he has a daughter. He would have liked a son, but a second child would have meant a fine of something like two thousand yuan and the loss of his ration tickets. Because he would also have been the target of public criticism from the village organization, Yan decided there was no point. Mao has disappeared from the walls of the room and been replaced by calenders and advertisements. The room is furnished, which was not the case previously, with bamboo chairs, an enamel spittoon, and a moleskin sofa, the ultimate in luxury for a Chinese family. On a low table are some old framed photographs, which seem to indicate, in a discreet way, that the cult of the ancestors has been revived.

The novelty, however, is at the level of rhetoric; Yan still remains a model peasant—but a 1987 model. The situation has not changed, and a real conversation is just about impossible. Yan dodges my questions, recites his official bits, and gives stereotyped answers except when I manage to take him by surprise. If he has problems remembering or fumbles, the head of the village, who is present at our meeting, quickly steers us back on course. Yan informs us that he is no longer a salaried wage-earner of the people's commune as there is no longer a brigade or a people's commune. All the lands, as well as small tools, were redistributed in Tuanjie in 1982 on the basis of 1.2 mous (one mou is about one-fifteenth of a hectare) per adult living in the household, plus a half share for the first child. Nothing is given to the subsequent children. Yan has received 3 mous of rice field, which is an irrigated area of about two thousand square meters demarcated by a raised earth boundary. Moreover, Yan's rice field is not all in one piece, as redistribution, to be equitable, took into account the quality of soil, breaking up each plot still further.[2]

At Tuanjie land distribution did not give rise to any quarrels, but this is far from the norm. Village chiefs in charge of reform often kept the best plots for themselves. However, if the reform came about relatively easily in Tuanjie and if subdividing rice fields there was not difficult, the large state farms under wheat cultivation made distribution almost impossible and perpetuated the old regime of collective farming. Tuanjie is thus a pilot commune; the reform is still in its experimental stages and far from complete.

# Freedom Under Surveillance

The new Chinese model cannot be called liberal, but rather a technical restructuring of the system so as to allow agrarian socialism to work. Yan Hansheng does not own the field he works on; it continues to belong to the state. He is only required to cultivate the land for a period fixed at 50 years. If the contract is adhered to and assuming no new political changes occur, the Chinese peasant can hand down to his successors his right to cultivate. But this right is relative because Yan Hansheng is not free to exercise it as he wishes. The village organization assigns the nature of the crop and the minimum quantity that he is to produce and deliver to the state shop. This local organization is merely applying the directive of the Planning Commission of the Province of Sichuan. For Yan Hansheng, the quota in 1986 was three hundred kilos of paddy at a price of 40 fens a kilo. In every region of China the fixed quota takes into account local traditions, whether for cabbages, wheat, apples, or ducks.

The exact nature of this arrangement is not always clear. Yan Hansheng is of the view that he is obliged to hand over a certain part, but the village chief calls it a contract and adds that, like all peasants, Yan Hansheng will take time to catch up with reform, unless, of course, official rhetoric changes. It is difficult to find out to what extent the contract is fulfilled. The village chief informs me that there is 100 percent compliance. Ten years ago I would have undoubtedly been told that the target had been surpassed because of the enthusiasm of the masses!

When all is said and done, the efficient execution of plan objectives is based on a series of disincentives and incentives that have been imposed on Yan Hansheng. If he delivers his quota the village organization will give him a bonus of ten fens per kilo over and above the price paid by the state shop. The village organization could also reward his diligence by making an advance payment, selling him tools at low prices, or giving him chemical fertilizers and high-yielding varieties of seeds. These advantages disappear if Yan Hansheng does not adhere to plan targets. Thanks to this complex system of incentives and disincentives, the authorities of Sichuan manage to feed the cities and build up sizable rice reserves, enabling China to reach agricultural self-sufficiency.

From the old popular commune to the new contractual system, the Chinese peasant has not moved from collectivism to freedom but from collective constraints to individual constraints accompanied by economic incentives. The manner in which reform has been applied is proof of this. The peasants are called on to prove their efficiency in the new system in the same authoritarian manner and in the same stilted jargon that condemned them to collectivization under the old regime.

But in this socialist cage the government has opened the door halfway, allowing the more dynamic peasants to move beyond the compulsory quota delivery to selling the surplus on the open market. Yan Hansheng, like all the other enterprising Chinese peasants, can also diversify his production to crops that are more remunerative. In May, he will grow oranges, Sichuan oranges being famous all over China. He transports his personal harvest, twelve kilos of oranges, by bus to Chengdu, about twenty kilometers from his village. There, after having sat the whole day on his haunches on a city footpath with his portable scales, he will get the best price. The city dwellers find the prices, one yuan a half kilo, high, but it's the only way they can get good oranges. The state shop, when it has oranges, does sell them cheaper, but they are not fresh. It has been a good day for Yan Hansheng; after much bargaining with the city dwellers, he has made about 80 yuan, one week's wages of a factory worker. Yan Hansheng returns home that night on foot, having bought for 1 yuan plastic shoes for his daughter from a state shop. Consumer goods, so despised at the time of the people's commune, have now become second nature. Yan Hansheng is still very careful about spending, especially since the campaign against bourgeois liberalism. He doesn't want to excite the jealousy, what the Chinese call the "red eyes illness," of his less enterprising neighbours.

## The Enterprising Chinese

The story of Yan Hansheng teaches us that there is no food shortage that the liberalization of agriculture cannot overcome. Fruit, vegetables, spices, and meat suddenly appear on free markets where only a few years ago there was not even a whiff of them in the state shops. Between 1980 and 1985 pork production has doubled, rapeseed production has trebled, and oranges, quadrupled! The Chinese experiment, unlike the green revolution in India and Indonesia, owes its success not so much to the introduction of new high-yielding fertilizers or irrigation techniques as to a new pattern of social organization. The peasant's individual interest and economic motivation seem to determine his output, making a mockery of the idea of the collectivist utopia and the fear of being swamped by the population of the Third World. China has managed to come out of the famine with its billion inhabitants intact for the first time in its long history. If starvation deaths in China have ceased, it is no miracle, but living proof of the universal character of enterprising individualism.

The peasant's income went up threefold between 1979 and 1985, whereas urban wages did not even double in the same period. At the time of the people's communes, the peasants were subsidizing the cities, which is typical in poor countries. Today, with reform, a new rural-urban balance has been created that benefits 800 million peasants. Perhaps therein lies the true nature of reform. It is not only economic but also introduces greater social equity in the socialist universe. Reform is the product of a long process of thought and reflection. Yan Hansheng's every act has been planned by the Chinese leadership. If the peasant is like a nightingale in a cage, China may be compared to a game of chess wherein the players are the Mandarins in power, who think and mediate at length before each step and never move a pawn without having pushed back another.

# The Strategy of a Mandarin

YU SWALLOWS HIS STEAMING HOT SOUP IN THE CHINESE MANNER, NOIS-
ily and in large gulps. Small, rotund, and lively with thin gray hair and
wearing a Mao blue canvas suit and velvet shoes, Yu Guangyuan is a survivor. In 1957, Yu wrote that part of Mao's famous speech, "Let a hundred flowers bloom, let diverse schools contend." This was considered to
be the first attempt to restore the freedom of speech in a communist
country. Like most intellectuals, Yu took his own rhetoric seriously and
criticized China's industrialization, a replica of the Soviet model. A year
later, he was in a labor camp with a few thousand scientists and writers
who were being punished for their rightist leanings.

But for Yu the worst was yet to come: the "great" Cultural Revolution of 1966. (The adjective *great* ought to be replaced by horrifying.)
Yu, already suspect, was deported to a distant province with hundreds of
thousands of intellectuals, a term covering just about anyone who had
pursued any kind of study, particularly teachers. For twelve years the
great economist raised pigs to renew his contact with the land. He is of
the view today, not without a certain amount of humor, that he is very
lucky because in Shanxi the conditions were not too bad for the pigs.

After the Gang of Four, headed by Mao's widow, Jiang Qing, were
discredited in 1976, the world learned that the Chinese per capita agricultural output had fallen below the 1949 level. For the first time in its
history, the Chinese government sought the help of international organi-

zations in its fight against famine. Yu Guangyuan had to cool his heels one more year before he was freed from his gulag, as the new regime did not immediately realize that it also needed economists. Yu, however, is disenchanted with neither communism nor Mao. Thirty years after the "Hundred Flowers" speech, he is happy to state in the *People's Daily* that Mao's sincerity had been betrayed by infiltrated leftist factions in the party and asks once again, "Let a hundred flowers bloom, let diverse schools contend," as if nothing had happened.

In China today the "Hundred Flowers" speech is the charter for research and the theoretical basis of the social science academies. It is to these academies, at Beijing and in the provinces, that all the retrievable economists have been posted—Ma Hong, Liu Guoguang, Jiang Yiwei, and Dong Furen being the most prominent. These men are over 60; their age confers on them an intellectual authority and freedom of thought unheard of in China even before the Cultural Revolution. The Central Committee, who made it known that economists were not implicated in the campaign against bourgeois liberalism, gave them the responsibility of drawing up for China a socialist blueprint that works. According to Dong Furen, director of the Economic Institute, that system exists nowhere else in the world. Once adopted by the Central Committee of the communist party, this model, conceived at the top, will assume the form of instructions, be relayed to all the echelons of the party and government, and then applied to one billion Chinese. There is no precedent in history for so vast a social transformation conceived by so small a group. This is also an ideological maneuver typical of Chinese tradition wherein intellectuals are rarely dissidents but Mandarins in the service of the state.

## Economists or Acrobats?

In these economic laboratories of new China, neither computers nor typewriters tick away. The highest technology available to the Academy of Social Sciences of Beijing and the Economic Institute, an affiliate, is a few telephones that work intermittently, between power failures. Competence is also in short supply. After Ma Hong and Yu Guangyuan, the Cultural Revolution created a void; an entire generation has been deprived of higher training, and the contribution of the thousands of Chinese students sent to foreign universities by the government has yet to be felt. Let us add that the training of traditional Chinese economists is far more political and philosophical than scientific. These economists are more familiar with the works of Marx and the Bulgarian economy than with neighboring Korea or capitalist Europe. The role of these economists is not to organize growth but to introduce techniques of development that comply with the nature of the political regime.

Such theoretical gymnastics are in keeping with a tradition that has developed since China first came into contact with the West. From the sixteenth century on, a long line of Chinese philosophers have ceaselessly debated whether to do away with the barbarians or to favor the osmosis between Chinese and Western cultures. Generally speaking, the Mandarins have always considered that Western science and technology were good but that our culture and morality were far below theirs. Can one dissociate the two?

Yu Guangyuan illustrates the difficulty in applying Western logic to China through four examples from (1) medicine, (2) the concept of freedom, (3) scientific methods, and (4) the exercise of power. (1) Chinese medicine considers the body as part of the universe whose disorders result from a disharmony between humans and their environment; Western medicine, in contrast, is mechanical and believes that if one part goes wrong, all you have to do is to repair that part. (2) Freedom, in Chinese tradition, is the quest for an agreement between the self and the external world and an adaptation of the individual to his surroundings. For the Westerners, however, freedom is acquired by changing the world. (3) The Chinese scientific method is holistic, considering the universe as a whole and not separating the individual elements, as Western thought does. This makes it difficult to combine logic and practical experimentation. (4) Authority in the West derives its legitimacy from the rule of law, but according to Chinese tradition, personalized authority makes for good government.

Without destabilizing the cultural edifice, Chinese economists are required to preserve socialism, though a Chinese socialism acceptable to all remains to be defined. For Professor Ma Jiaju of the Academy of Peking, "Socialism is growth with justice!" If this is the yardstick, then several capitalist countries are more socialist than China. Chinese socialism is first and foremost Chinese, a Sinoization of Marxism that is largely the work of Mao. But China is truly a socialist country, for in addition to traditional constraints, it now has to live with ideological taboos, particularly the denial of the right to private enterprise, reform or no reform!

Endless cups of tea are consumed at any brainstorming session of Chinese experts. The surroundings, whether in an institution, academy, administration, or enterprise, are identical. The meeting rooms are uniform and uncomfortable, with enormous sofas and moleskin armchairs with lace-covered arm- and headrests, low tables along the walls on which hot water thermoses of colored plastic sit side by side with tea cups and green tea leaves. The decor is unchangeable, as is the heady stench of the toilets.

Another constant is that no tête-à-têtes can take place. The room is usually crowded and you don't know who's who because the name plates don't reveal the participants' functions. The true picture emerges only during discussions where the speakers' authority is reflected in how they express themselves. The answers to specific questions are couched in such generalities that they leave you none the wiser, and such answers are rarely off-the-cuff, but the subject of lively confabulations within the group before the interpreter is called on to translate the edited version to the foreign visitor. Chinese economists, like their colleagues from the socialist camp, tend to rely on figures for their explanations and arguments. Given the paucity of the statistics-gathering mechanism in this gigantic country, it is likely that most of the figures are false, but that doesn't stop anyone from reeling them off, down to the last decimal point.

Lest the reader get the impression of a stifling atmosphere, one must add that these debates are lively affairs, full of animation and humor. When the heat gets unbearable the participants remove their shoes and roll up their trousers. One sips the steaming tea trying not to swallow the leaves floating on top.

## One Billion Guinea Pigs

Chinese economists do not claim to have any magic formula for a perfect new society because theory must be rooted in reality. Such reality must be and is, above all, the Chinese reality, but the authors of reform looked around them and drew some of their inspiration from the socialist world. At one point in time they were enthusiastic about Yugoslavia and its self-managed workers' cooperatives, until they realized that the results were catastrophic. Subsequently they fixed their attention on Hungary, which thus could be considered the starting point of their inspiration for the evolution of reform. To date there is no definitive document, but a collection of directives that emerged from the internal debates of the Central Committee as well as from exchanges between economists and the leading members of the committee. The pace of change thus depends on power plays within an extremely small group. The liberals, however, are trying to favor the producers and the intellectuals in a bid to thwart supporters of the bureaucratic line of thought.

One rare declaration that mentions the general philosophy of reform dates to October 1984, when the Third Plenary of the Central Committee adopted a resolution on economic structure:

> History has shown us that egalitarian thought is a serious obstacle to the implementation of the principle of division, each according to his work. Naturally, a socialist society should guarantee to its members progressive improvement of material and cultural life, and collective prosperity. But collective prosperity cannot and should never mean absolute egalitarianism. The standard of living of all the members of a given society cannot be raised simultaneously at the same speed. If one interprets collective prosperity in terms of absolute equality and simultaneous prosperity, not only will our goals not be achieved but such a direction will lead to collective poverty.

On the basis of interviews and observations from March 1986 to May 1987—before and after the student demonstrations of the winter of 1986—I would like to suggest a personal interpretation of a movement that is often elusive to the foreign observer.

The first principle of reform has to do with its experimental nature, which might seem banal, but is quite extraordinary. It is not often that ideologists rally around empiricism and that economists use a society of one billion men as a laboratory. Reform was not intended to be applied instantaneously to the whole of China, but to enable comparisons on the basis of results achieved. This idea of progression is applicable to both space and time. Thus in 1987, seven years after the redistribution of lands, the task is not yet complete in all the territorial districts of China. Similarly, the reformers in the same regions are trying new property forms, like cooperatives and reinforcing factory manager's authority, and then studying the consequences before using these methods on a wide scale all over the country. Sichuan is such a favored laboratory, and one must be careful not to generalize from the observations that have been made for a single province. But the progressive character of reform is also a means to gauge the reaction of the bureaucracy. Economists tend to qualify such resistance as practical difficulties; to me they seem political and ideological.

The second principle is decentralization. China is moving from imperative national-level planning to indicative and regional-level planning. This is an attempt to perceive reality better, not a conversion to the market economy. In a country where the study of economics is still floundering and where public accounting systems are elementary, statistics random, computers rare, and economists scarce, the imperative plan is a figment of the imagination. But one wonders whether the plan, other than its economic functions, is perhaps the translation in modern terms of traditional social control that dates back to the Chinese classical era. Civilian society has always had to obey the stringent rules imposed from the top. The new planning process, conceived and executed at the level of each province, is henceforth a statement of economic policy rather than a series of quantitative goals. Specific production targets are set only for state enterprises, not for workers' cooperatives. Along with geographic decentralization comes the decentralization of economic power. The autonomy of production units and the roles of heads of enterprise have been emphasized, at least in official rhetoric. Generally speaking, reform tries to substitute the notion of hierarchical authority with that of the contract. The plan is a contract between the government and the production units; the commune concludes a contract with the farmer, and factory managers in turn conclude a contract with the community of workers.

The third principle is the progressive deregulation of prices, so complex a transition, that even the Chinese are lost. Thus in Beijing markets a ceiling price is imposed by the administration on most essential food items like rice and oil, but not on vegetables. Conversely, in Sichuan, all retail food prices are freely set, but the intervention of the state shops enables price stability. Clothes are sold as freely in Beijing as in Sichuan. Small kitchen utensils, a few items of furniture, and trinkets of all kinds are sold on the open market without any kind of price constraint, as are some services, like bicycle or watch repairing. More important items, like radios, televisions, and bicycles, can only be bought at the fixed price at state shops. Paradoxically, some items, such as watches, produced in Sichuan in excess quantities, are sold on the free market at a minimum compulsory price! A fall in prices would cause the small producer to disappear. Finally, both free prices and controlled prices can coexist for the same product in the same place. For example, the Sichuan peasant must sell a quota of rice to the state at a fixed price, but can sell the rest on the free market. Similarly, state factories, beyond the compulsory fixed-price production quotas, are free to surpass their targets and sell the surplus on the market. The coexistence of free prices and controlled prices based on product or regional considerations gives rise to a thriving black market and tempts enterprises or peasants to produce for the free markets on a priority basis. That is why Sichuan was short of rice in 1985, the peasants feeling that it was more profitable to turn to fruit and vegetables. At the Economic Institute of Beijing the consensus is that eventually free prices and controlled prices ought to coincide and all controls disappear. This observation would hold true in the context of the perfect market, but reality always lags far behind.

The fourth principle of reform is the diversification of property, with state enterprise still the most important principle, covering 60 to 99 percent of all industrial production, depending on the region. The percentage also varies depending on how strongly the speaker is in favor of reform. Such state enterprises are henceforth to face the competition of collective enterprises, a kind of workers' self-managed cooperative that brings together state capital, private savings, and, finally, individual enterprises, which fascinate foreign observers who are constantly on the lookout for a capitalist renaissance. Such enterprise, however, only represents 2 percent of industrial production and is allowed to develop only in the trade sector or for modest services.[1] In the normal course of events, an individual entrepreneur cannot employ more than a dozen wage earners but this figure can be manipulated. The main constraint to Chinese capitalism is qualitative in nature, as privatization has been limited to peripheral activities. The typical entrepreneur of Chinese reform is a small trader, a restaurant owner, a repairer of bicycles, or perhaps even a traditional doctor, who is free to fix his consultation fee, generally 10 fens. Capital accumulation is not for tomorrow!

The fifth and the last principle of reform, the most important and the most difficult to translate in reality, is the creation at the national level of a labor market.

## To Break the Iron Bowl

"China," observes Jiang Yiwei, "is infinitely more centralized and bureaucratic than the Soviet Union." We leave it to this venerable professor of the Academy of Social Sciences to answer for his judgment. It is a cold Beijing morning, and Jiang, in his office, has kept his warm blue coat around him with his head buried in a cap that covers his ears. Despite his somewhat fantastic appearance, the man commands respect, for he has made Chinese history and, subsequently, become a victim of that same history. A secret member of the Chongquing Communist Party before the revolution, Jiang fought against the Kuomintang and the Japanese before he was removed in 1959 for drifting to the right. He was only recalled in 1978, after the Gang of Four had been crushed. Like all the militants of his generation, his life had been obliterated for twenty years by the Cultural Revolution. Now his age and suffering grant him the freedom of expression lacking among the younger generation. Jiang Yiwei's reputation in Beijing is that he speaks the truth (do others hide it?).

Jiang Yiwei's last battle is trying to persuade the Central Committee that a labor market in China would be compatible with both Marxism and efficiency. In today's system (that Jiang Yiwei calls in anticipation *the old system*), each state enterprise is allotted its number of workers by the local labor office, a number that bears no relationship to the needs of the company. If an executive has to be recruited, the decision could go up to the ministerial level, but the basic principle remains unchanged. The job is guaranteed for life; the company cannot refuse the employee who has been thrust on it.[2] Nor do the wage earners have any choice in the matter. Firing personnel is practically unheard of, and the wage earner can only change his production unit with the consent of management. To avoid discrimination, enterprises receive an equal number of workers of both sexes, whatever the job. Industrial employment is often hereditary, with a worker who retires having the right to pass on his job to his son or daughter. Wages are generally fixed, not by the enterprise but by the administration, and are more or less uniform for the entire country and for all sectors of activity. The gap between the base and the top salary is extremely small.[3] The bonus that goes with the wages and that supposedly takes performance into account is often identical for everyone in the same factory and is fixed at four months' wages by the state. Beyond this ceiling, the wage earner has to pay a progressive tax. This rigid system is called the *iron bowl* because it guarantees (in principle) the basic food requirements to the worker. Thus unemployment does not exist in China, overemployment is a general phenomenon, and the enterprises are unmanageable.

Jiang Yiwei's new system, the basic principles of which were adopted in 1986, lays down three new rules: that life employment be replaced by a five-year renewable contract, that jobs be no longer passed down from father to son or daughter, and that bad workers be fired. To counterbalance these new freedoms, Chinese enterprises are to finance a social security regime for their wage earners. Only new wage earners are affected; the others continue under the old system.

Jiang Yiwei notes that the debate on the labor market centers, as often is the case in China, as much on terminology as on substance. Have we the right to speak of the labor market as if labor were some kind of merchandise? Will the workers be able to accept working under contract when they are, in theory, the owners of the means of production? Two Chongqing factories were selected on an experimental basis, after having secured the agreement of their workers, to inaugurate the new system in 1987. One important constraint in the experiment was that only the workers were affected; the degree-holding executives and the military continued to benefit from the life employment scheme. Considering the arrogance and the mediocre training of the young degree holders, I noticed that the manager of the enterprise was often more pained to receive an executive than a worker. Although some Westerners believe that China is moving back to the path of capitalism, China is actually going through a phase that can best be described as one of *theoretical transition*, to use Ma Jiaju's term. Practice lags behind even further.

## Shanghai, 1930

Ordinarily a two-hour flight would get you to Shanghai from Beijing. But one is traveling in China. In China the airline, a state monopoly, is governed by the mysterious rules of *guanxi*, a concoction of influence and corruption. You can only get a reservation if you have *guanxi*, so that those who hobnob with the higher-ups fly away, leaving lesser mortals to stand and wait. You cannot purchase a return ticket; tickets can only be purchased from the place you are leaving! (It helps to have a well-placed relative at the other end.) Computerized reservations are unheard of. Perhaps computers could destroy *guanxi*. Once in the air, the journey is somewhat bumpy; the army, which controls air traffic, shows great indifference to wind pockets.

But who has not dreamed of visiting Shanghai? The city looks just like it did in the black-and-white films of the 1930s. On the Whampoa River a succession of tarpaulin-covered barges blow their foghorns. The sky is always overcast; rain the year-round gives this Asian city a whiff of London. The quays remind one of the Thames with Victorian constructions—the old stock market, the chamber of commerce and the Hotel of Peace—on either side. The British seem to leave such gems of residential architecture throughout the course of their colonial travels. The residential areas, previously reserved for Europeans, contain the villas of the Norman British style. The old servants have taken their masters' place and divided these buildings into many small apartments, one family to an apartment. In the midst of this gigantic agglomeration, the old city remains unchanged from when travelers discovered it in the nineteenth century. In a labyrinth of narrow streets, where legend has it that without a guide one could get lost, one has to jostle through thronging crowds, step over mountains of refuse, nimbly move out of the way of bicycles, endure the smells, and get used to the shrugging and the shouting. The inhabitants of Shanghai are noisy, undisciplined, boastful, and always ready for a laugh. Each dwelling has long bamboo poles for drying clothes. Families live in dingy, dark holes with no water and almost no light. Depending on your taste and mood, you will see the corbelled houses as either picturesque or sordid. The footpaths have been annexed by housewives, who wash their clothes and their dishes in a collective sink; by old people sitting on tiny bamboo armchairs; and by the countless cardplayers and tea, soup, and noodle vendors. In Shanghai people are always eating hurriedly on the streets.

In the midst of this hustle and bustle is an old teahouse set in the middle of a small lake, the silent center around which this metropolis of eighteen million inhabitants seems to gravitate. Pensive old men, their chins resting on their canes, spend their day sipping out of a delicate cup of green tea and listening to the nightingale singing in its cage.

The enterprises are in the image of the city—outdated, unchanged— it is hard to believe that the Shanghai of 50 years ago was one of the capitals of the industrial world. But here too, reform is under way, at least in the slogan, "Free Your Minds, Take Initiative!" A vibrant appeal addressed to pipe factory workers. The slogan, as is customary, is drawn in beautiful golden pictograms on a red background and is displayed at the entrance to the workshops. The factory employs sixteen thousand people, considerably more than its production would warrant, as can be seen by the idleness of the workers and the card games going on in the workshops. The technology is archaic, and the buildings are crumbling from a general lack of maintenance. Some furnaces go back to the 1930s; the trains, to the 1950s; and the workers make the parts by hand. Nonetheless this factory has been taken up as a model for reform. The factory only manufactures two kinds of pipes—thick ones and small ones. Thus the state plan has assigned it a simple production quota. Over and above the quota—and herein lies the innovation—the factory is free to sell to clients of its choice at a price to be negotiated directly with them. This liberalization is supposed to force the factory to improve the quality of its products and to discover the techniques of marketing. Although the rationale behind this move seems liberal, it is meaningful only if the clients can choose their suppliers. This, however, is not the case. The factory has a monopoly over the production of pipes for the entire province in a market characterized by scarcity. It has no competitors and thus has steady sales of its products, whether of good or bad quality, on the free market at a price higher than that fixed by the plan. The clients, generally new cooperatives, are obliged then, to grease the palms of some intermediary or other, *guanxi* at work.

But the inefficiency of the pipe factory and the Chinese economy in general is aggravated by the behavior of the bureaucracy. Bureaucratic meddling has effectively subordinated the enterprise to a plethora of administrative rules and regulations. The pipe factory, with its sixteen thousand wage earners, must employ 2,400 management-level people whose main occupation is to keep the authorities happy at three levels:

the central state at Beijing, the provincial government, and the Shanghai municipality. The Ministry of Industry in Beijing fixes the long-term production plan of the factory for both the quantity and the variety of the products. Then the steel and iron department of the province allocates energy—a rare commodity and essential for such production. Lastly, the municipal authorities control the company's management and look after the departments of iron and steel, budgetary affairs, industry, trade, planning, and general economy. Each one of these municipal departments requires a corresponding office in the factory.

Despite reform, officials maintain an arbitrary authority over the enterprises. Thus in Shanghai, the provincial Ministry of Economy constantly varies the taxes on profits (over the last three years, they have fluctuated between 77 and 86 percent). Moreover, tax rates are not usually known in advance; in May 1987, factory management did not know what share of profits would be retained as taxes for that financial year. Under such conditions, taxation of Chinese enterprises has less to do with fiscal technique than it does with administrative extortion on profits, the amount to be negotiated.

Once again we encounter the central paradox of reform: the liberalization of management without the corresponding dismantling of bureaucratic authority. Government servants are expected to adopt behavioral patterns that are the exact opposite of those they have been accustomed to for the last 30 years. A spontaneous renunciation of authority is even more improbable, given that the economic administration has taken into its ranks several army officers who were considered too rusty to adapt to the new military strategy. One such officer, who was reabsorbed by the Planning Ministry in Beijing, explained to me that reform was so significant and so complex that it was necessary to recruit even more bureaucrats to apply it correctly!

Add to this dependence on local authorities the power of the communist party, which is present at all levels of administration and production. Also, keep in mind that we are in a socialist country and that the workers are powerful. The general assembly of elected delegates meets four times a year and exercises pressure on management.

This climate of uncertainty and subservience nearly obliterates the responsibilities of management and leads to the constant adoption of short-term policies on a systematic basis. The profits earned on the free market are either confiscated through taxation or distributed to the workers in the form of social benefits and allowances. Little remains for investment, and there is no long-term strategy for taking a Shanghai factory out of the Middle Ages. Returning to Beijing, I asked to see, as a contrast to Shanghai, what modern Chinese industry had to offer. I was thus taken on a visit to the East-Wind factory where two thousand workers assemble television sets under a Japanese license. An air-conditioned room is reserved for impressive quality control apparatus, also imported from Japan, that one can only enter after having removed one's shoes, but the machines are not working. When the factory manager goes to give a demonstration, he realizes that his chief technician is absent and that there is no electricity!

In the capital another model enterprise, the iron and steel combine of Beijing, is cited to me as an example of high-tech industry. Steel production has doubled in the space of ten years, reaching three million tons in 1986. But Feng Zhongmao, the manager, takes as much pride in the beauty of the surroundings as in the production figures, assuring me that 28.3 percent of the combine is a green belt and that 92.47 percent of the water used by the factory is recycled. In a nutshell, a factory garden! As I had just read in the official *China Daily*, published in Peking, that one-third of the steel produced in the country is unusable and has to be re-melted, I asked Feng how much his company has lost. "Our steel is 100 percent good," he protests. Then why does China have to import twenty million tons of ordinary steel every year?

As for rural industry, the performance did not seem much more convincing.

## Reform or Leap Forward?

Along with opening up the free market in towns, the peasant was called on to set up his own enterprise in his village with his savings, which is the most spectacular change in China's economic landscape. In the heart of Tuanjie, which we have already visited with our friend Yan Hansheng, a huge brick chimney, belching black smoke, symbolizes the new Chinese way. Madame Zheng, the head of the village (the choice before the electorate was limited to a single list), proudly invites us to visit the two local enterprises, which make bricks and beer bottles. Out of an atmosphere thick with coal dust and toxic gases, heaps of bottles pour out of the factory onto dusty little lanes before they are delivered to the breweries. When there is electricity, activity is hectic, for the speedy development of rural cooperatives has created a serious energy shortage, with working hours subject to the availability of electricity. But Madame Zheng, by approaching the local authorities and using *guanxi*, manages to get what she wants at the expense of state enterprises. The architects of reform did not foresee the contradiction between planning and the opening up of initiatives at the grass roots.

All the villagers who have reached the age of sixteen take turns at the cooperative in conditions that the extreme heat of the furnaces makes unbearable. Such work, in principle, is not compulsory, as was the case at the time of the people's commune. But few are likely to abstain for fear of social consequences. Some Tuanjie peasants, however, have set up cigarette stalls at the exit of the factory rather than exert themselves inside. The melting of the recovered glass and the blowing and the molding into bottles are carried out with devices from another age, from factories that long ago abandoned them. The end product is mediocre, going by the large number of ill-shaped bottles which are thrown in the rubbish heap.

The inhabitants of Tuanjie have no training, and the technical management of the glass factory, as in the case of the neighboring brick kiln, had been handed over to retired workers from Shanghai. The man who built and supervised the glass factory in Tuanjie is venerated with the same fervor that is usually reserved for the aged in China. But his appointment, however worthy, means that sixteen-year-old apprentices learn methods and techniques from the Shanghai of the 1930s. Madame Zheng sweeps aside such objections, asserting that the cooperatives not only produce bottles but also further the cause of socialism and that the glass factory employs people who, without it, would have been idle and tempted to migrate to the cities.

For those regions of the Third World where disguised unemployment in agriculture and rural exodus are common features, rural cooperatives seem an intelligent response. Tuanjie charms Western ecologists, amateurs of appropriate technology, and others indulging in fantasies they would not want for their own country. Cooperatives are, in fact, part and parcel of the Third World myth that small is beautiful. But what is small and technically backward is not necessarily viable. One wonders how long this Chinese adventure, devoid of economic logic, rationale, or accountability, can last! It is almost impossible to determine who actually runs the cooperative. Belonging neither to the individual nor to the capitalist mode of ownership, the ownership pattern is undoubtedly socialist (at least everybody is clear on that score). Some say that the glass factory is public property owned by the commune of Tuanjie; others, that it is the collective property of all the inhabitants; and still others, that it belongs to the workers.

The system of management is as hazy as the ownership. The manager is theoretically chosen by the wage earners, but, in fact, his nomination depends on Madame Zheng, who represents the party. The supervisory role of the authorities is even more ambiguous. In the beginning, the Tuanjie cooperative was exempted from tax on profits, but since it started making money, it has been taxed arbitrarily and prohibitively by the Chinese government, whose view is that the rural enterprises are developing too quickly and consuming too much energy. What remains of the profits, after negotiation, is broken up into funds for wage earners, subsidies for the improvement of habitat, a ten-yuan bonus for pigs sold to state shops, reimbursement of children's medical expenses, and funeral charges borne by the state. Nothing is left to invest. The peasant workers of Tuanjie prefer pocketing the profits immediately—the first result of the system where no one is responsible for the future.

How not to recall that another great leap forward took place in 1958, when it was deemed necessary to produce steel at any price, and blast furnaces mushroomed all over the country. The experiment ended the following year when it was discovered not only that the steel in question was unusable but that the countryside had been hit by famine, the peasant-farmers having been marched off to work at the blast furnaces. Despite this disastrous experience, the Chinese authorities still seem to hold the view that technology can be replaced by the mobilization of workers. In this light, reform is more a new leap forward than a step toward economic liberalization, which is what the West wants to believe.

This comparison excites the anger of Chinese economists but they apparently have given some thought to the matter. Thus according to Chen Deyan of the Economic Institute of Sichuan, what is happening at Tuanjie is that, unlike the great leap forward, the reform of the 1980s has been initiated at the grass roots level to percolate to the top, not vice versa, and is governed exclusively by economic considerations, not ideological ones. One week later, two thousand kilometers away in Beijing, Liu Guoguang, vice-president of the Academy of Sciences, observed that, far from being a great leap forward, the reform of the 1980s is a grass roots movement. Whenever the Chinese go in for such jargon, it implies that a solution has not yet been found for dealing with a major concern.

## Why Is the Chinese Awakening So Slow?

Whether high tech or low tech, rural or urban, industry is remarkably uniform in China. Technical backwardness is everywhere and the lack of training a universal phenomenon. A general sense of laxness pervades, with quality being sacrificed at the altar of quantity for goods and services. Academy economists, on the whole, agree with this observation. But who is to blame? history, national culture, or the socialist regime?

For Dong Furen, the economic backwardness of China is due to the absence of clear-cut, corporate decision-making mechanisms. No progress can be made until responsibilities are clearly allocated and a hierarchy is established among the three competing powers—the company managers, the party, and the workers' assembly—within each organization. Only a law on factories could enable the technocrats to win over the politicians. But do the economists wield the kind of power necessary to bring about this revolution within a revolution? To date, the party prefers a socialism that does not work to a socialism that will work without the party!

I fear that for a long time to come the factories of Beijing and Shanghai will suffer for want of investment and management. I also fear that the rural cooperative of Tuanjie will never become an efficient unit; in addition to the many inconsistencies that riddle public enterprise, the cooperative further complicates matters because wage earners will never take decisions against their short-term interests. Even in the agricultural sector, reform is beginning to peter out. The peasants prefer selling their produce on the free market rather than sticking to their contract with the State, thus jeopardizing town supplies. Moreover, the division of land slows down technical progress and marketing. It is as unthinkable of going back to the system of community farming as it is to allow the free sale of land.

The Chinese authorities, as well as travelers who are inclined to believe that China is on the move and in the process of change, will be quick to refute my pessimistic conclusions. It is true that Beijing telephones have begun to work, that the capital experienced its first traffic jams, that hotels are painfully coming up to international standards, and that the first credit cards have come into circulation. But these are only stray techniques copied from the West, seen in large cities and free trade zones with a view to attracting foreign capital. The instruments of central, civil, and military power are being modernized in China but only to consolidate the power base, not to affect the development of the society as a whole.

For the moment, China does not offer the Third World a system of development but a model for managing scarcity and an ideology for power—it is more like a cage with solid bars than a gilded one.

I doubt that the next generation will fully open the cage. Thousands of students shouting "Democracy" in Tiananmen Square [This was written in 1987; the author has not modified his original text here to consider 1989 events.] does not mean that China is awakening. I think that this postrevolutionary generation is protesting against the establishment because it is in a hurry to take over the reins of power from the gerontocracy. From the University of Business and International Trade, a new Beijing establishment that recruits the nation's elite, I discovered that the best students rush toward the economic ministries of the capital to manage reform. These students are the new Mandarins of a China where the party has replaced the son of the soil and Marx, Confucius. Why destabilize an old order to launch a path of growth whose social and political consequences are unforeseeable? The Chinese prefer indulging in their traditional civilization and the doublespeak of Marxism to maintain stable order rather than a creative disorder. Let us now turn to another group of Third World countries who, searching for a new reference point, see liberalism, or rather what they claim to be liberal, as an alternative.

# Did You Say *Liberalism?*

FROM THE ARGENTINEAN PLAINS ON OUR WAY TO BOLIVIA, OUR AIR-
plane climbs higher and higher, winging its way through arid mountain
chains, as a lunar landscape of lakes and craters unfurls itself. The La Paz
Airport, aptly named El Alto, is, at an altitude of four thousand meters,
the highest airport in the world. Before leaving the aircraft, our pilot
tells us to take deep breaths and walk slowly toward the airport, preferably with nothing in our hands, for there are a thousand depressing anecdotes about passengers who, stricken by the oxygen deprivation as they
climb down the gangway, have to be taken back to the valley by the next
plane. (As soon as you let it be known in Buenos Aires or São Paulo that
you are going to La Paz, everybody looks at you with commiseration.)
The first steps on the tarmac are a trial; my feet feel as if they are made
of lead, I am short of breath, and my heart beats fast. A delegation awaits
me and is watching my reactions closely. I do not feel too bad until the
minister remarks that I am looking pale. I then yield to the ministrations
of an aide, who rushes to my side with a bottle of oxygen and authori-
tatively ties the mask around my face. Why on earth have I come to
Bolivia?

A small country, six million inhabitants, Bolivia has nothing in common with either Brazil or Argentina, but has nonetheless played a unique
role in history. It was Bolivia, particularly the Potosi mine, that provided
Europe with large flows of gold and silver in the sixteenth and seventeenth centuries, which was a decisive factor in the industrialization of

that continent. Five centuries after the Spanish conquest, Bolivia is still one of the poorest countries in the world, unchanged since 1825 when Simon Bolivar described it as "a beggar sitting on a golden throne." This paradox was my first reason for going to Bolivia.

The second reason, and the one that swayed me, was that the president of Bolivia had turned into an adept of liberal capitalism. Such news would seem hardly out of the ordinary on the Latin American continent, where words are of little consequence and the ideology in vogue changes all the time, had not this Bolivian president espoused the capitalist cause. Why Paz Estenssoro had for a long time been the symbol of socialism for Latin America. Head of state since the 1950s, he nationalized mines, expelled the tin king, Antenaor Patiño, from the country, confiscated land from the aristocracy, which he redistributed to the Indians, paid no compensation, and packed off his bourgeois enemies in what are today referred to as concentration camps. This man set everybody's imagination aflame ten years before Castro and Guevara. Paz Estenssoro, a liberal? I had to meet him.

## The Second Life of Paz Estenssoro

La Paz is a geographic aberration. Even the slightest movement in this rarefied atmosphere is no mean feat. Only *matecoca,* the national drink, brings some succour against *soroche,* or height sickness. The Indians of Altiplano and the Aymaras have always known that, to survive at this height, one must chew coca leaves, walk slowly, and not think too quickly. Everything in La Paz goes on at a leisurely pace. In their bowler hats Indian women sit on their haunches on the footpath waiting for a customer to buy a pack of cigarettes or a lama fetus from them. (The lama fetus is a lucky charm the Bolivians seal in the foundations of all new construction.) This slow pace is interrupted by innumerable festivals, half Christian, half pagan, with repetitive dances to monotonous music that go on day and night until the drunken dancers fall. We are very far from the Parisian atmosphere of Buenos Aires or the New York environment of São Paulo.

Paz Estenssoro rules over this strange country, where since the time of the Spanish conquest, no more than a 100,000 Europeans replaced the Incas and dominate the Indians. The president lives in a palace that would make an excellent set for a light opera, guarded as it is by soldiers in white trousers, red flannel coats, and vast leather belts.

The colonel, the chief of protocol, invites visitors to share his daily routine. First, he gets his shoes polished—a sign of respectability in Bolivia—by a roadside shoe shiner. Lingering over his morning coffee, he pours over the local daily. At eleven o'clock, a much-awaited hour, *salteña*, a turnover stuffed with meat, is brought by the officer on duty. Thus time trickles by slowly in the silent antechambers.

The president receives his visitors ensconced between two electric heaters that work all the time. But the worn-out body of this man of 83 (who claims he is only 78) contains a sharp mind, for he has the reputation of being as cunning as a monkey, the nickname given to him by his people. He is aided by Jacobo Libermann, a mysterious counselor who ostensibly has no function other than being a friend of the president. Libermann, thin, brown-haired, lively, and of an undefinable age, is a poet, a writer, and the author of a biography of Bolivar that runs about fifteen hundred pages. The son of a Polish immigrant, he renews, in this faraway land, the European tradition of Jews at the court acting as counselors to the king. Libermann, then, is the liberal adviser to the president, a former leftist.

Paz Estenssoro succeeded, in 1985, in coming back to power after an election that foreign observers described as democratic,[1] and he is doing his best to undo all that he did over the last 35 years. For three years he was the most openly committed leader to the market economy in the whole of Latin America!

Let us judge the results. When he returned to power, inflation had reached a staggering 18,000 percent per annum, a record without a precedent for a peacetime nation. A pack of cigarettes cost three million pesos, and the smallest purchase required a suitcase full of bank notes. Bolivia did not have a mint capable of keeping up with the rate of inflation. Bank bills, purchased from Brazil, had become the third largest import item of the country! Hernan Siles Zuazo's government, which preceded Paz's, printed bank notes of one and ten million pesos to facilitate transactions. But now Paz Estenssoro has managed in three months to wipe out the price hike by strictly adhering to the International Monetary Fund's recommendation—the state should spend only what it receives, not print money to cover the deficit. Inflation was controlled overnight, Bolivia being a perfect example of the relationship between the price rise, money creation, and public debt. In line with monetary orthodoxy, Paz Estenssoro unfroze prices in 1986, something that neither Alfonsin nor Sarney had dared to do in their respective countries. The scarcity on the capital market disappeared and all consumer goods were once again available—but only while the Bolivian bourgeoisie has money.

Paz tells me that 25 years ago one had to be socialist, that one had to eliminate the land-owning oligarchy as well as the mine oligarchy to save the country from guerrillas and communist revolution. It was in Bolivia, he reminds me, that the adventures of both Che Guevara and Regis Debray, the French leftist intellectual, came to an end. But today socialism is outdated, nationalization absurd, and anti-imperialist rhetoric grotesque. Liberalization is the historical necessity of our times and will hold good, according to Paz, for the next 30 to 40 years.

Such an economic rationale calls for wiping out state and public sector deficits, which for the most part are Comibol's, the mining company of Bolivia, which runs the tin mines that the president nationalized in 1953. Comibol's trade deficit constitutes three-fourths of its turnover. Every time it exports a hundred dollars worth of ore, it imports four hundred dollars worth of equipment. Thirty-five years ago Paz would have attributed these losses to Western imperialism, but now he explains that the drastic fall in prices is the expected economic consequence of the end of the tin cycle. He blames Comibol for its bad management and its inability to adapt to the new world demand for gold and silver, which abound in Bolivia. The mine reconversion implies tendering for international capital, putting 75 percent of Bolivian miners out of a job. Paz has appealed to multinationals and called on unions to form cooperatives to manage their own decline. The unemployed can then return to traditional agriculture in the unoccupied lowlands to the east of the country.

The colonization of virgin territory is the future that the liberal president offers his people, which might be acceptable if it were possible to effectively colonize the lowlands where the only profitable crop has been coca. Paz Estenssoro's appeal will send the Indians of Altiplano not toward a brilliant future but toward certain physical disintegration. The Bolivian forest is uninhabited because it is uninhabitable. The mosquito of this region spreads Lechmariose, a terrible disease, whose symptoms are similar to those of leprosy. From time immemorial, this parasite has gorged on the limbs and faces of those who dared to venture into the lowlands. In the Lima museum are mummies with neither nose nor ears, the stigma of the illness contracted centuries ago. Studies conducted by the Biological Altitude Institute of La Paz under Philippe Desjeux, a French doctor, show that of the populations trying to colonize the forest—either in Bolivia or in Brazil—*half* of them catch this disease. There is no vaccination, and a medicine exists but most patients are not treated. This cruel reality masks the appeal to individual initiative made by an irresponsible and savage state.

## A Time for Recovery

Paz Estenssoro's policies have nothing liberal about them; they are totally reactionary. On the Latin American continent, the new song is intonated by the great feudal leaders, who have decided to let nothing come between them and their absolute power. Such is the case in Brasilia. General Ivan De Souza, director of information services—a mysterious title that hides the persistent influence of army men in the government—indicates to me that army officers are all liberals which means, for him, against extremists, especially leftist extremists. In the office adjacent to General Ivan's, Jose Sarney, the president of the republic, the chairman of the senate under the military dictatorship, and the head of state since the return to democracy, full of bonhomie and cunning, explained to me at length that he too has always subscribed to liberalism "even before it was in fashion." I would have had no reason to doubt Sarney if I had not known that he scrutinizes each and every government appointment, however low the level, to ensure political allegiance to his regime.

Such is also the case in Mexico. At the Cortez Palace, the minister of planning, Carlos Salinas de Gortari (he became president in 1988), assures me that privatization is on the move because in 1986 the government sold back to the private sector two hundred state enterprises—the smallest ones—and, for the first time in history, closed down a public sector foundry at Monterrey that was running at a loss! The minister observes that until recently to criticize the public sector was unheard of, in fact, taboo.

Such is also the case in Buenos Aires. The secretary of state for economics of the Radical government, Adolfo Brodersohn, tries to convince me that the Argentinian state will not loosen its control on what it has, but that "growth shall be privatized." But where is the growth?

Why have all these powerful men resorted to a liberal vocabulary? Why do they insist on privatization, the spirit of enterprise, market forces? This rhetoric is partially imposed by the quasi-bankruptcy of governments, which are then condemned to seek from private capitalism what they can no longer find in state coffers. But more than anything, this rhetoric is intended for foreign consumption—to reassure international organizations and banks and to attract foreign investment. These speeches are often drafted by international experts.

For Africa, an additional explanation was supplied to me by Senegalese president Leopold Sedar Senghor, who now lives in Paris. He considers that Africans want to please us and say what we wish to hear. When the West was socialist, Africa was socialist; now that Europe, like the United States, has switched over to a free market policy, the Africans have in turn changed their tune. (We shall look into the deeper reasons for liberalization in Africa a little later.) In the meantime, let us not forget Senghor's comments lest we fall prey to our own foibles; let us not be victims of our own categories. Imbued with Senghor's words, then, I listened carefully to Mohammed Zahwi when I went to Cairo.

## Islam, Open Door

Equally comfortable in English or French, President Mubarak's youthful secretary of state is a perfect blend of Egyptian classical refinement and modern technocracy. If Zahwi is to be believed, Egypt has at last shed the socialist fantasies of the Gamal Abdel Nasser era. Its middle-of-the-road policies protecting it from the eventuality of an Iranian-style revolution, it has embarked on the path of economic development in the liberal mold. According to Zahwi, Egypt has been liberal since the French brought their language, culture, and civil code to the country. Socialism is viewed as a historical accident caused by the ineptitude of the West. The United States virtually pushed Egypt in the arms of the Soviet Union by refusing to finance the Aswān Dam and by not taking into account the legitimate nationalist aspirations of the Egyptians. The country was steered back to its original course, thanks to *infita*—open-door policy— of Anwar as-Sadat, for whom liberalization and privatization were key words. Since then the Egyptian state has devoted itself to the tasks traditionally reserved for the state: the development of an infrastructure, public transport, and telephones. Although the gigantic public sector has not been dismantled, it faces competition from private, national, and foreign capitalism. Foreign firms called on to invest in Egypt are offered a whole range of benefits, tax exemptions, and sometimes even certain labor law dispensations, which is quite extraordinary. International trade is once again being encouraged. Autarchy and austerity are things of the past, and the Egyptians' right to establish private enterprises and banks has been restored.

Zahwi recognizes that Egyptians have not been the best managers and entrepreneurs in the world, but they are not to blame. The system offered no incentives, the bureaucracy was stifling, and prices and exchange rates absurd. As Zahwi is telling me how he has controlled all the economic parameters, the call for midday prayer resounds and smothers his voice, as if the muezzin were in his office. The loudspeakers fitted on the minister's balcony make such a racket that Zahwi is forced to shout to me the virtues of his plan, which envisages a growth rate of 6.3 percent per annum for Egypt. Statistics and the muezzin's hoarse invocations rattle with each other, and suddenly Allah seems to overshadow economics.

Listening to Zahwi reeling off statistics to the last decimal point, I recalled an interview I had with Ismail Sabri, chairman of the Egyptian Employers' Association. Ismail was of the view that 60 percent of Egypt's economic activity is clandestine—activities that escape the purview of Zahwi's plan—and that $40 billion of Egyptian capital is invested abroad. This figure is ten times higher than Egypt's annual export figure.

I would like to believe what Zahwi says, to be persuaded that Egypt is on the path of liberalization and development. I would also like to be convinced that the April 1987 elections were a clear verdict that the Egyptian people have given their assent to this open-door policy, that the 80 percent of favorable votes cast were valid, and that socialism, fundamentalism, and Wafd party conservatives have been sidelined.

## Islam, Closed Door

Ismail Abdalla is skeptical; unfortunately his skepticism is not unfounded.

A former minister of the Nasser government, a militant communist in the old days, and a progressive non-Marxist today, Abdalla played a significant role in the socialist revolution era. This was 30 years ago and, as Abdalla is only 54, we are reminded that most revolutions are the work of the very young. His fate, he thinks, accurately reflected the life of an intellectual in the Third World. On three occasions Nasser threw him into prison, and three times he was pulled out to be nominated minister, following the ups and downs of the Rais's relationship with the communists and the Soviet Union. Today, in opposition to Hosni Mubarak and the open-door policy, Abdalla plays a role familiar in the Third World—a dissident tolerated and financed by an international organization. The United Nations entrusts him with research assignments on the future of the Arab world.

Ismail Abdalla's analysis is diametrically opposed to Zahwi's, each representing one of the two major schools of thought on development, which we have already seen at work in Santiago, Chile. Ismail Abdalla claims to be an adept of both Prebich and Nyerere. He is the Egyptian representative of this Third World international.

For Ismail Abdalla, *infita* is aptly named because this laissez-passer brand of liberalism has become a joke; the door has been opened to all manner of excesses and corruption in private and public life. The state sector, which no longer has any goals, has been handed over to techno-crats and military men recruited for their loyalty, not for their compe-tence, who manage companies as it suits their personal interests. As for the Cairo upper classes, they have managed to rebuild their immense fortunes, thanks to international transactions and speculation on the dollar!

Since *infita*'s adoption ten years ago, Egypt's total income seems to have gone up significantly, but the figures cover only external resources: Suez Canal payments, oil sales of the Sinai, and wage transfers of Egyp-tian workers who have been exiled in the Persian Gulf. No additional wealth is being generated by the Egyptians in Egypt, and the new bour-geoisie are not investing; this bourgeoisie does not even have virtue of being capitalist and pays practically no tax at all! For the citizen on the street, the most obvious results of *infita* are the indecent display of ill-gotten luxuries by the nouveaux riches and the increase in consumer prices. The state has done away with subsidies for items of daily use so it can repay its debts, which were created for the most part through misap-propriation of funds by political leaders and the bourgeoisie!

Ismail Abdalla's criticism is not misplaced, but tends to overlook the circumstances that led Egypt to its present state. The country is totally bureaucratized because the Nasser regime nationalized practically every-thing, scared the entrepreneurs, discouraged private investment, and was responsible for the flight of capital. Egyptian companies are unman-ageable because the labor laws of Nasser's time gave the unions full power. The administration is ubiquitous because Nasser's constitution obliges the state to recruit anybody with a university degree.

Another Rais policy that seems designed to place the country in a labyrinth of poverty is bread prices, an explosive issue that has been the downfall of several governments. For the last fifteen years a loaf of bread in Cairo has cost one piastra, much less than its value. Bread is thus so cheap that peasants buy it to feed their hens, for it is less expensive than seeds. The state subsidy for bread is intended to help the poor, which is a noble intention indeed! But who is paying for the subsidy, if not the Egyptian people? Selling bread for one piastra impoverishes those who have to finance the state deficit through an imperceptible mechanism. To reduce the deficit, the Mubarak government is trying to raise the price of bread incrementally so as not to cause riots comparable to those of 1977, when Sadat made the first foray in this direction. For Ismail Abdalla it is indeed a great temptation to compare Nasser's state, which cared for the poor, to the savage liberalism of Mubarak.

# How to Rebuild the Pyramids

One cannot really blame Ismail Abdalla for refusing liberal solutions that have been badly implemented or for looking for alternatives. The spectacle of Cairo alone justifies his concern. Cairo, a capital, like many other cities of the Third World is accumulating the disadvantages of technical progress as well as those of mass poverty. A jungle of noise, dust, dirt, obstacles, and an architecture badly suited to its climate, Cairo combines the worst of the East with the worst of the West. The Cairo of yesteryears, probably was an astonishing city. Around the Turkish citadel that dominates the old quarters, you can still visualize a harmonious landscape of small streets and sand-colored domes and minarets. Probably from the upper part of the city you could see the Nile and toward the West, a string of pyramids and the Giza plateau. This is what it must have been like before the suburbs engulfed ancient Egypt, before the banks of the river had been swallowed up by the tidal waves of cars, and before the monstrous American hotels had blotted out the old view. Cairo today is the capital of ugliness. In saying this, I am not speaking as a nostalgic tourist; the tourist will always be endowed with the selective blindness that allows him to contemplate the Sphinx and conveniently obliterate the surrounding horrors. My compassion is not for the visitor—he will pay Cairo but a fleeting visit—but for the inhabitants of Cairo, who are going to spend their whole life in this city. How can the Arab people, so attached to their identity, endure so much disorder and so much pollution, their present-day decadence standing in stark contrast to the splendor of the past.

There must be a way out. But although the criticism of Ismail Abdalla is well-founded, the model that he offers is outdated and no longer of any use to the Third World. Ismail's model is based on the idealization of history, the socialist mobilization of the masses, and Nasserism without Nasser—gathering an entire population to move it out of the vicious circle of poverty, a vast plan for progressive Islamic society the historical model for which is the awesome Aswān site.

## The Aswān Site

Abdalla reminds us that for more than ten years 35,000 workers and engineers worked day and night to construct this massive dam. The Egyptian workers were at the time the best in the world, and Aswān is the pyramid of modern Egypt! Without moral solidarity and the unity of the masses, the Third World cannot progress, according to Abdalla.

A mythical vision? a utopia? undoubtedly, yes. Abdalla feels that the Third World must create its own utopia. Without a utopia, Egypt, the Arab world, the entire Third World will run out of breath trying to imitate the West without any hope of ever catching up with it.

These two visions of development—Zahwi, the liberal realist, against Abdalla, the progressive dreamer—are not exclusive to Egypt, but illustrate the debate going on in the Third World over the resurgence of liberal ideas. In another Muslim country, Pakistan, I encountered exactly the same arguments. As was the case in Egypt, after the socialization of the country by the Bhutto regime, the pro-West General Zia ul-Haq, in the name of free enterprise, has allowed 22 traditional feudal families to rebuild their fortune. This pseudobourgeoisie does not invest any more than its Egyptian counterpart, limits itself to trade, undertakes no new ventures, and reinvests all its profits abroad. Let us add that in Pakistan, like Bolivia, drug trafficking is a major economic activity. Estimates are that some five billion dollars worth of heroin has been exported from Pakistan, the poppy being cultivated in the north of the country as well as in Afghanistan. One market that no economist will integrate in a plan, its principal virtue is that all those involved stand to gain—the farmers, the transporters, and the sellers. The People's party under the leadership of Benazir Bhutto opposes General Zia, idealizes her father's regime, and wants to return to the ante-Zia period through a vast surge of the whole society and a mobilization of the masses. Thus the Third World comes on, buffeted between a liberalization of intention and an empty ideological rhetoric far removed from social reality and revolutionary myths.

We have up to now, I think, explored all the pitfalls, and readers who have been following us may have begun to despair. But having remained with us for so long, they will be rewarded because the next chapter deals with the answers to these problems. For the most part these answers are based on two principles: the state of law and the respect for the individual. This is a true model of liberal inspiration.

# ELEVEN

# Song of Hope

AS SOON AS SANDHU CATCHES SIGHT OF ME, HE WAVES ENERGETICALLY and acts as if there were nothing more natural than this meeting. I had been present at the winter sowing in his village of Shikopur and vaguely promised that I would come back when the wheat was grown. But how did he know that I would be there, at that very moment, at the end of the road that leads to Shikopur from an offshoot of the Delhi highway? Sandhu was bubbling with joy, in a state of exultation. Had he smoked a little too much of his pipe, seasoned with a pinch of hashish? for he forgot to ask me about my children, who are as numerous as his. Even the traditional welcome refreshment, *lassi* and the aromatic curry plus *chapati* with goat's cheese, could wait. First, I had to go and see the field to admire the new wheat!

I do not know much about agronomy, but this short-stalked wheat with big ears is growing straight and thick, the irrigation canals are perfectly maintained, and there is no trace of weeds or insects. Sandhu had experimented with a high-yielding variety of wheat seed that he managed to get from a pilot agricultural center instead of taking the seed from his harvest as had been the practice in Shikopur from time immemorial. Although Sandhu had taken a considerable financial risk in buying these seeds, he was expecting a harvest three times that of the previous year, or about 80 quintals per irrigated hectare. (He sowed one of his five acres of land with traditional wheat seeds for personal consumption because the new wheat did not taste as good as the old.) For centuries, in this village in Haryana in northern India, each person has been, according to his or her caste, assigned a specific task. The landed peasants produce enough cereals, vegetables, and fruit to meet all food needs, including those of the landless castes, the untouchables, and the artisans. A few enormous black buffalo housed in the courtyard supply milk, which, when fermented, constitutes, with *chapatis,* the basic meal. The few pieces of furniture and domestic utensils are all made within the village, of terra-cotta, wood, or rock, with great technical ingenuity. A special caste's exclusive occupation is to braid vegetable fiber. Another caste looks after cotton weaving, and another, the silk from the mulberry trees. Women stack cow dung cakes in symmetrical pyramids, and when they see a foreign visitor they hide their faces behind their saris. Shikopur also has Brahmin priests and a doctor who only uses ayurvedic remedies from local plants. The inhabitants of Shikopur never bought from or sold to the outside world until the Green Revolution came. (This term was coined by the World Bank to describe the spectacular success story of Indian and Pakistani agriculture.)

## The Gene that Shrank

When Sandhu sowed this high-yielding seed that was going to change his life, he did not know that it had been invented in Mexico twenty years ago by the American agronomist Norman Borlaug. The link between Borlaug, a Nobel Peace Prize laureate in 1970, and Sandhu is one of the most astonishing scientific adventures of our times.

Our story begins in nineteenth-century Japan when American agronomists found on the rich land of Hokkaido peculiar varieties of wheat. The height of this wheat stalk never exceeds 60 centimeters, and the ear can thus grow heavy without falling on the ground. This dwarf wheat strain, which has no equivalent anywhere in the world, owes little to the vagaries of nature, but was the result of centuries of patient crossbreeding and selection by Japanese peasants. These farmers had found an answer for all cereal planters: a heavy ear whose weight does not bend the stalk. This dwarf wheat left Japan for the first time in 1867, thanks to a Frenchman, Dr. Mourier, who handed over a few seeds to the Jardin d'Acclimation de Paris. In 1880, his diary records that the wheat from Japan bloomed three weeks before it was due. It was marketed as a botanical curiosity until 1904, at which time the shrinking wheat gene faded away without its secret being revealed.

But another promising line of thought was being developed: A semidwarf wheat, the Daruma, was crossed in 1917 with an American wheat strain, the Fultz, in an experimental center near Tokyo. This crossbreeding gave rise to the fourteenth generation of the Norin 10 strand, which has a 52-centimeter stalk. The Norin 10 cultivation revolutionized Japanese productivity from 1945 onward, when it was adopted for large-scale use. Ten years later, an American agronomist, Dr. Salomon, who had accompanied the Occupation Army, found these peculiar wheat stalks in a research center north of Honshū. Salomon immediately realized the significance of his discovery and sent the seeds by air to the United States; Borlaug stepped in to carry on the good work.

In northern Mexico this young agronomist, financed by a Rockefeller Fellowship, was striving to improve the strains of wheat or maize traditionally used by the Sonora peasant, but making no headway. Each time he tried to increase the output through better fertilizers and irrigation, the ear became heavier, spluttered, and rotted. Borlaug then shortened the stalk by crossing Mexican wheat with Norin 10. But Mendel's genetic laws cannot be circumvented. The creation of a new strain through crossbreeding requires fourteen years unless—and this is the second Borlaug brain wave—it was possible to have a biannual harvest. Mexico's diversity of climate, altitude, and exposure to light proved to be ideal for such an experiment. Borlaug thus alternated the pattern of crop rotation between the northern and southern parts of the country, achieving in a single year what should have taken two years. The new strain the Mexican dwarf wheat Sonora 63, which was to revolutionize the agriculture of the poor, appeared in the seventh year.

About the same time, in the early 1960s, India was going through its severest famine since World War II. Dr. Swaminathan of the Indian Agricultural Research Institute, having heard of Borlaug's work, invited him to come immediately to Delhi. Borlaug told me how he caught the first available plane, taking with him only his attaché case full of Sonora 63 seeds. When he met Prime Minister Indira Gandhi, he persuaded her to experiment with his seeds. The Mexican variety, which had been grown alternately in varying climates and light, proved well suited to Indian conditions. The Sonora seeds are remarkably resistant to infection and offer the additional advantage of not belonging to a pure strain. As they were a hybrid, the Indian agronomists of the Ludhiana University in Punjab were able to use their genetic reservoir to create new, better varieties more suited to local conditions. Having traveled from Japan to Mexico and then to India, these wheat strands carry the HYV1 and HYV2 shrinking genes.

Sandhu is the last link in the Green Revolution cycle that, in the space of twenty years, has taken the monsoon-dependent Asia out of the grip of chronic famine. Today India's wheat surpluses equal those of Canada and the European Economic Community. The Green Revolution has generated sociological, economic, and ideological literature, each of which interprets such a transformation in a different way. The issue has become even more complex because the Green Revolution was initiated and became a great success in the Punjab region of India and because its momentum has been sustained by a singular religious community, the Sikhs. Are the Sikhs alone capable of such progress? Are the Hindus and the Muslims not up to the task?

The Sikhs seem to feel this is true!

## The Jews of India

The productivity of the Sikh Punjabi peasant is comparable with that of U.S. farmers of the Middle West. In the space of twenty years, wheat production in the state has gone up eightfold, rice production threefold, and potato production sevenfold. Thanks to Punjab, in less than one generation, India moved from starvation to abundance: with just 6 percent of this state's total land under cultivation, it accounts for 60 percent of the country's wheat production.

Half seriously, half ironically, Khushwant Singh says to me that the Sikh peasants were bound to succeed because they are Sikhs and Sikhs are the Jews of India. Refugees who share the same faith and for whom ritual is stronger than belief, the Sikhs are gifted with a proven talent for economic success and are by nature both proud and timorous. The Sikh religion, as revealed by Guru Nanak in the fifteenth century, is based on the concept of one God and no caste system. Predestination has no place in this religion, which favors individual initiative and equality. A Sikh never shaves and keeps his hair long, twisted into a bun under his turban. He and his dagger are inseparable, for his dagger symbolizes that he belongs to the community.[1] Khushwant Singh, a historian and an editor, is well known in India for his nonconformist stance. He stretches the comparison between Sikhs and Jews by hanging a mezuzah on his door that he brought back from Jerusalem, where he had been warmly welcomed. (The head priest of the Sikhs recognized the state of Israel long before the Russians or the Americans.)

After the partition of the subcontinent, the Indian government distributed land to the Sikhs that they built into a community of small enterprising individual owners who learned how to use all the available resources and put agricultural innovation and irrigation to the best use.

Water has certainly been the decisive factor in Punjab's Green Revolution (Punjab means the land of five rivers), but water had to be brought to the fields, which required that each peasant dig a well and buy a pumpset in those places where there was no collective irrigation network.[2] The traditional Sikh traders did their bit by ensuring a regular distribution of seeds and fertilizers in all the villages of Punjab. Fertilizers were expensive, and the peasant had to be willing to take new risks, which would not have been the case if he had stuck to traditional agriculture. The government also deserves its due, for since 1965 it has guaranteed a minimum procurement price. This was the handiwork of L. K. Jha, who informed me that the main opposition came from Soviet advisers, who were very influential in government circles at the time and saw Borlaug as part of an American conspiracy. Had prices remained low, however, the Sikhs would certainly not have shown any inclination to invest in the Green Revolution.

What did the trick? The Sikhs, the Mexican seed, water, small holdings, or a guaranteed minimum procurement price? Can the Green Revolution spread elsewhere in other conditions? Thus the stakes in Sandhu's harvest at Shikopur were showing the world that the Green Revolution can succeed elsewhere.

## Return to Shikopur

For Dr. Singh it is anathema to be told that the Green Revolution has succeeded in Punjab because the Punjabis are Sikhs. He is not Sikh, but an agronomist at the Institute of Agricultural Research in Delhi who belongs to a family of Hindu peasants. He feels that custom and religion played no part in Punjab and that only objective conditions count; namely, seeds and irrigation. To prove his point, Hindu villagers had to switch from traditional agriculture to high-yielding varieties. Singh chose Shikopur for his pilot project because the village had many wells and was made up of small landowners who would have a direct interest in producing more and marketing the surpluses. All that remained was to convince the peasant through practical demonstration, Singh's motto being, let results speak for themselves.

After having persuaded the Shikopur *panchayat* (municipal council) to place at his disposal some acres of common land, he planted traditional seeds as well as selected seeds of wheat, mustard, and radish. The schoolchildren helped out in the experiment by using class time to sow both the old and the new seeds.

The first year, the differences in output, for equal amounts of work, fertilizer, and water, were spectacular, but not spectacular enough to dispel the peasants' doubts. It took three years of this wondrous technique to convince the peasants that the new seeds would not be destroyed by insects and gave them time to calculate their cost benefits (there is no point in producing more if the expected profits are to be pruned by the cost of new seeds, fertilizer, or extra work). At the end of the three years, Sandhu, who Dr. Singh described as a progressive peasant, opted for change.

After visiting Sandhu's field, we drank the much-awaited glass of *lassi*. Lying under the shade of a fig tree on string cots, the men of Shikopur chat and pass around the water pipe. Each one pulls deeply and lets out puffs of thick, aromatic smoke. It is the women brightening the green fields with the lively colors of their saris, who mix the dung, feed the buffalo, remove the weeds and make the *chapatis*. Sandhu, who catches my disapproving look, observes that he was responsible for the Green Revolution as it was he who had sown and he who shall reap. Economic growth in Shikopur has not brought out the best in men and done little to improve women's lot.

I shall probably never meet Sandhu again, for my journey in India came to an end in the spring of 1987. But I shall never forget Shikopur. This village is a perfect example of how modernization is possible in any civilization, including the most conservative. Here we learn that the Third World can feed itself and absorb its population growth, provided sound agricultural techniques are used. The village population has doubled in the past 30 years, but is no longer haunted by the specter of famine. Shikopur's Green Revolution will bring about changes in social organization and create new forms of inequality; some landowners will get richer than others, but the entire village will reap the benefits of this newfound prosperity. Shikopur also represents all the uncertainties and slowness of development; this experimental program is taking place in only one of the 600,000 villages of India. All the villages do not have water, and Dr. Singh's experiment is as remarkable as it is isolated. To spread the Green Revolution, the Indian government must work resolutely and spend more money on it. Even more important, qualified agronomists, engineers, and technicians trained at Indian universities should quit their offices and laboratories and go work in the villages. For the most part they refuse to do so, which is an attitude characteristic of the new elites of the Third World, who prefer to devote their time to basic research and theory in an urban milieu. Singh, perhaps because he is the son of a peasant, proved to be the exception.

The "Song of Hope"[3] of the Green Revolution can be heard in several villages of the Third World, and even in India, the miracle has been reproduced in other provinces without Sikhs, like Tamil Nadu in the south of the country. New rice seeds have also appeared in Thailand, Indonesia, the Philippines, and Korea. Mainland China has drawn from this reservoir of techniques accessible to all, and Bangladesh, which has been a prototype of famine for a long time, has achieved remarkable progress in the spheres of rice and wheat. Practically the whole of Asia now abounds in cereals and is discovering the hitherto unknown problems of storage and surpluses. Asia is no longer the continent of famine,[4] as any village in Asia that has adopted improved techniques has been embraced by the Green Revolution.

In 1967 two famous agricultural experts, William Paddock and Paul Paddock, published a remarkable book entitled *Famine, 1975* (Little Brown), which was devoted to the inevitable tragedy of Asia. The question of Africa was not even mentioned, as at the time Africa was still self-sufficient. Twenty years later, the situation has changed, and it is Africa's production that can no longer keep up with population. Why hasn't Africa benefited from India's kind of progress? Ostensibly because of nature's harsh treatment and agricultural traditions: fragile soil, large variety of crops, difficult climate, ignorance about irrigation, and archaic forms of subsistence agriculture. But such natural obstacles could have been overcome in most cases if faulty policies had not thrown research off the rails.

## The White Gold of the Savannas

Soon after its independence the government of Ghana destroyed all agricultural research centers and cast to the winds specimens and samples carefully collected over a period of 30 to 40 years. This kind of revolutionary gesture is meant to wipe out the memory of the colonial past. The slow, meticulous process of genetic selection, however, requires years of patience and peace, which has been unknown for a long time in the countries south of the Sahara. In contrast, the steady research work done in the Ivory Coast both before and after independence illustrates that nothing in Africa's natural habitat prevents it from achieving an agricultural miracle.

Thus in the Ivory Coast cotton output has gone up from one hundred kilograms per hectare in the 1950s to eight hundred kilograms per hectare, thanks to the introduction of ISA 205, a new improved variety selected by the Institut des Savanes in Bouaké. Under the guidance of Claude Angelini for the last 45 years, this institute has achieved for cotton in Africa what Borlaug did for wheat in Mexico. The Ivory Coast has become the largest producer of African cotton, a variety that does not require water. At the time of independence, it was thought that cotton would not be suitable to the ecosystem of the country. Cotton is, in fact, the white gold of the savannas; it supplies oil, fiber, and textiles, and, if one desires, protein. The Institut des Savanes has developed a glandless variety that can be used to make flour and cakes, thus providing an inexhaustible food reserve.

Anticolonial critics of the Green Revolution lament that Africa concentrated on cash crops to the detriment of subsistence crops. There is, however, no contradiction between these two types of crops because the same plant can feed the peasant and its surpluses be sold. Moreover, the African peasant grows sweet potatoes and cotton or cocoa in the same place for the most part, and if one crop is well looked after, the others will benefit. The time has come for African peasants to get out of this poverty syndrome that has condemned them to a vegetative existence. Africans, like everyone else, are looking for more than mere survival and they too want development. But development is impossible if they have nothing to sell and grow only subsistence crops.

# We Know Enough to Be Able to Feed the World

At 64, Borlaug has a midwestern accent and gnarled peasant hands. The means he has at his disposal today are a far cry from the rudimentary methods that led him to Sonora 63. Even though he is no longer officially in charge, he continues to be the driving force behind the Centro Internacional de Mejoramiento de Maiz y Trigo (Cimmyt), part of a huge research network, financed by the World Bank in Washington, whose main branches are located in Manila, Nigeria, India, and Syria. Guy Vallaeys, the chairman of Cimmyt since 1986, is an agronomist from France. This network is one of the greatest success stories in international cooperation in the Third World. One hour away from Mexico, near the great pyramids of Tehotihuacan, the Cimmyt experimental fields are impeccably maintained, irrigated, and straight and a striking contrast to the disorder of the nearby Mexican farms whose landscapes consist of cactus and rock. In an air-conditioned building, a genetic bank houses several thousand germoplasms collected from all over the world, an international data bank of agronomic knowledge. Each one of these seeds has specific properties not found in any other; some are the products of nature's haphazard selection, whereas others have been scientifically chosen and developed.

Even more impressive is the scientific community who works at the institute. The agronomists and geneticists, who learn how to cross the strains and perfect them, come from more than a hundred countries— from China, from Africa, from the Arab world, as well as from all over Latin America. Once they return to their countries, it is their responsibility to adapt the Cimmyt seeds to their specific agricultural conditions. Research has gone far beyond shortening the wheat stalk or the maize stalk to selecting cereals resistant to insects and virus that are far more devastating than any drought. A whole host of harmful worms are bred to infest plants, thereby allowing the resistant plants to be identified. More than 150 years after Darwin, at Cimmyt the struggle for life has become synonymous with that of wheat against the locust.

But what is the use of creating new seeds if no effort is made to popularize them with farmers and consumers? Why talk of insects alone? Food habits can also prevent the extensive cultivation of a cereal. There is no point in inventing a maize that has a higher protein content than milk, such as Opaque 2, which already exists, if the flour's color and consistency does not appeal to the peasant of Central America. What good is it to invent a new cereal—the very first created by man, the tritical, a cross between wheat and rye—if the Indian peasant cannot make *chapatis* out of it to his liking? One novelty at Cimmyt is that you can, in the presence of white-coated scientists, make bread, cakes, paste, and doughs with the new cereals and then get a briefing about their color and taste.

In 1986, Borlaug demonstrated the unlimited possibilities that Cimmyt's technology could open to Sudan. On four hundred unirrigated, experimental fields scattered all over the country, he was able to get a rye harvest six times greater than the traditional peasant's. Explains Borlaug,

> It was easy. In the first year all I had to do was use good seeds, good fertilizer, and a good weed killer as well as a good watering system. On the basis of the results obtained, I changed the proportions and the next year I doubled my output. All that's left for me now is to persuade the Sudanese government to distribute fertilizers to the peasants six weeks before sowing, give them necessary credit to buy fertilizer required for harvesting, which will be paid back after the harvest, and to fix a minimum procurement price for rye, allowing them to pay back their loan.

Elementary, my dear Watson! Herein lies a solution to the problem of famine in this part of Africa, but the governments of Ethiopia and Sudan are too busy making war on each other.

According to Borlaug, between Cimmyt and the International Rice Research Institute of Manila there is enough knowhow available to make it possible to feed the Third World and face the challenges of the unprecedented population growth. Borlaug points out that, since the Green Revolution, which affected only a small part of the country, 700 million Indians eat better than they did a generation ago, when there were only 350 million to feed.

## Malthus Defeated

Borlaug's remark will surprise those with preconceived notions about overpopulation. The past 25 years have witnessed not only an unprecedented population explosion but many agricultural miracles as well—a coincidence that invalidates the laws of rarefication of natural resources as postulated by Malthus, which governed the thinking of the Club of Rome, an international group of economists who launched the debate on zero percent growth in the 1970s. The unprecedented population surplus, far from leading to famine, which experts thought inevitable ten years ago, has seen an improvement in the overall food situation and in the health standards of the poor.

If undernourishment persists in the Third World, it is not due to a scarcity of agricultural resources but to low incomes due to underemployment. This basic distinction shows the necessity for a development policy that goes beyond agriculture.

The only real famines that persist in the world are not due to overpopulation but to war or underpopulation as in the Sahara and on the Andes plateau. Also, overpopulation does not lead to impoverishment. The new industrial countries of Asia—Korea, Singapore, Taiwan, Thailand—are among the most densely populated of our planet. The poorest countries of the world, Tanzania and Bolivia, in contrast, are relatively underpopulated.

We must thus revise our assumptions about the relationship between population, hunger, and poverty. For example, overpopulation does not lead to famine, but could result in moving from extensive agriculture to intensive techniques. The natural corollary, then, is that underpopulation does not prevent famine, but could, in fact, aggravate it because it would not allow the necessary threshold to be reached for intensive agriculture. All this is well known to the concerned populations.

In the villages of black Africa that I visited, whether in Senegal, Tanzania, or the Ivory Coast, peasants regretted not having enough children to spread their fields further. Procreation in Black Africa is not reckless, but linked to the underdevelopment of the people. If parents choose to have (on average) six children, it is not only for cultural or religious reasons (as frequently mentioned), but because it guarantees more labor for their old age.

Experts argue that these peasants only consider their immediate interests and have no idea of the disastrous consequences that their irresponsible behaviour brings on the community as a whole. The price, however, is not really so high, given the scant resources that Third World countries allocate to education, health, and housing; an extra child is not an expensive proposition and, in fact, will soon become a factor of production, which will add to national wealth. Moreover, the young generations, by looking after their old parents, are helping the state economize on the collective cost of social security for the poorest; the large family is the Third World's old-age pension. The major problem with Africa is not that it is experiencing a population explosion, but that it is currently a continent of children, with 45 percent of the population under eighteen. A people in the making! The challenge is in educating and training this youth. On the whole, the economic rationale on which birth control policies have been based over the last 25 years seems rather tenuous to me. It is impossible to prove that the decline in birth rate leads to development because the opposite is true. Development brings about a decline in the birth rate, as shown by the experience of the newly industrialized countries. The slowing down of population growth in Southeast Asia is a result of the economic takeoff and urbanization, not its cause. The bourgeoisie brings about new attitudes leading to a smaller family, not the opposite. This is why all population policies, which have claimed for the last 25 years to be one step ahead of development, have proved, without exception, failures.

In the light of such evidence, one wonders why the governments of the Third World, in particular those of India and China, with the help of international organizations, persist in their brutal birth control policies. The answer does not seem to be entirely economic, but, I tend to think, has more to do with a desire to control society as a whole. China presents a most worrying example. Childbearing is not a natural right, but requires an authorization of the production squad to which one belongs. Any infringement is punished with a fine and the withdrawal of ration tickets, the right to go to school, and social services, not to mention the public censure of "mass organizations."[5] It is difficult to understand how the one-child per family policy serves the cause of development. The Chinese authorities, however, have begun to realize that this policy is leading to profound psychic disturbances and that the new generation in the Beijing schools is unmanageable because as only children, they are extremely spoiled by their parents.

India also illustrates to what extent population control is used as a scientific alibi to rationalize the bourgeoisie's fear of the teeming masses. Listening to Delhi's high society on the subject is revealing: It is always "Oh, the poor have too many children"; never the Indians. The Indian leaders' hysteria reached its height with the compulsory sterilization campaign of 1976. Today the bourgeoisie is feeding itself new myths for miraculous solutions. The latest of these comes from Professor Talwar, director of the Center of Immunology in Delhi, who in 1987 experimented on some female guinea pigs with the first antipregnancy vaccine. (It has been said that this extremely eminent researcher is secretly working on a cream for men that will be both erectile and spermicidal. Pleasure will automatically annihilate fertility!)

If Indian leaders were really keen to curtail population growth, they ought to take inspiration from Kerala, a state in their own country. Here the birth rate is much lower[6] than the rest of India, but the population is literate, and girls go to school. Among the reasons for this are that Kerala is traditionally a matriarchal society and that the local government—a communist majority—has invested a lot of money in education. If the Indian government wishes to bring down the birth rate, why not follow Kerala's example and spend four times more on education than it does on defense?

But even though India and China can, thanks to the Green Revolution, feed a growing population, are there not inextricable situations where Malthus holds good? A case in point is Egypt. The Egyptian population is growing at the rate of a million inhabitants every ten months, creating panic among its leadership. "This youth," says Ali Loutfi, the former prime minister, "is like the wide-open mouth of the lion which swallows all that one throws to him, all the while trying to escape from him." Today more than 50 million inhabitants are huddled together on the narrow banks of the Nile in the same space where only 12 million lived 50 years ago. The population of Cairo has gone up in 25 years from 2 to 12 million inhabitants, and this city has become a vast human traffic jam. The gap between food production and consumption is widening; every year Egypt imports half of its cereal intake. The Nile peasant, who was previously considered one of the most efficient in the world, cannot keep up with the ever-growing demands. How does one stem the tide? "My government," says Loutfi, "decided to reduce population growth from 2.7 to 2.4 percent per annum." How? "I set up a commission to go into the question with all the circumspection that Islamic and Christian faiths require."

But another solution is at hand. Just as in India, where Kerala offers a far better answer than Professor Talwar's or any family planning center, so in Egypt one should go to Ten of Ramadan, a newly built city in the heart of the desert between Cairo and Ismailia with a hundred thousand inhabitants and the most modern factories in Egypt. This exemplary achievement illustrates that Egyptians can successfully irrigate and colonize the desert. Egypt will be able to house and care for its large population the day it decides to exploit its real wealth. Its neighbors in Israel have managed to do this without the waters of the Nile. At Ten of Ramadan I became convinced of the universal fallacy of Malthusian logic.

Birth control policies are nothing more than an admission of failure; they have removed neither hunger nor poverty. Only through the development of the economy and education will families of the Third World voluntarily accept having fewer children. Techniques to put an end to mass poverty, particularly famine, exist and are available. The real question is, Why are they not used?

# TWELVE

# Hunger, A Thing of the Past

FELUCCAS, WITH THEIR TRIANGULAR SAILS PUSHED BY NORTH WINDS, take their consignment of wheat toward Upper Egypt. Sleepy-looking fellahin trot along on their donkeys, light-hearted and full of jest. A young cow turns a heavy wheel attached to a rope that brings the waters of the Nile up to field level. The landscape and traditions are little changed since the time of the pharaohs, although cement parapets have begun to replace the traditional brick because the government ordered that the clay of the valley be used only for agricultural purposes. Ahmed is a Nile peasant whose family has most probably lived at Chebin-el-Kanatir for thousands of years. Ahmed's concession to the West is wearing laceless tennis shoes and an old American gabardine coat on top of his djellaba.

In 1956 his father, previously a landless peasant, became an owner when Nasser evicted, without compensation, all the large landowners and redistributed the land to the fellahin. Since then the Egyptian population has swelled to such numbers that Ahmed's entire family has to live on a *fedan,* about half an acre. This soil, enriched by the waters of the Nile, is some of the most fertile in the world, but Ahmed cultivates his field, divided like a kitchen garden in small plots, in the same way as his ancestors. His field has been irrigated on fixed days ever since the Aswān Dam regularized the floods of the river.

Thanks to agrarian reform, Ahmed has managed to escape the quasi serfdom of his father, but he is still not a free peasant because property in Egypt, as Ismail Abdalla, a former minister of the Nasser regime, clarified, is not governed by Roman law. Property only has a social function and is meant to serve the interests of the entire community. Thus, the large landowner was replaced by a bureaucrat in the Ministry of Agriculture who tells Ahmed to plant wheat, maize, cotton, and sugarcane, even though these might not bring Ahmed more money, because the government deems it to be in the national interest. Ahmed must then sell his harvest to a cooperative, which is a part of the Ministry of Agriculture, at a very low price. Ahmed is exploited by the state so that the town population can be cheaply fed.

This system, which was introduced by the Nasser government, seems reasonable until you see it in action in Egypt, where the first consequence of low procurement prices was a rural exodus. The population of Cairo shot up from two million to twelve million in 25 years. Add to this the emigration to the Persian Gulf, and you find an overpopulated country like Egypt short of labor in the rural areas, which leads to considerable losses at harvest time. One look at Ahmed's field, however, and we realize that he is growing vegetables instead of the cereals the government told him to grow. Ahmed breaks the law because he can sell vegetables on the Cairo market for much more money than he can wheat or maize. He does have to pay a fine, but he will negotiate the sum with an official from the Agriculture Ministry who is so badly paid that he has to strike such deals with the peasants to survive.

Ahmed's greatest ambition is to acquire a motor pump that will enable him to draw water directly from the Nile to ensure a steady water supply rather than depending on the administration, which provides water only on fixed days. This again is illegal, but nothing is impossible with baksheesh. Their palms greased, the officials readily turn a blind eye, but Ahmed assures me that he still stands to gain, given the small amount of baksheesh and the low cooperative prices.

One consequence of all this is that Ahmed grows very little wheat and that more for the straw than for the grain because he sells the grain to the cooperative but the straw on the free market, where it is in much demand as cattle feed. Unlike all the other peasants in the world, Ahmed chooses longer-stalked wheat of the thickest possible variety, harvests his crop late in the season, and is even willing to lose considerable amounts of grain. It is estimated that in Egypt one-third of the potential wheat harvest is thus wasted! The food deficit in the country is considerable, and wheat imports, massive.

So lives Ahmed, the peasant of the Nile, in fear of the official on whom his fate depends. His economic behavior is extremely harmful to the national community, but from his point of view, perfectly reasonable.

Whenever the governments of the Third World refuse to take such logic into account, they are starving themselves and their people. The tragedy of Egypt has not been the expropriation of huge, often badly run properties, but the refusal to allow the creation of a peasantry not dependent on political power. The fear of all authoritarian regimes is the creation of a class of small owners who are free and enterprising (the old kulak myth). It is not so much the natural conditions but the desire to control the peasantry that explains the food scarcity of the Third World. Theodore Schultz, a Nobel Prize laureate and an economist from the University of Chicago, proved this in a systematic manner.

## The Rational Peasant

"Even a peasant who cannot read, knows how to count and that in any language and under any climate," says Schultz. "Each and every peasant is a rational being."[1] If he can foresee material and personal gain from working and producing more, he will do so. If his gains are not so perceptible, he will be content to produce at a subsistence level. For Schultz, the peasant of the Third World is thus a capitalist on a microscopic scale, capable of combining the rare resources at his disposal to obtain maximum benefit and how to measure the value of his time. Schultz adds, "What many economists fail to understand is that the poorest are not less concerned than the rich about improving their own as well as their children's lot."

Schultz's truisms have been ignored for the last 50 years by all those governments that have been trying to train, collectivize, and thereby squeeze the peasants to produce more. Not treating the peasant as a *homoeconomicus*, according to Schultz, has starved the Third World, and it is only the rediscovery of the motivations of enterprise that will breathe new life into Chinese and African agriculture. Such an analysis means that one must invest in the people, particularly their education, because they are the most efficient factor of agricultural production. All information accumulated by the rational peasant is transformed with utmost certainty into additional production.

Schultz's hypothesis enables us to look at the villages of the Third World in a new light and to understand the attitudes of the peasant population, whatever civilization they belong to. I have often tried the Schultz method in environments where language and cultural differences made any other conversation impossible, but understanding was perfect when

it came to things material. Thus, ostensibly incomprehensible, even aber-
rant behavior suddenly becomes clear if examined under the microscope
of rationality.

The refusal to innovate, frequently encountered among the peasantry of the Third World even though the techniques are available, is often
interpreted by Western observers as a sign of cultural retardedness. This
is patently absurd, for Schultz teaches us that this apparent archaism actually obeys a very coherent logic. Traditional agriculture offers the peasant a regular harvest; without changing his techniques or his seeds, he
will produce, come what may, enough to ensure subsistence and survival
for his family. If he were to innovate, the profits would perhaps be considerable but the risks equally high. The Third World peasant often has
nothing to fall back on. For him, innovation could mean the loss of his
land, the necessity to migrate to the city, or even famine. Because he is
rational the Third World peasant is particularly reticent about innovation, but this same rationality allowed him to enter into the spirit of the
Green Revolution.

More than water, more than seeds, more than climate, it is the peasant's relationship with his soil that determines the level and quality of agricultural output. In China a change in the ownership pattern, that is,
moving away from collective farming to family farming, has enabled the
peasant, within seven years, to transform the agricultural sector of this
huge country. But the restrictions on ownership have slackened this
progress. Family ownership appears to be the most profitable mode of
cultivation for both the individual and the society. Such has been the experience of the developed and the developing world alike. Most of the
countries I visited, however, do not seem to recognize this principle. For
historical reasons land is often concentrated in the hands of a few large
owners, but ideological considerations more than anything else go against
the notion of individual property: land ownership is the center around
which all Third World politics revolve.

## For a Liberal Revolution

This individualistic and capitalistic interpretation of the poor peasant
radically differs from another theory that held sway for a long time,
the so-called moral peasant theory, where the farmers are presented as
altruistic beings who are inclined to unite under a collective banner.
Schultz's theory, however, is based on direct observation; he is one of the

rare economists who have managed to strike the right equation between fieldwork and theoretical reflection. Like Adam Smith, Tocqueville, and, more recently, Hayek, Schultz is first and foremost a great traveler and a perceptive observer. Even today, at the age of 80, this solid man with white hair and light eyes, unassuming and cheerful, only stops over at his home in Chicago between journeys. Faithful to the liberal tradition, he turned to theory only after watching firsthand the real-life experience of men and women. His fieldwork, especially his comparison of behavioral patterns of peasants in India and Guatemala, enabled him to move from the particular to the universal. But having been dismissed as a crank and reactionary for a long time, he is now hailed as a prophet and his travels to India and Africa viewed as triumphant journeys. The theory of the rational peasant, which derives its strength from its simplicity and clarity and is revolutionizing Third World agriculture, illustrates that ideas have a much greater impact on the economy than do natural conditions.

Let us make no mistake; Schultz's conclusions do not reflect the views of the establishment. He is talking about a liberal revolution with the creation of a bourgeois peasant—peasant owners who will innovate because their right to property will be legally guaranteed and their labor rewarded at its just value by the market. Remunerative prices and the right to property will answer the growing food needs of the Third World. The path of liberalism generally leads to agrarian reform and the creation of a peasant bourgeoisie, not an uprooted proletariat. Such liberal agrarian reform is possible, and at least one model has been identified.

# The Bourgeois Peasant in Taiwan

Kang Lieu San has bartered his Chinese straw hat for a baseball cap, which in Taiwan is a sign of economic prosperity. Although Kang is not rich, his Japanese car and television set do place him in the Taiwanese middle class, but he regrets that he did not switch to raising asparagus or snails like some of his neighbors from Taoyuan who only grow for export. At 64, Kang is too old to grow anything but rice on his two-hectare farm.

Kang has not always been this well-off. Until 1949, in fact, he lived like any poor Asian peasant, a life of poverty and insecurity. A sharecropper, as were his father and grandfather, he had to give half his meager harvest to the village chief, who could at any time snatch his land away. Nothing motivated Kang to produce beyond what he required for his own subsistence, and he was content to follow the example of his ancestors and watch history go by, a history that was engulfing Taiwan. In 1949, however, Kang's fortune took a swing in the right direction. First he witnessed Japanese colonization and then the liberation by the Kuomintang armies. But when the communist party took the Chinese mainland and Chiang Kai-shek realized that he would never see Beijing again, Kang suddenly became a significant factor in the rivalry between the two Chinas. How could the Kuomintang hope to reconquer the mainland if it could not prove the superiority of its model for society? Between Nationalist China and communist China, the armed struggle was coupled with an ideological confrontation, with the peasantry the main stake. The fate of the oppressed peasant, as it has been since the days of feudal China, was the key reference point for any comparison.

Mao chose to liberate the masses by exterminating landlords and collectivizing lands. On the other side of the strait of Formosa, Chang Kai-shek remembered the dictum of Sun Yat-sen, his guide, philosopher, and mentor: "Land belongs to he who cultivates it." A simple formula, a good formula, but difficult to implement as long as one is dependent on the bourgeoisie and landowners. This policy bore fruit, however, and within the space of ten years brought about complete agrarian reform. Unlike Mao, Chang Kai-shek sold the land to the peasants and compensated the owners.

Kang, then, in 1949 was granted a lease that was to be registered for at least six years and then be renewed and the owner's share brought down from two-thirds to one-third of the harvest. That same year, Kang was democratically elected to a village committee where farmers, sharecroppers, and owners were called on to evaluate the entire harvest. In 1953, all owners who did not cultivate their own lands and who held more than three irrigated hectares or six nonirrigated hectares were obliged to sell those lands to the state. The state handed them over to the peasants for a price fixed at 2-and-½ times the value of the annual harvest to be paid over a period of ten years. There were 300,000 families who bought land. The entire operation was facilitated by registers that had been drawn up by the Japanese colonizers, who also left behind an excellent irrigation network and roads in perfect condition. One reason for the success of this program was the relative absence of corruption among the officials in charge. Companions of Chang Kai-shek who had fled the mainland with him had no ties to local landowners. In Taiwan, unlike India and Pakistan, life is not a series of dubious deals, or *benami* transactions, concluded by former landlords to maintain control of their property![1]

Agrarian reform in Taiwan finally resulted in about one hectare of land per family on an average, without the former owners being unduly penalized. In fact, they were immediately compensated by the government with coupons they could use to buy everyday items as well as shares in prosperous public enterprises confiscated from the Japanese. This privatization of state capital encouraged even the old landowning bourgeoisie to redirect its investment into industry. Not all former landowners became captains of industry, although an active minority did accept the challenge, and several industrial families owe their fortunes to agrarian reform.

In 1987, Yen Chia Kan, former president of the Republic, successor to Chang Kai-shek, and the architect of the agrarian reform, explained to me, "The despoilment which generally accompanies the very idea of agrarian reform is a political and economic absurdity." Owners, he observed, did not cultivate the land, but, as in any other traditional society, fulfilled three essential functions: (1) they looked after the upkeep of their estate, particularly the irrigation network, (2) they were responsible for marketing seeds and grains, (3) and they guaranteed finance to all because agriculture cannot work without credit. Agrarian reform in Taiwan is a success because it was not limited to the transfer of property and because it reassigned the owners' duties to farmers' associations. There are about three hundred of these associations on the island, and each one elects its own council and president. The council then engages a manager who is paid and who looks after irrigation, marketing, and credit.

When Kang became an owner, he started innovating and was willing to take risks. He gave up traditional seeds for the new shortened rice stalk, developed in the Philippines, that was more responsive to irrigation and fertilizer. On the same plot of land where in the 1950s Kang produced two thousand kilograms from three harvests, he now produced twenty thousand kilograms from only two harvests, a record in Asia. The government guarantees a high procurement price to maintain national production levels. Without remunerative prices, agrarian reform serves no purpose at all!

Because Taiwan is producing enough rice for national consumption, Kang's four sons have left the rice fields for the factory. Agrarian reform, an economic, political, and psychological precondition for development, guarantees a constant supply of food to the country, as well as an export surplus, and its success cannot be dissociated from the rapid industrialization that followed. This liberal revolution, based on the principle of ownership and remunerative prices, seems universal. One hopeful sign for the Third World is that this model is beginning to find its way onto the African continent, undoing 50 years of agrarian socialization.

# The Three Lives of Mahmadou Faye

The subprefect of Gandiaye has on the battered door of his modest office the following decree: "It is forbidden to beat the tam-tam between the 15th of June and the 15th of September." When I asked for an explanation, he said that the sound of the tam-tam might keep the rains away from Senegal.

Gandiayen women draw water from deep wells, their hands sawed by the ropes as they exchange village gossip. The marabout makes the children, gray with dust, drone out verses of the Koran that they do not understand a single word of. The village elders sit and chat under the shade of the baobab tree. Hens, goats, and buffalo move between the straw huts looking for stray bits of food. On the dusty track, venerable old buses race madly toward Dakar, bursting at the seams with laughing passengers, cotton bales, and sheep. The office of the subprefect, the school, and the baker are reminiscent of the French era. Mahmadou Faye, a peasant from Senegal who has never stirred out of Gandiaye, feels as if he has lived three lives: colonized when he was young, collectivized when he reached adulthood, and an entrepreneur after the age of 50.

Mahmadou retains a certain nostalgia for those early years, fondly remembering the good old days when one hundred kilos of groundnuts from his field bought him two hundred kilos of rice, with fish, his staple diet. Forty years later, how things have changed! Today he needs two hundred kilos of groundnuts to buy one hundred kilos of rice. After independence, when Mahmadou's second life began, President Senghor explained to him that he had been exploited by colonizers and that socialism was going to replace the large French companies and the Lebanese traders who bought his produce at arbitrary prices.

Thereupon Mahmadou Faye fell victim to the community myth, which was much in vogue with the ruling elite of his country and with the European left-wing intelligentsia that supported decolonization. In this scheme of things, Africa, with its tribal civilization and traditional solidarity, was, to a certain extent, ideally suited for agrarian socialism and cooperatives. Private property and economic individualism were perceived as alien to the history of Africa and therefore ideologically obnoxious. Since 1972, Mahmadou Faye had been obliged to sell all that he produced to the Office National de Cooperation et d' Assistance au Développement (ONCAD), the state monopoly, which went bankrupt and was dissolved in 1982. Poor Mahmadou! ONCAD was his only source of seeds and fertilizer. Seeds were distributed by the local cooperative's president, a bureaucrat of the Socialist party, to his political allies and the corrupt, and the fertilizers were given out far too late to be of any use. At the time of procurement, officials often underweighed Mahmadou's produce. At the time ONCAD employed some six thousand officials and paid the peasants with a promissory note that they then had to negotiate with moneylenders. Often the only way Mahmamdou could make money was to clandestinely crush seeds to make oil and sell it on the black market or sell part of his crop to intermediaries, who would in turn sell it in Mali or Mauritania at a price above the official rate. Senegal claimed to be the victim of drought and the international price fall. True as that may be, Mahmadou was crushed by a bureaucracy who wore African socialist colors and aggravated the effects of falling world prices rather than trying to find means to support them.

In 1985 Mahmadou began his third life when he was able to leave agrarian socialism behind, thanks to the new agricultural policy of Abdou Diouf, Senghor's wise and thoughtful successor. Now Mahmadou buys his own seeds, instead of getting them free, and if he runs short, he gets them directly from the oil mills or from the new, democratically run cooperatives. Private traders can once again buy his crop from him (although they are obliged to stick to the official rate, nothing stops them from offering Mahmadou a few candles or bags of fertilizer under the table). Competition is back, the drought is over; although prices remain low, they are guaranteed by the state. Such measures have changed the old economic equation between villages and towns that kept the purchasing power of the farmer below that of the urban dweller.

Mahmadou now feels responsible for his land. He alone made the decision to limit his production to groundnuts and market garden produce in the lean season. In the humid valleys, now that he has the necessary capital, he grows tomatoes and paprika, which bring the same profit margins as groundnuts. He works more now than he did during the agrarian socialism phase; he would produce even more, had he more children. Only his four sons, he told me, are of an age to be able to help him; his two daughters have refused to toil in the fields ever since they started watching serials on television and giving themselves city airs. Only this shortage of labor slows down the development of his farm. Land is the most freely available factor of production. This resurgent Africa has everything: the soil, the labor, and now judicious policies.

Mahmadou's story is not an exception on the continent. The independence generation has gradually given way to a less charismatic but more reasonable set of leaders. Thus the bureaucratic myth has begun to recede. In Tanzania, when Julius Nyerere voluntarily gave up the presidency in 1985, he left behind a tragic situation. For the first time since the country's independence, the shops in Dar es Salaam were completely empty. Nyerere's successor, President Ali Hassan Mwinyi, re-established supplies by resorting to the oldest economic method in the world—opening up the food grain market. Peasants are no longer forced to sell their produce at throwaway prices to the state monopoly, but can once again trade with Indian intermediaries, who have reappeared in the countryside. Production has been resumed, surpluses are pouring out of the granaries, and cities are well stocked. President Mwinyi's liberalization is a carbon copy of Turgot's model, which was developed in France two centuries ago. Turgot among the Bantus works for the same reason; the underlying principle is universal!

## Charity Begins at Home

Africa is ceasing to be the continent of famine. According to the 1987 Food and Agriculture Organization report (and this organization is generally pessimistic), only three countries—Ethiopia, Mozambique, and Angola, all revolutionary regimes in a state of civil war—will require food aid from abroad. Elsewhere, except in times of crisis, the African peasants have once again begun to feed their people. This is not only because of the rains, as we hear so often, but because the new agricultural policies give the individual peasant a better deal. Thus Africa, like India and China, has come out of its famine in about ten years through the application of sound agricultural techniques and an economic system that offers incentive.

Meanwhile, several obstacles—drought, locusts, wars, and revolutions—have come in the way of these favorable developments. Food aid from abroad thus remained a necessity, but the problems cannot be solved if agriculture is not liberalized. Aid, being such a tricky business, can be nothing more than a last resort.

What thought could be more alluring than transferring the agricultural surpluses of rich countries to the meek of the earth? But this beautiful symmetry is an optical illusion; our surpluses do not correspond to their needs. We do not all eat the same things, and changes in people's food habits often lead to total dependence on imported foodstuff that is impossible to grow on native soil. Even more serious is that food aid has often contributed to the destruction of local crops that are more expensive than foreign products, thus forcing the peasant to migrate to the city and live on charity. These risks are further compounded by trying to ensure that aid does reach the truly needy. In practice food aid is channelized on a government-to-government level, but Third World governments sell back food aid to their own people, thus destroying traditional production circuits and sales outlets. (The poorest people who live in the remote parts of the country suffer the most.) Profits thus earned by the state should theoretically be earmarked for agricultural development projects; in reality, bureaucracies and intermediaries embezzle such funds somewhere along the line. Aid is also often distributed by the governments of the Third World for partisan or trivial considerations and thus becomes a political lever used at home (Tanzania) or can lead to civil war (Ethiopia). Thus food aid rarely reaches those for whom it is intended. Aid must remain the exception and not become a substitute for agricultural development. I believe that this principle holds good for all forms of aid.

## Aid Despite Everything

We have only briefly mentioned aid for development handed out by a fleet of public organizations, private institutions, international officials, experts, and volunteers. Such aid has nothing to do with development but a lot to do with ideological preferences and military strategies. In the name of aid, governments happily confuse arms deliveries and support dubious but friendly regimes with generosity and cooperation.

Some forms of aid defy classification. For example, how do we classify folding hospitals, made in Germany and financed by the French government, delivered in cartons to Madagascar? These cartons, with their sophisticated equipment, were dumped in villages with neither water nor electricity nor, of course, doctor. In Tanzania, on the banks of Lake Tanganyika, stands a glass factory financed with European funds. Five years have gone by and it still hasn't been commissioned because no one knows how to operate it. In Egypt, agricultural machinery centers called Mubarak stations, financed by the World Bank, are constantly being inaugurated, especially during the electoral season. But this equipment is unusable because the fields are too small and the agricultural prices too low to make the machines economically viable. With no one to run these stations, they have fast become derelict. These are just a few of the many cases where Western aid is fostering poverty.

Even after 25 years, no Third World country has ever developed because of aid. The example of Tanzania is most telling: this African state receives the largest number of gifts; it is also the state that is getting poorer the fastest because its institutions are defective. Aid in this case helps strengthen a regime whose policies are harmful.

It would be tempting to get the most virulent critics of aid together under the banner of the British economist Peter Bauer, for whom all aid, by its very definition, reinforces the status quo and aggravates under-development. His critique is directed not so much at private associations as toward public aid and international agencies. A state naturally tends to strengthen another state, even if it is not quite respectable, whereas private associations, untouched by the hypocritical solidarity of the strong, can generally function at a people-to-people level. But private associations are not above suspicion simply because they are private; several are nothing but a replica of the bureaucracy of international agencies in miniature and like them, imbued with redemptionist revolutionary zeal.

Bauer's analysis and those similar to it, however, seem to skirt the issue. Because economic and humanitarian aid is not so much a factor of development as a recognition of the West's responsibility and the need for solidarity. Such acts of humanity protect helpless people from the indifferent tyranny of their own leadership. Our ultimate act of solidarity with the Third World is to admit that the solution to mass poverty can only be found in the Third World itself, not in our countries. The only nations that have escaped mass poverty over the last 25 years—Korea, Taiwan, Singapore, and Hong Kong—are proof of this; they adopted a model for growth and relied on their own strength.

# THIRTEEN

# The New Conquerors

AT THE AGE OF NINETEEN, ANNIE LAN IS TERRORIZING NORTH AMERICA and Europe. She is making our industries go bankrupt and invading our markets, as in a broken-down warehouse of a suburb of Taipei, capital of the Republic of China (Taiwan), bent over a Singer sewing machine, her long, spindly fingers moving without respite, this frail Chinese woman stitches the thousandth buttonhole of her long working day. The blouses she makes are sold at six dollars a piece by Cannontex, the company that employs her, to the fashionable shops of Los Angeles and Dallas. Annie Lan does not take her eye off the job for a minute, and her five-hundred-odd colleagues are equally skillful and diligent. All of them are about her age and perform extremely specialized tasks. Division of labor is one of the secrets of productivity and quality at the Cannontex factory.

For 9-and-½ hours of work a day, six days a week, Annie Lan earns about three hundred dollars a month. Added to this are a few extra dollars when she overshoots the very high production target set by her boss, In Lung Chu. She is entitled to one week's vacation every year; the number of holidays increases with every year of service. Like most unmarried working girls, Annie Lan lives in a large dormitory on the factory premises and is given all her meals at the canteen. If she falls sick or is hospitalized, the entire expenditure will be covered by insurance; the company pays 80 percent and she 20 (about six dollars a month). Such working conditions are good compared with other countries of industrialized Asia; Annie Lan's wage is much higher than it would be in Korea, Thailand, or even the Philippines. If Cannontex were to scale down its operations, Annie would be out of a job. Unemployment insurance is unheard of, for according to the Taiwanese, it would imply an attack on the work ethic. Growth is so sustained, however, that over the last twenty years the case has never arisen.

The productivity of the Taiwanese worker is the highest in the world. Nowhere else, not even in Japan or Korea, have I come across such dedication as I did in that Taipei storeroom. Annie Lan and her companions' spirit of fierce determination can perhaps be explained in terms of anticipated material gain, a desire to escape poverty at all costs (a still not too distant memory), and the feeling of belonging to a community threatened by its huge communist neighbor. She works quietly, without a murmur of protest or union activities, and with great respect for the boss. Smiling and ubiquitous, In Lung Chu is the benevolent but authoritarian father, a key figure of the Chinese civilization as perpetuated in Taiwan.

The superiority of Cannontex on the world market has nothing to do, according to In Lung Chu, with low salaries. It is the newly industrialized countries of Asia—Malaysia, Thailand, Indonesia, and more recently communist China—where wages are really low! In Lung Chu says sadly that in Taiwan unbridled capitalism ceased to exist when the Kuomintang government fixed a compulsory minimum wage. Thanks to the quality of his products and his capacity to adapt to all the whims of the fashion market, In Lung Chu has an edge over his competitors. Although he is an engineer by training, he did not go in for a high-tech option, preferring old Singer machines with which he produces made-to-order collections that satisfy the idiosyncrasies of U.S. designers with all the economies of scale. Strictly complying with the models his clients send him, each garment is subject to constant quality control. Neither the large Korean factories, which are far more modern, nor the Indonesian ones, which are far less expensive, can do this. For these exclusive clothes, price is of little consequence; in the courtyard of the factory, China Airlines containers are waiting to carry the clothing to California. The U.S. consumer will not wait.

In his disorderly office, which is cluttered with trinkets from all over the world (I even espy a miniature golden replica of the Eiffel Tower), In Lung Chu has accumulated an impressive collection of U.S. books on management. For In Lung Chu, it all boils down to motivation and organization; the secret of success in Taiwan lies more in management than in technology.

Annie Lan and In Lung Chu are taking Taiwan out of the orbit of the Third World. Thanks to their work and imagination, their country's wealth has gone up twelvefold in the last 25 years; per capita income increased during the same period from two hundred to more than two thousand dollars per annum. The annual growth is about 7 percent, putting Taiwan at the top of the list of nations catching up with the rich countries at a faster pace than the former have ever achieved in their history. Such phenomenal growth, when expressed in figures, seems neutral and cold and is difficult to translate into real terms. But just consider the changed status of women in Taiwan. Annie Lan's mother spent her life being subjugated to her father, her husband, and her son. She met her husband for the first time a day before her marriage, which was arranged by her parents. Annie can choose her own husband. Her mother lived in a village without water, electricity, doctor, or leisure. Annie lives in Taipei; she has no nostalgia for her childhood in China. She loves Taipei.

## The Other Capital

Take your time when you visit Taipei. Although the wooden houses of ancient China have given way to urban highways, sleepy Taoist temples beckon at the end of forgotten small streets. There are charming teahouses and even a few merchants who sell snake's blood, which they claim has aphrodisiacal properties. But it is the restaurants, the hundreds and thousands of restaurants open at all hours of the day and night, and the big shops that make the city throb with life. Taipei is a mixture of noise and people in a hurry, Chinese, Japanese, American. Keep in mind that Taipei claims to be the capital of both Chinas and expects the Kuomintang troops to seize power over the mainland any day. In the West, we have a tendency to consider that this is an obsessive illusion; not so in Taipei. Everything reminds you of the real China: the avenues are named after provinces and capitals of the continent, the public monuments are a hodgepodge of the Beijing Palace, and the tomb of Chiang Kai-shek is a miniature of the Forbidden City. Most symbolic, however, is that Taipei's national museum has preserved the artistic wealth of China. When, in 1949, Chang Kai-shek gave up the struggle against Mao, his army transferred the art collections of classical China to Taiwan. (That a million soldiers on the retreat had nothing more to do than save Ming porcelain and Tang statuettes seems surprising.) But the conservation and display in Taipei of these jades, bronzes, artifacts, paintings, and lacquer work makes obvious the claim to sole national legitimacy. This political determination cannot be dissociated from the economic success of Taiwan.

## The Sons of Sun Yat-sen

Before I met Ma Ying Jeou, the general secretary of the Kuomintang, I shared the common Western prejudices against the party. The Beijing government has more or less succeeded in making us believe that the Communist Party of China has been moving in the direction of history and that Chang Kai-shek was nothing more than a puppet, a fascist dictator, in the hands of the Americans. André Malraux is one of the people most responsible for the bad reputation of the Kuomintang, for it was he who in *La Condition humaine* created the archetype of upright militants in conflict with Kuomintang thugs. We have since learned that the Chinese Communist Party was not ideal, but we should also revise our judgment on the Kuomintang because this party has developed as rapidly as Taiwan's economy.

Ma is the living proof. A rising star on the political scene, he is too young to have experienced decolonization and the anticommunist struggle. Ma was born in Taiwan, never met Chang Kai-shek, and has never seen mainland China, which his parents fled in 1949. His degree from Harvard Law School proves his success, and he seems to have brought with him the neat, clearheaded, high-tech ways of American lawyers. He was able to complete the long and expensive law program thanks to a scholarship granted to him by the party. How could Ma not be grateful to his party? At the age of fifteen, his intellectual qualities were noticed, and one of his professors asked him to join the Kuomintang. Currently engaged in the search for new talent, his "agents" scout campuses and select students for training abroad. Labor leaders and village peasants can be chosen as well, thus depriving the opposition of party cadres! Ma Ying Jeou's most recent initiative has been to rejuvenate the grass roots–level organizations, making it possible, among other things, to get free driving lessons with the Kuomintang card. The results, the general secretary assures me, are excellent. The youngsters flock to the party, though Ma is quick to point out that the young do not only join for material benefits, but because they are idealistic and want to carry on the historic work started by Sun Yat-sen to liberate the Chinese people.

Ma Ying Jeou begins most of his sentences with "as Dr. Sun said" and asserts that Sun Yat-sen is the greatest thinker of the century. Sun, who overthrew the Manchu dynasty in 1911, has written little; only his pithy sayings remain, which makes it easy to adhere to his three principles: nationalism, democracy, and the welfare of the people.

For Taiwan, these three principles constitute an ideological alternative to the mainland's communism. By constantly comparing it with the communist party, Ma defines the work of the Kuomintang. He does not allow the Beijing Chinese to monopolize ideology; the Kuomintang offers the Chinese people material prosperity, equality of opportunity, and, according to Ma, democracy. The Kuomintang, he adds, is not the only party in Taiwan; it is the only *dominant* party.

The electorate votes regularly in the Republic of China, but only to re-elect local authorities and representatives of the sole Taiwanese province to the National Parliament. The other legislators (at least 80 percent of them) were elected in 1949 to represent the provinces of mainland China. Age, however, is progressively eliminating them, and those who die will only be replaced after the liberation of the homeland. Waiting for this, the surrealistic parliament, made up of the survivors, nominates a president of the republic. Election campaigns are free, but are strictly limited to a period of fifteen days, and the opposition does not have the right to form a party or to question the right to reconquer. [Some of this has changed since this chapter was written: the 1989 elections were opened to the opposition parties.] The press is ostensibly heterogeneous and thriving. Ma states that Taiwan has 31 newspapers and three thousand magazines, but most of them are controlled by the Kuomintang. The three television channels are heavily dependent on the government and the army. Direct pressure on the voters, the opposition, or journalists, however, is seldom exerted, and when instances are reported, they give rise to public scandals. But self-imposed censorship is a permanent feature of life, and journalists in particular, knowing full well that discretion is the better part of valor, do not take up what they call sensitive issues.

The youth of Taiwan, which has never known scarcity, is no longer satisfied with this paternalistic regime. Each year thousands of students trained in the United States come back with dissent and democracy in their hearts, and the opposition, circumventing legal prohibition, has formed a political party. The island seems to be in a demand cycle that stems from growth as well as exposure to the Western world. But Ma Ying Jeou asserts that the Republic of China on Taiwan is the most democratic regime that the Chinese people have ever known and that it is certainly far more democratic than the Beijing regime. But he concludes that Taiwan is not the Philippines, that the Kuomintang has brought prosperity and security to the island, and that its destabilization would suit Beijing very well. In Ma Ying Jeou's rhetoric this argument seems to clinch the issue; in fact, it seems the only one worth entertaining.

## Against Bad Luck

Let us imagine a poor country that is destined to remain so. It is very small with a huge population that has it bursting at its seams. Let us say that the density of population is four hundred inhabitants per square kilometer, with one of the highest rates of population growth in the world, around 3 percent. Let us deprive this country of all natural resources, especially oil and ores! Let us assign this country a static civilization with a conservative religion that invites the people to passiveness. Add a bit of feudal tradition and a value system based on contempt for trade. Eighty percent of the population is illiterate and, to complete the picture, has a language that has nothing in common with any other language, thereby rendering communication with the outside world impossible. The people have no industrial tradition, having always practiced an ancient form of agriculture and having never received economically active foreign minorities. Compounding the woes of this unfortunate country are exploitation by a rude colonial foreign power, a world war that partitioned it, and then a civil war that threw half the population at the other half's throat. We leave on the field two million killed, and almost half the available housing destroyed, as well as all the roads, bridges, and dams. Let us not forget to give our model a very hot summer and a very cold winter and then situate it in an isolated corner of the map. To put the final touch and to remove all chances of allowing such a country to come out of its sorry state of affairs, our subject is the target of military threats on one hand and foreign bases on the other. This permanent tension obliges our guinea pig to spend one-third of its public money on defense.

Well, you must have guessed by now that our unfortunate country does exist—that we have faithfully drawn the contours of South Korea. Until 1961, no expert could go wrong by predicting that this country was doomed. At the time, out of 74 underdeveloped countries, taking into account criteria like per capita income, Korea occupied the 60th position. One-fifth of its population was unemployed, and people could only survive with the help of food aid from the United States. Twenty-five years later, Korea has climbed up to the 9th position and its annual growth rate remains higher than 7 percent. What magic potion did the Koreans take!

# Out to Capture the World

In the port of Ulsan overlooking the Sea of Japan, Korean workers at the Hyundai shipyards climb the steel skeletons and beams of gigantic ships. They work eleven hours a day, six days a week, with no more than a two-hour break, and take their meals and rest at the shipyard itself. Off the coast, huge oil tankers undergo sea trials before they are handed over to their new Norwegian, Greek, or Arab owners.

The Hyundai factories are the symbols of modern Korea's civilization and prosperity. The shipyard is like a gigantic Erector set where steel parts are assembled to form a majestic structure. The workers bustling about are like the individual components of such ships, with each individual having meaning only in relation to the whole and obeying a strict, almost military-like, hierarchy. This giant pyramidal organization is part of a scheme where everything is measured down to the last millimeter, be it steel plates or flower beds. The Ulsan shipyard was constructed twelve years ago, along with the first ship, as banks refused to finance workshops that did not have at least one order in hand. Such industrial daring is typical of Hyundai, today the second-largest ship builder in the world, having delivered 54 ships in 1986. Korea still lags far behind the Japanese in terms of technology and organization, but as Chung Joo Young, the chairman of Hyundai, points out, "The Japanese began a hundred years ago."

The day I visited Hyundai, news had just come in that British shipyards were letting one-third of their staff go. Hyundai initially structured itself on the British model; in 1970, Chung Joo Young, because he had not the faintest knowledge of shipbuilding, sent 50 of his engineers and technicians on a training program to Great Britain. "We know how to copy," Chung Joo Young tells me, "but we also know how to improve and very soon we will know how to invent." The wages of the Hyundai worker are one-fourth of his British counterpart's, but as in Taiwan the edge the company has over its competitors is not lower prices but its capacity to meet deadlines. In Ulsan, commitments to ship buyers the world over are always respected, something that is not true of Europe. Workers, following the example set by their chairman, do not count the hours of labor they put in.

Chung Joo Young's life is inextricably linked to the development of his country. The leading industrialist of his country, he has the weather-beaten face of a peasant combined with the authority of a billionaire. Legend has it that in the 1930s Chung Joo Young, the son of a poor farmer from the north, came on foot to Seoul because he did not have the means to buy a train ticket. At the time of the Japanese colonization he was a car mechanic and then a delivery boy with a rice trader, where he learned that credit held the key to success, a lesson he applied to his venture and that inspired the Korean economy. In 1947, Chung established his own public works enterprise, Hyundai, which means modernity, and thus actively participated in the reconstruction of the nation. From that time on he never looked back. He built barracks during the Korean War, the first highway after peace, aviation fields for the Americans in Vietnam, more roads in Thailand, buildings in Alaska and in Australia, and the metro in Seoul as well as entire cities in Saudi Arabia.

An entrepreneur in every sense, Chung loves his profession and feels that any enterprise is just a question of putting things together. Thus after you put bricks together, the next step is to assemble pieces of steel and produce ships and cars. At the age of 70,[1] Chung, the owner of a company that employs 100,000 people with a turnover of more than $10 billion, embarked in 1985 on the assembly of microprocessors. Although he did not go beyond primary school and has only a vague idea of how computers work, he lured back Korean engineers who had emigrated to the United States, bought patents, launched into the production of 64K random access memory circuits, and now competes with the world leaders, the United States and Japan. Chung embodies the dichotomies of the Korean temperament: a workaholic who doesn't look down at bar hopping in the capital late at night, individualistic yet authoritarian, cordial but commanding complete respect from his employees, ascetic but reigning over an industrial empire from the rooftop of the most luxurious building in Seoul.

The giant shipyard at Hyundai is the antithesis of the Cannontex textile factory in Taipei, although Western analysts tend to clump the two countries together. But their economic patterns of growth are radically different. On the Korean side is a policy of power based on a few groups—the Chaebols—operating at an international level backed by the state; Taiwan is a myriad of small, independent enterprises carried along by the inventive genius of their creators. Nothing can be more different from the rigorous organization of a shipyard at Ulsan than the confused and not very clean workshops of Cannontex. Hyundai's motto is Think Big; Cannontex's is Think Small: military order versus creative disorder.

The Korean shipyard workers, like those of the nearby Pony automobile factory, live in Hyundai accommodations, their children go to Hyundai schools, and they all do exercises together that have been specially conceived by Hyundai to keep them in excellent physical and moral shape. Worker participation is fashioned along Japanese lines, with quality circles and negotiating committees, which in principle are elected bodies, but the representatives have not changed since 1974. The selection is approved by Chung and the government to ensure that they are anticommunist. Korea has known few strikes and hardly any labor trouble. But this is due more to the ruthless nature of the political system than to worker passiveness and devotion to duty. Whenever there is trouble, the police get rid of the leaders, who are always suspected of being on the payroll of North Korea.

In the heart of the Ulsan stands a column that bears the inscription Beware of Spies! I am told that this warning is no longer necessary, but it has yet to be erased. Hyundai is by no stretch of the imagination a concentration camp. The atmosphere is relaxed, the wages good, and the social benefits better than average in Korea. Job switching is quite frequent because workers are not hesitant about changing employers. This individualistic attitude of labor stands in sharp contrast to the attachment of Japanese workers to the *zaibatsu* who employ them.

More than anything else, all those who contribute to Korean industry are bound together by fierce nationalism. Every day at five o'clock sharp, the national anthem resounds through shipyards, in offices, and in factories across the country. Everybody stops and stands at attention for two minutes, an act that seems to come from conviction, not simply a desire to conform. The South Koreans have a profound feeling of belonging to a nation of resistance workers, for they have withstood the trials and tribulations of Japanese colonization and the communist revolution. The other Korea, whose border is 50 kilometers north of Seoul, is an obsession.

# The 38th Parallel

From the suburbs, you have to cross barricades and security checks to reach the capital, Panmunjon, the place of the 1953 armistice where frontline movement was halted. The war seems to have stopped only temporarily. All along the 38th parallel U.S. army personnel, U.N. observers, and Korean soldiers keep watch, in a state of full alert. At the watchtowers, behind barbed wire fortifications, U.S. sentinels scrutinize the demilitarized zone with their binoculars as if they were expecting to see hordes of barbaric warriors appear. Hardly anything is known of North Korea. The adversary is a mysterious, almost theocratic regime where the cult of Kim Il Sung and his son hold sway. North Korea, in consonance with its hermit kingdom image, is closed and inward looking.

At Panmunjon blank shells are fired at fifteen-minute intervals. On

Sundays families separated by the war gather at the uncrossable border and shout the names of those who disappeared and who perhaps live on the other side of the line. But over the years, restaurants, cafés, and souvenir merchants have crowded behind the trenches, transforming the border into a vast military Disneyland where American soldiers guide groups of Japanese tourists. The briefing of the visitors by officers as well as the war museum near the border gives the communist regime larger than life dimensions. A diorama enacts in technicolor the incursion of a group of soldiers from the north in 1976. A child from South Korea is shown being assassinated for shouting, "I hate Communists." All this would be a show if every family in Korea had not lost at least one member in the 1950 war that claimed two million lives.

This nation of fighters is also a nation of survivors who resisted the communism of the north and survived the Japanese colonization.

## The Art of Being Colonized

The Japanese, from 1910 to 1945, transformed Korea into a vast enterprise industrialized in the north and agriculturalized in the south, in service of the Japanese. More than a conventional economic and political domination, this colonization was an attempt at cultural extermination. The Japanese wanted to annihilate Korean individualism from a civilization they judged to be inferior. The use of the Korean language was prohibited in public places, administration offices, and schools. During World War II, the Koreans were forcibly enrolled in the Japanese army and systematically sent to the front or deported to factories in Japan to replace the workers enlisted for battle.

However, even as they were destroying their culture, the Japanese were also educating the Koreans. An entire people was snatched from the feudal era and taught how to work à la Japanese, learning modern techniques for rice growing and industry. Production during the colonial era grew at a spectacular average of 10 percent per annum, a growth rate comparable to that of modern-day Korea. The Japanese exploitation required the active participation of the local elite; estimates are that in 1945, Korea had some 7,000 executives, 28,000 technicians, and more than 2000 enterprises that were entirely Korean. The most gifted young people, often the sons and daughters of the old aristocracy, were sent to the University of Tokyo. After the 1945 liberation, a majority of the new Korean leaders had been trained in Japan.

Thus, when the Japanese left, Korea was endowed with an impressive industrial setup: factories, hydroelectric dams, roads, and irrigation networks. The Koreans discovered that their products were exportable, an idea further strengthened by the return of those who had been deported, and thus 2-and-½ million Koreans willy-nilly discovered the Asian continent. Finally, as the colonizers did not belong to a race or a culture very different from those of the Koreans, the latter concluded that if the Japanese had dominated Asia, they could too.

Although the Japanese legacy seemed to have been frittered away by the end of the Korean War in 1953, only physical capital had been destroyed. Human resources and memories remained intact and were to constitute the basis for future development.

# A Nation of Cavalrymen

The tragic destiny of Korea and her desire for revenge seem epitomized in the immense blue wooden emblem of the First Manchu Cavalry, the regiment stationed at the demilitarized zone. Dominating the U.S. encampments and facing North Korea, its motto reads In Front of Them All. For the Americans, these words signify Communists wherever they may be. But for the Koreans *all* encompasses a much vaster universe: In Front of the West, in Front of the East is the manifesto of a great nation who did not allow itself to perish.

For Korea not only is an Asian peninsula where docile, cheap labor produces VCRs and shirts, but is first and foremost a great civilization. (Korea, wrote the Indian poet R. N. Tagore at the beginning of the century, is a lamp that has for long enlightened the world and shall continue to do so.)

Explains the Korean artist Nam June Paik,

> It is impossible to understand the economic success of modern-day Korea if one does not know that my people are the torchbearers of one of the most ancient cultures of Central Asia. The Koreans are the inheritors of the Huns and Genghis Khan, the nomadic hoards which, for centuries before settling down on this peninsula, roamed Asia and Europe, from Seoul to Budapest. We have nothing in common with the Japanese, a community of fishermen, or with the placid Chinese peasants. The Koreans are cavaliers, and our language, like our music, is closer to that of Hungary than our immediate neighbors.[2]

It is not in the archaeology or monuments that we should look for Korean continuity. (In any case, the few carved wooden doors and palaces that have survived are drowned in the urban chaos of modern Seoul.) No-madic people, Paik tells me, carry their culture with them and do not feel the need to preserve a legacy rooted in time and space. Because Korean culture has been internalized, it has been able to resist the Japanese, who only succeeded in destroying external symbols.

Paik is himself a bit of a nomad. A painter with an international reputation and the best-known Korean abroad, he lives and works in a New York loft in a state of indescribable disorder that reminds one of a Mongolese camp. "My country," says Paik, "is where I am." His art is just as pragmatic, a new form of expression that uses videotape. At his editing table, facing 50 screens, he creates the mind-boggling pictures for which he is famous. A combination of absurd, psychedelic, line images, live canvases of constant movement and sound, this ultramodern art form is for Paik the pursuit of the Korean tradition of sign and abstraction. According to Paik, his fame in the 1960s owed little to hippies and psychedelic effects. The happenings were in fact a modern transcription of shamanistic ceremonies in which he had participated as a child and an attempt to communicate, through song, dance, and cries, with telluric forces, a practice still prevalent in Korea. In the same way the Koreans invented the Mongol alphabet and the first metal printing characters, Paik creates new modes of communication based on modern Korea's televisions, videos, and computer programs. Samsung, the major Korean manufacturer of television sets, obligingly supplies him equipment, old sets and cathode tubes, which he transforms into monumental sculptures and aquariums. These objects that the world identifies with Korea are objects of derision for Paik, Korea's most provocative son. This tradition of dissidence, concludes Paik, this cavalier temperament that refuses to bow down to any kind of authority, explains the current violence that cannot be dissociated from modern-day Korea.

## The Rites of Violence

When Seoul smells of tear gas, Yeong Hang is to blame. She is a tiny, very determined, Korean woman who pursues her studies at the University of Seoul and unleashes political agitation on the campus with equal seriousness. In class, she demurely takes down the words of wisdom dictated from above by the professor, in keeping with the Mandarin tradition. The Korean university is a school of discipline and obedience, not a place for critical reflection. As soon as she leaves her class, however, Miss Hang begins tearing the system apart. This dissident student as well as her distant professor symbolize two aspects of Korean tradition: (1) the spirit of rebellion that comes from the Kirgiz Steppes and (2) Confucian order nourished by centuries of Japanese and Chinese domination.

Miss Hang's job as a member of the clandestine organization Minmintu is not to face the police; that is left for the boys. She disapproves of those excitable students who burn themselves with kerosene shouting Down with the United States. Miss Hang would like the democratic process to gain momentum. Besides, the university obligingly places at her disposal a room in which she holds Minmintu seminars. The professors also attend these meetings as silent spectators. During these long and confused sessions we try to define the ideology of Miss Hang and her dissident companions. The themes derived from Third World rhetoric and the Western left of the 1960s, include the following: Korea is a proletarian nation that has been exploited by the capitalist camp, and its development, peripheral. The Americans are imperialists, the Japanese, neocolonials, and Washington is abetting military dictatorships. Echoes of these lines—neutrality, antinuclear sentiments, and a vague aspiration for the reunification of the two Koreas—can also be heard in divided Germany.

Miss Hang terms as *capitalist* and *American* all that is associated with the rapid modernization of her country. She weaves around North Korea nostalgic fantasies for a lost civilization, imagining it to be a sort of ecological haven for the age-old tradition of inwardness. All these complex feelings are summarized for Korean youth in the word *democracy*. Democracy will solve all the problems and give Korea independence, freedom, and civilization, cleansing the polluted air of Seoul.

For Miss Hang, one man, Kim Dae Jung, represents all these confused aspirations. Kim, whose fame has crossed the borders of Korea, for the last 25 years has led the opposition to the military regime of Seoul and become in this part of the world, the symbol of democracy.

## The Legend of Kim Dae Jung

Kim Dae Jung was sentenced to death by the North Koreans in 1950; barely managing to escape, he was kidnapped in Tokyo by the Secret Service of his country and slipped out of their hands just as they were going to stab him. Sentenced once again to death in Seoul for some obscure reason, he was finally pardoned through the intervention of the United States. His status when I met him in February 1987 reflected the ambiguous nature of the political regime in Seoul: martial rhetoric and propaganda mixed with dissidence in prisons, a relatively critical press, and the freedom to enter and leave the country at will. Before the people took their demand for democracy to the streets in June 1987, Kim was denied any political rights; he was under house arrest in his modest Seoul residence, but that did not stop him from receiving journalists from the West as well as his followers. The authorities discouraged such visits but seemed content to photograph his visitors secretly. Kim Dae Jung, feeding his own legend, asserts that four hundred spies watch his house, follow his car, and tap his telephone. His program contains nothing formidable, being based, for the most part, on the redistribution of wealth through taxation, the protection of the environment, and upgrading health and education. He feels that democracy would dissipate student agitation and automatically improve the quality of teaching. But he also adds that weakening the state is out of question; a strong state is indispensable to be able to face North Korea on equal footing. In fact, Kim Dae Jung condemns the Korean government not because it is authoritarian, but because it is a military government. For him democracy is, above all, power to the civilians, not a reflection on the nature of power and the preponderant role played by the state in the Korean society.

Kim Dae Jung uses Western jargon skillfully, but belongs to another culture. At the end of our interview, the politician gave way to the calligrapher as, with meticulous care, he prepared his silk brushes, thinned his ink in a black stone cup, and drew for me, in Chinese characters, The Strength of the Soul is Invincible. He signed it and presented it to me as a gift, humbly apologizing for the clumsy execution, which was, in fact, perfect. (In Asia calligraphy has always been a sign of authority.)

It would be wrong to interpret the violent incidents in Seoul as a revolution breaking out. The clashes between the police and the students are brutal, but follow a specific code, and for the most part the capital's citizens remain indifferent. When an excess of tear gas forces them to move around with handkerchiefs over their faces, they complain as if it were pollution or bad weather. For the time being, the Confucian sense of order in Korea does not seem threatened by the cavalier spirit, although the pressure of the United States might speed up the transition toward more modern authoritarianism. In the ultimate analysis, the political model most likely to suit Korea, like Taiwan, is that of Japan rather than any Western democracy. As in Japan, a single party uninterruptedly monopolizes the government with opposition checks.

If this *is* to be the pattern of development in the newly industrialized countries of Asia, we have here not only a new form of economic growth, but also a novel political system that we may describe as overtly authoritarian. This overt authoritarianism is capable of integrating change as well as foiling any internal or external destabilization attempt.

From Hong Kong to Singapore, the success story is the same. Along with Taiwan and South Korea, these countries have accomplished what no other nation has in the history of mankind: overcoming mass poverty in the brief span of 25 years. The West and even the Third World, however, tend to view this achievement with condescension rather than genuine interest and poke fun at or speak of these countries as inhuman workshops where robotlike workers are exploited by American or Japanese capitalism. Conversely, the apostles of the market economy lump them together ideologically and exaggerate the successes of such a capitalist strategy.

In reality, deep cultural differences separate these nations and the paths they have chosen to tread. More than their economies, what unites the four dragons is the commonality of their destiny. The four Asian dragons are both survivors and fighters. But where does their determination and moral strength come from?

The dilemma of development is a question of choice. Should one attach more importance to race, religion, customs, resources, foreign aid, or the nature of the political system? The obvious explanations, those that derive their strength from the nature of things, are the most popular. But evidence suggests that these are less effective than the development strategy theory.

# FOURTEEN

# The Good State

IF THERE IS A FATHER OF THE TAIWANESE MIRACLE, IT IS SURELY DR.
Tsiang Shoh Chieh. Now 84 years old, Tsiang has the ivory complexion
and serenity of wisdom synonymous with old age among the Chinese. He
comes from a unique intellectual family, completely Chinese yet completely international, whose members are constantly on the move from
one country to another. For the past 30 years Dr. Tsiang has served simultaneously as professor of economics at Cornell University in New
York and as the most highly regarded economic adviser to the Republic
of China. This cosmopolitanism, typical of the overseas Chinese intelligentsia, lends a universal value to Tsiang's economics lesson.

Let us begin at the end of the 1950s, when Taiwan found itself
caught in the classic underdevelopment trap: on the verge of fiscal collapse and strangled by bureaucratic controls. The country had, up to that
point, unimaginatively followed the mainstream of the economic thought
of the era. The overvalued currency allowed the Taipei bourgeoisie to
import consumer items cheaply, and the country lived under the protection of high tariff barriers, ostensibly to facilitate the growth of national
industry. To maintain the rate of investment, the government kept interest rates low. This import-substitution strategy was *the* prescription for
the underdeveloped world during the period of decolonization. In effect,
the island continued to subsist as it had before the war by exporting rice,
sugar, and bananas to Japan. These agricultural exports accounted for

80 percent of foreign exchange earnings. Until 1960, Taiwan was a neo-colonial economy, bolstered by U.S. aid that financed the reconstruction of its infrastructure destroyed by the war. By dint of his nonconformism, Tsiang reversed this situation by reorienting his government along a path that, a generation later, other poor countries would try to follow.

## Through Saving and Through Work

Tsiang started with the assumption that his compatriots were reasonable people. If the banks offered interest rates well below the rate of inflation, savers logically preferred to invest in land or real estate. Therefore, the profits earned by the agro-export sector could in no way promote the growth of industry. Tsiang's second postulate was that Taiwan would not grow rich without pursuing its comparative advantage, offering what its rivals did not. The island has no natural resources, but possesses a labor force well-trained in the Chinese tradition and available as a result of technological improvements in agriculture.

This analysis led to a complete shift from an import substitution strategy to one based on export promotion. Because comparative advantage implies competitive prices, devaluation was necessary and was effected in 1958. In Taiwan, as in all successful economic experiments, monetary reform was the prerequisite for development. Tsiang's most original contribution was to persuade the government to adopt interest rates systematically in favor of savers. Since the end of the 1950s and in spite of occasional hesitancy, interest rates in Taiwan have exceeded price increases, which at times reached 125 percent per annum. Positive results were immediate; savings flooded into the banks and inflation declined rapidly. Inversely, each time the government was tempted to bring interest rates down below the rate of inflation, savings dried up. A fair return to savings thus proved a good way to both finance development and fight inflation. After a quarter century of fiscal stability, each Taiwanese saves a third of his or her income, a world record.

Therefore, the high level of savings cannot be attributed to some innate frugality of the overseas Chinese. Appropriate policies are required for this tendency to manifest itself and steer those savings into official channels rather than toward traditional hoarding. The proof is that the rate of saving, which was barely 5 percent of total income in 1952, did not surpass the U.S. or British rate until 1963 and, Japan's until 1971. It was also in 1963 that U.S. aid virtually ceased. It might be suggested that,

since that date, the economic development of the Republic of China has
been undertaken by the Taiwanese themselves and owes nothing to foreign aid. We might add that the island exports more capital than it receives and invests elsewhere in the Pacific region.

On the basis of this experience, we may deduce several propositions
that owe more to economic analysis than to Chinese culture. Tsiang in
fact believes that one can speak of a Taiwanese model only to the extent
that it is based on universal theoretical principles, and that this particular
model favors monetary stability and private savings. Another aspect, less
well-known, but as remarkable as Taiwan's rapid rate of economic growth,
is the equalization of incomes. Tsiang's ambition was to reconcile development with social equality.

## Adam Smith Versus Marx

According to socialist-inspired economic doctrines, capitalist growth
spurs inequality and, worse yet, cannot prosper without injustice. The
scientific version of this conventional wisdom was formulated by the Rus-
sian-born U.S. economist Simon Kuznets. On the basis of the experience
of the early industrializing nations—Great Britain, the United States,
and Japan—Kuznets showed that, in its initial phase, capitalist growth
impoverishes the lowest strata of the population. But Kuznets also showed
that in the second phase of development, beginning, for example, in
1860 in Britain and 1920 in Japan, incomes expand rapidly in all social
categories and more rapidly among unskilled workers than among other
professions. Kuznets's second phase is often ignored in favor of his first,
which corresponded with the publication of Marx's works. However, if
Kuznets's theory is indisputable for the first generation of capitalist countries, it is false for the newly industrialized nations. In Taiwan, but equally
in Singapore, South Korea, and Hong Kong, growth did not at any time
impoverish anyone. On the contrary, from the start economic growth enriched the poorest most rapidly. This can be shown using the Gini coeffi-
cient, which measures the income gap between the richest 20 percent
(quintile) of the population and the poorest quintile. In Taiwan, the gap
between the two groups grew until 1964, when rapid growth began. This
growth in equality is contrary to the standard image of industrialization
based on exploitation, whether the nineteenth-century model or the contemporary model used in developing countries like Brazil and India.

Tsiang puts forth a series of explanations that do not focus on circumstances peculiar to Taiwan, but that seem generalizable. First, agrarian reform, by suppressing ground rent, overcame the major obstacle that in poor countries locks the peasantry in destitution and perpetuates the wealth of the landed aristocracy. Second, monetary reform, by favoring the saver, allowed the emergence of a middle class capable of seeing to its own economic security. Thanks to constantly positive interest rates, there were no ruined peasants! Third, contrary to the Brazilian or Indian models, Taiwan's comparative advantage, which is based on labor rather than capital, allowed the dissemination of the benefits of growth to the whole population.

The fourth equalization factor is mass education and its social role. Taiwan, South Korea, and Singapore have become meritocracies (Japan has been one since the beginning of the century). Status is a function of effort, not of landed property and its attendant privileges. This goes for women as well as for men, and Taiwan is one of the rare Third World countries where women hold public and private office.

This principle of equality is confirmed by the case of South Korea, although its income gap is somewhat more significant. That country's economy, which was ravaged by inflation from 1975 to 1981, is dominated by giant corporations that have long enjoyed state protection. The period of inflation aggravated social inequalities, thereby underlining the importance of monetary stability as a factor promoting equality.

Tsiang notes that income equalization in the newly industrialized countries of Asia was obtained without income redistribution. Social welfare systems are more or less unknown; minimum wages either do not exist or are of recent date, as in Taiwan; progressive income taxation is marginal; and taxation systems are generally weak because they do not finance a welfare state. Nevertheless, the income distribution of these four countries is more egalitarian than Sweden's. Thus the market not only creates wealth but also allocates it between the strong and the weak, men and women, more effectively than public policy does. By attenuating the difficult first stage of development, which is based on exploitation, the four dragons thus constitute a new cagegory within capitalism, belatedly supplanting the views of Karl Marx with those of Adam Smith, author of *The Wealth of Nations*, who posited that economic growth promotes equality.

Beyond this, one cannot fully understand what occurred in Taiwan without noting a peculiar characteristic of its demography: Two peoples have coexisted there since independence, which provides a further clarification of Tsiang's strategy.

## Two Peoples—One Island

The first wave of migration, which came from the south of China in the nineteenth century, colonized the island and made it prosper. This civil and peaceful community, preoccupied primarily with individual economic well-being, makes up nine-tenths of the population and speaks Taiwanese. The second wave came from all the provinces of mainland, the first time in 1945 to supplant the Japanese occupation, then in 1949 when Taiwan became the refuge of Chang Kai-shek's defeated army. These Mandarin-speaking mainlanders (Mandarin became the official language of the republic) were soldiers, politicians, and bureaucrats preoccupied, above all, with reconquering the mainland.

These two groups are not in open conflict; in a generation intermarriage has become common. This is not to deny that a division of the spoils exists, the state to the mainlanders and the economy to the Taiwanese. The universal conflict between the public and the private sectors thus took on a quasi-ethnic dimension. Taiwanese civil society controls small private enterprise and foreign trade—the dynamic economic sectors. In turn, the continentals dominate political life, the Kuomintang, internal trade, and the public sector. Contrary to the widely held, ultraliberal image of the Taiwanese economy, the public sector incorporates not only natural monopolies such as transport and telecommunications, but also banking and insurance, petrochemicals, sugar refineries, synthetic fibers, steel, shipyards, and even construction firms that compete with the private sector. This immense public sector is run by former high government officials and military officers, remunerated accordingly by the state.

Taiwanese entrepreneurs oppose subsidizing an inefficient state and public sector. In its defense, however, the state does have some rare and essential virtues: It costs little, only 18 percent of the national product (making it one of the world's cheapest), half of which is devoted to defense and security. It seems, by Third World standards, relatively honest despite certain traditional practices such as the remittance of *red envelopes* to certain officials. Its perennial nature permits Taiwanese entrepreneurs to invest in the long run without incurring major risks. It guarantees security of incomes and protects savings via nearly complete price stability and positive interest rates. Finally, it ensures territorial defense, without which Taiwan would long ago have been absorbed by the People's Republic.

These Taiwanese characteristics enrich Dr. Tsiang's lesson. The Taiwanese model does not arise from a stateless liberalism, a laissez-faire, laissez-passer, that seems never to have existed anywhere but Hong Kong. Taiwan, on the contrary, illustrates the dualism necessary for the proper functioning of any economy, the coexistence, which is by nature conflictual, between a state and a civil society.

We shall see that in the case of Singapore, even more than in Taiwan, the state plays a dominant role in development.

## A Government of Competition

I remember the Singapore of twenty years ago as a city of smells. The traveler landing here was immediately surrounded by a curious mixture of exhalations from fermented fish and the acetylene lamps lighting the streets. But the street vendors have disappeared, and Singapore no longer smells of anything. Also gone are the Victorian stucco facades encrusted with tropical moss, the cycle rickshaws with their opiated and skeletal drivers. Vanished are the unhappy people living beneath tarpaulins on moored boats. Of British, Chinese, Indian, Arab, and Malay architecture of old Singapore there remains only stretches of wall lost in a marble, glass, and steel panorama. Singapore is no longer exotic; its government is obsessed with modernity and cleanliness. The atmosphere is more that of Dallas than of China; the humid heat itself is forgotten, banished to the outdoors by the air-conditioning of buildings and automobiles. Only the billboards asking the populace to refrain from spitting remind us that old Chinese habits have not yet been eliminated by this purge of tradition.

Goh Keng Swee, president of the Central Bank and former prime minister, is unanimously considered to be the architect of this transformation. He is a short fellow with the dark complexion of South China, a pair of large prominent ears, and an extraordinarily lively intellect. Like most of the founders of modern Singapore, Dr. Goh is an intellectual in the British tradition, a former student at the London School of Economics, which has sent forth as many liberals as Keynesian economists. "We were and still are a handful of Chinese," he notes, "two million when the British departed, isolated in a Malay and Muslim sea." This Chinese minority, threatened internally by a communist insurrection and externally by Malay domination, in 1965 chose independence and made Singapore a unique city-state.

At first (and again recently), Singapore was even worse off than most Third World countries: not one natural resource on this marshy, four-hundred-square-kilometer islet, a largely illiterate population, no administration, a tradition of commerce but no productive enterprises, old displaced servants of the British crown, and mass unemployment further aggravated by the closing of British military installations during the post-independence period. The impossible task confronting the nation's founders was to organize simultaneously state, national defense, and economic growth as the basis for coexistence, with the Chinese majority, of a million Malays, Arabs, and Indians. Dr. Goh's responsibility was to define a strategy.

He rejected the Hong Kong model despite the demographic and geopolitical similarities. For one thing, Hong Kong was not a state; its administration was assured by the British, thus permitting the local entrepreneurs to capitalize. More important, the origins of the populations were not the same; Hong Kong had welcomed an entrepreneurial elite fleeing Shanghai and Canton, who brought with them their capital and their technological mastery of the textile industry. This small initial group joined itself to six million Chinese predisposed to work under conditions of low wages and poor accommodation rather than to endure rule by Beijing. In Singapore, however, the population, receptive to communist propaganda, could not be employed under the same conditions. Goh considered the Taiwan strategy to be equally impossible. Singapore's entrepreneurs had no experience with industry or exports. Finally, it was impossible to base growth on protectionism because Singapore had no internal market. All that remained was to turn to the outside world; only foreign companies could create jobs immediately and on a large scale. Multinational corporations would be welcomed without reservation and would provide capital, jobs, expertise, and markets. Singapore would become the global factory.

With hindsight this way of proceeding seems self-evident; yet it presupposes that a government that had just gained independence would resist the temptations of nationalism and autarchy. It required all the cosmopolitanism of the overseas Chinese to acquire such an understanding without undue delay. This government also had to show itself capable of offering the multinationals a stable and functional framework in which they would be tempted to establish themselves. The leaders of Singapore accomplished this by setting up a no-holds-barred command economy. This unexpected blending of the state and the multinationals constitutes Singapore's originality and a rather uncommon case study in liberal development.

# At the Service of the Multinationals

For Singapore to become the economic backbone of the region, its government, led since independence by Lee Kwan Yew, had to transform the old decadent colony into a perfect multinational city. Thus Singapore, with its profusion of hotels, hygienic conditions beyond reproach, the best airport in Asia, freeways lined with frangipani, and incomparable golf courses offers impeccable service for the demanding executive. These managers also expect a well-heeled labor force, and the state provides it. The government imports contract workers from Malaysia who are expert at assembling electronic components and trains semiskilled personnel in the local schools and universities according to rigorous selection criteria.

This taste for perfection even verges on eugenics. In 1983, the government offered specific forms of assistance toward the birth of a third child if the mother held a postsecondary diploma. Protests in Singapore as well as the foreign press led to the abrogation of this form of discrimination, but that such a notion gestated in the mind of Prime Minister Lee reveals his conception of the role of the state. He relapsed in 1987, regretting that the demise of traditional polygamy prevented the most intelligent men from expanding their progeniture.

Goh's strategy was brought to fruition by a world market that required Singapore's services. Singapore became a factory for the cheap assembly of U.S. and Japanese goods, particularly semiconductors. In addition to gaining newfound prosperity based on the exploitation of labor, Singapore also became the service depot for all of Southeast Asia. This second stage of the Singapore model is not indicative of laissez-faire; the state went directly into business, transforming the ancient British docks into naval shipyards and repair centers for the regional oil industry. The government itself developed subsidiary activities—transportation, telecommunication, and finance—around this initial core. But Singapore's public sector enterprises are still administered by contract managers, never by bureaucrats, and all are profitable. These massive public interventions are financed in a manner for which I know no parallel. Taxes on income and profits are set at a very low level in order not to discourage foreign investment. Wage earners, however, are required to save 30 percent of their income through a public institution, the Central Providence Fund (CPF); employers remit 25 percent of wages to CPF to which employees add their contribution of 5 percent. These amounts are deposited in the wage earner's name. Each citizen thus possesses a sort of obligatory savings passbook on which she or he holds the right of withdrawal. But wage earners can only use their savings for certain expenditures: a retirement fund turned over at the moment of retirement, medical expenses, or the purchase of a home. Thanks to CPF, the population of Singapore has been housed under conditions of exceptional quality for such a recently developed nation. Although there is no unemployment insurance, savings deposited in CPF cannot be used during a period of unemployment; this would be contrary to the work ethic. Thus, CPF controls considerable capital, which is invested in state enterprises and outside of Singapore.

Dr. Goh's strategy therefore contains a great deal of suspicion regarding the economic virtues of Singaporeans. Whereas Tsiang appraised the Chinese as frugal and entrepreneurial, Goh regards them as irresponsible and spendthrift; he doubts their entrepreneurial abilities and prefers the multinationals. Goh judges the Chinese to be incapable of spontaneous saving and therefore manages their earnings on their behalf. This efficient system is not, however, immune to failure. In 1985, for the first time since independence, there was zero growth and only a slight recovery the following year. Was Goh's method the source of prosperity or had he simply benefited from propitious circumstances: a cheap and able work force, an unprecedented global demand, a strategic location at the heart of Southeast Asia, and the prosperity of the oil industry? The recession of 1985 illustrated the limits of state intervention in the development process. This conclusion was not drawn by Goh, but by the new generation in power, especially Lee Hsien Long.

## In Search of State Excellence

Lee has short hair, wears a look of certitude, and is a perfect product of modern Singapore. Graduated from Cambridge in the physical sciences and from Harvard in political science, he has been, in succession, a military officer in the national army, a colonel at 32, and minister of industry at 35. One of the few ministers in the world to have a computer terminal on his desk and to know how to use it, Lee owes his career to exceptional intelligence and panache; add to which, he is the son of Prime Minister Lee Kuan Yew, who he will probably succeed. The prime minister therefore has entrusted the revision of the Singapore model to his son.

For Lee Hsien Long, the crisis of 1985 does not cast doubt on Goh's strategy, but is only a momentary failure in public management due to a high wage policy. Contrary to all the governments in the world that were trying to slow down the rate of increase in salaries, Singapore had since

1979 allowed wages to rise faster than productivity. Only those entrepreneurs capable of keeping up with the new wage rates could survive in Singapore; those who could only survive on the basis of cheap labor were forced to leave. By the same token, the immigration of unskilled workers had ceased. This great leap forward, coinciding with global recession, forced the multinationals into a large-scale transfer of their activities to cheaper countries like Thailand or Indonesia. The government had wrongly believed that it could counter world market forces.

Since 1986, Singapore, with Lee Hsien Long at the helm, has responded to the market's verdict, but, as always, in an authoritarian manner. Wages have been frozen, the regulations on savings have been eased, and taxes on businesses have been reduced. Many observers see this only as an alignment with the liberal model of the 1980s, but in reality, Singapore has not changed its strategy, but is trying to improve its mechanisms of state control of the market. "We are," says Lee Hsien Long, "searching for state excellence, and Singapore remains an antiliberal paradigm."

Singapore is, in effect, an embarrassment for the partisans of an unreconstructed free market economy. Confronted by this economic success, an exception to all the rules, they are tempted to resort to metaphors. "Singapore is not a real state," I was told by Milton Friedman, "it is an enterprise which manages three million inhabitants according to the principles of a free market economy." But Lee, Jr., does not agree; the state of Singapore is not an enterprise seeking to maximize profit, but is guided by the national interest. The citizens of Singapore are not employees but shareholders because they have the power to change the managers at each election. Lee believes that if Singapore troubles Friedman, it is because Singapore proves that a state can be productive and well-run.

A good state is managed by a good government, and if Singapore's is good, says Lee, it is because it is in the hands of the best. The selection of future bureaucrats begins when they are eight years of age and continues through high school, where, at around the age of fifteen or sixteen, the brightest will be given scholarships to study abroad. In return, they owe eight years of service to the state in either administration or public enterprise. They are better paid than the cadres in the private sector, but corruption is punished with extreme severity.

Singapore, then, is not an anti–free market paradigm (to borrow Lee's expression) unless one believes that a free market is synonymous with laissez-faire. Like Taiwan, Singapore demonstrates the necessity of running government and business in a stable manner. Once the framework—infrastructure, individual and property rights, public services—

devised by the state—is predictable, private enterprise can undertake long-term investment. Although the enterprises in Singapore are foreign, this does not affect the analysis; the multinationals have done nothing but obey the logic of the marketplace. In the history of modern economic growth, the lesson of Singapore is that a good state is required to achieve a good economy. This is confirmed by the case of Korea.

## The Virtues of Ginseng

In the high-tech offices of the Blue House, the seat of the Korean presidency, cups of ginseng tea are ubiquitous. The Blue House is a modern fortress, part hospital, and part barracks, and the bitter caramel-tasting root is supposed to maintain the physical and intellectual vitality of the state's servants. The high consumption of this national infusion seems to be an activity encouraged by the government. Everything at the center of Korean power is controlled in intricate detail. Ministers and counselors are guarded by a rigid and deferential protocol run by hordes of secretaries, assistants, and so many security controls that it verges on the absurd. The decor is of modern Korean, spare and comfortable. In these presidential offices, as in all Korean bureaucracies, the only signs of rank are the silk borders surrounding (or not) the doorknobs and telephones. On the walls, in calligraphy, President Chun's authoritative maxims provide the watchword of the hour: National Security, Diligence and Frugality, Law and Order, Technological Improvement, Olympic Games. I don't know whether this Korean administration is the best in the world, as it maintains, but it is one of the most self-satisfied.

If one were to believe Sakung Il, economic counselor to the president and, as such, charged with the nation's development strategy, the entire country is behind its administration, bent on economic progress based on the national interest and fusing public and private initiative. The Blue House, then, is the engine of development, and Sakung Il, its chief technician.

Sakung Il, wrought of a typically Korean Confucian alloy of civility, is quick-witted, intensely authoritarian, and given to U.S.-style efficiency. Like most U.S.-trained economists, he is not far from believing than economics is the end of politics and reminds me of his distant cousins in Chile, the Chicago Boys. Sakung Il is a Korea Boy, with all the virtues and all the arrogance of Asian technocracy, and in fact, is the leader of a veritable cult of this technocracy. In a work published by Harvard University, Sakung Il explained that in the early 1960s, Korea adopted a quasi-military development strategy whereby all means were focused on the pursuit of one goal, economic growth. No delays or hesitations are permitted in the execution of policy; decisions are rapid and usually correct.

This political scenario began in 1961 with President Park Chung Hee, who ended a thousand years of isolationism, united with the traditional enemy, Japan, and chose exporting for his people's national goal. A historical precedent is Japan's Meiji emperor opening up his country to the wider world in 1868. But Sakung Il informs us that it was Germany that inspired Park, when he discovered, during a visit to the Federal Republic, a situation comparable to Korea's: a nation divided by war and ideology. Ludwig Erhard, then minister of finance in Bonn and a European disciple of free market economics, first gave President Park a vision of what had to be done in Korea. Since its inception, Korean development has been grounded in a sort of enlightened despotism, steering a recalcitrant and sometimes rebellious private enterprise. The tools of this strategy have been the plan and the *chaebols*.

In Korea, unlike Taiwan and Singapore, according to Sakung Il, public opinion and an isolationist tradition prevented reliance on foreign investment; Korean capitalism had to be national. But initially, Korea had neither the savings nor the entrepreneurs to embark on an industrialization program. Must the state then substitute for private enterprise by creating public sector industries? Unthinkable! that would be socialism, North Korea, the absolute evil. The solution was *chaebols*, private conglomerates forged by the state using a group of select bosses. To them, and only to them, for a period of 25 years, the Korean government reserved all public contracts and preferential credits. Finance was based on foreign debt as a substitute for inadequate domestic savings. But unlike Latin America, the amounts borrowed were productively invested in the country and scrupulously repaid.

This strategy of enlightened state-guided development was not entirely free of Mandarin distrust of corporate directors. Sakung Il believes that many Korean bosses could not have launched their businesses without the black market or some illegal investments. He thinks that the directors of the chaebols are too strict and authoritarian with their employees and that their decisions are more often based on speculation than on the national interest. These sentiments, a rather banal anticapitalist diatribe, do, however, reflect a certain distrust between public and private sectors that is unknown in Japan, for example. Thus the image of Korea as another Japan, where business and the state move forward in perfect harmony, does not correspond to reality. Korea is conflict-ridden, both at the top as well as at the bottom—in its labor relations as well as in the interpretation of its own history. This scenario of Sakung

Il's, although it is systematically propagated by the state communications apparatus, is vigorously challenged by the bosses and many economists.

## The Chaebol's Strategy

Kim Woo Choong proposed an entirely different interpretation of Korea's development to me whereby the state played a much more marginal role. Kim,[1] president of Daewoo, a commercial empire ten years in the building, is a second-generation chaebol, not a crafty peasant who succeeded by dint of sheer force like Chung, the director of Hyundai. But Kim too is a legend in his own right. His company, founded in 1967 with eighteen thousand dollars, became in just twenty years the fourth-largest conglomerate in Korea, with one hundred thousand employees and more than $8 billion of business. Daewoo, which originated as an exporter of knits to Singapore, has become synonymous with advanced technology and heavy equipment, making and selling chemicals, computers, hospitals, nuclear power plants, fiber optics, pianos, aerospace components, highways, trucks, and trousers. These enterprises date back to the period of Korean economic expansion in the late 1960s that was characterized by healthy exports and a shift from assembly industries to advanced production. Kim Woo Choong, a brilliant and eloquent intellectual, one by one demolishes all of Sakung Il's arguments.

For example, the plan was nothing more than a series of haphazard documents hastily assembled by the economists of the Korean Development Institute (KDI, a public institute and Korea's principal economic research center) to rationalize Park Chung Hee's policies. To illustrate, Kim tells the story of the wigs. Korea has traditionally been a hair exporter. At the beginning of the 1960s, Korean merchants noticed that this export went mainly into American wigs, which they then decided to manufacture themselves—a wise decision because wig manufacturing uses cheap skilled labor and low capital investment. Soon, wig exports became Korea's second largest behind veneer! American demand exceeding supply, Korean entrepreneurs turned to synthetic hair and developed a synthetic fiber industry. At no time did the plan ever refer to wigs or, consequently, foresee the conversion from human hair to synthetic fibers. In fact, no serious planner even contemplated such an industry. If the goals of the early plans were met, it was not due to good planning, but rather to starting from a small base, the needs being so great that any plan would succeed.

According to Kim, Korean industrialization does not owe a great deal to planning, but everything to its comparative advantages: a disciplined and well-educated labor force, low wages, and access to Japanese and U.S. markets. The state's most important contribution to Korean development was not planning growth, but rather creating a solid infrastructure, including roads, ports, telecommunications, and a good educational system. Korea's productivity is so high, according to Kim, because 95 percent of its employees are college graduates. Social relations are stable because one can have a dialogue with an educated populace. *That is how the state contributed to growth.*[2]

Kim's speech reveals the new economic cycle unfolding in Asia under the influence of American ideas. Company directors now find governments an encumbrance, with excessive military expenditures, pipe dreams of reconquest, and a public sector poorly run by retired officers. We need less government in Seoul, we need a Korean Reagonomics, Kim maintains. Such language, commonplace in the West, constitutes a veritable call to revolution in this part of Asia. "You know that they no longer respect the bureaucrats?" Taipei's secretary of state for the economy said in hushed and shocked tones.

In place of the ideal technocrat, Kim proposes the ideal corporate executive, for these Korean entrepreneurs have shown exceptional talent during the last 25 years. In spite of their large size, chaebols have been able both to invest and to disinvest rapidly, a flexibility that accounts as much for the resilience of Korean enterprise as it does for Japan's. Since 1960 the Hyundai group has thus gone from heavy construction to shipbuilding, from automobiles to microprocessors, seizing any and all opportunities on the world market. Chaebols also manifest an astonishing geographic agility. During the Vietnam War, Hyundai was building roads and barracks, but as the war wound down, Chung sought alternative markets and won his first contracts in Saudi Arabia even before the oil boom in 1973. The date is important because the Korean government subsequently sought to portray this redeployment in the gulf as a response to rising energy prices. Legend has it that the Saudi king, startled to find workers laboring after dark, was told that these were Koreans who always meet their deadlines. The king then demanded that more contracts be awarded to this extraordinary people.

Daewoo has evinced the same adaptability as Hyundai. Kim Woo Choong can divest himself in an instant of an unprofitable factory by selling it to its employees, who reinvest their termination compensation in the repurchase, lower personnel costs, and resume production. This ability to disengage has allowed Daewoo to react smoothly to shifts in the world economy by moving from one sector or market to another. Indeed, Daewoo is a prime example of how chaebols have been able to pursue long-term investments; on average, 15 percent of their budgets is devoted to research and development, four thousand Ph.D.'s will be recruited by 1990, and two hundred cadres each year are sent to U.S. universities for additional training. In the most recent initiative, chaebols have been luring back those Koreans who settled in the United States; Lucky Gold Star was thus able to launch its personal computer division by hiring Korean engineers who had worked for IBM.

The rivalry between Daewoo and Hyundai also illustrates the parallel strategies followed by Korean firms to overcome the increasing threat of international protectionism. Chung's method consists in publicizing Hyundai as a high-quality trademark to maintain consumer preference. Kim Woo Chung, however, prefers to keep the Daewoo name under wraps, instead associating with U.S. or Japanese firms to slip through the tariff net.

Thus in 1986, Hyundai launched Excel, the first Korean car on the U.S. market, and sold one hundred thousand in its first year. "Perfectly understandable," says Chung, "since it is the world's best car." Chung invested several million dollars to familiarize Americans with the Hyundai name, even suggesting that it rhymes with Sunday (although this is not the Korean pronunciation). Every personal computer sold by Chung in the United States is proudly inscribed Made by Hyundai. A little later, when Daewoo cracked the U.S. market, Kim Woo Chung sold his car—designed in Germany by Opel, the General Motors subsidiary—as Le Mans. Similarly, it is practically impossible for the American buyer to know that his Model D computer comes from Daewoo.

For Kim Woo Chung, Korean development is a function of firm-level strategy, not the reverse. His interpretation and that of Sakung Il, however, are less mutually contradictory than consecutive. Korea today is in its second growth spurt, a new phase in which decentralization of investment decisions plays a more predominant role than in the previous phase. For each phase, there has emerged an appropriate strategy.

## Can Miracles Be Repeated?

Is the experience of the four dragons unique or can it be repeated in other Third World countries? The response of Kim Man Je, vice prime minister of Korea and reputable economist, is that the question is poorly phrased and that the four dragons have been the beneficiaries of both internal and external circumstances specific to their time and place. These factors—culture, Japanese colonialism, East-West conflict, U.S. aid, and receptive markets—are not reproducible. Nevertheless, according to Kim, this chapter in the history of economic development, however closed and unique, does hold some valid lessons for the Third World as a whole.

The first and most important lesson is that always and everywhere man is a *homo economicus,* motivated by material incentives, which means the acceptance of a bourgeoisie, but most Third World governments repress this class for ideological reasons or for fear of the social tensions that might erupt with a larger income gap.

The second lesson is recognizing the key role the state apparatus has in development, provided that it concentrate its resources in areas suitable to its capacities, for example, education, infrastructure, and, in the early stages, ensuring productive investments where private enterprise fails to respond to obvious comparative advantages. This notion of phases is vital. Thus the Korean government during the early years of development maintained a selective aid to industry policy (not without error), but later gave way to market forces.

The concept of comparative advantage is vital. Kim Man Je believes that all nations have such an advantage at their disposal at any given moment, provided that they turn toward external markets, adopt a reasonable rate of currency exchange, and do not hesitate to promote exports. There is no country, maintains Kim, that does not have some advantage on the world market. One example is Bhutan, the world's leading exporter of broomsticks.

But is competing on the world market for everyone? Although it has served the Asian countries well, has it not turned against Africa by flooding markets for the goods it exports? Kim Man Je thinks that the market is not at fault, but rather that the Africans have failed to grasp its workings. The market is not some system of social security guaranteeing each country a constant stream of income. Had Taiwan or Korea continued to export the same products for twenty years without improving both quality and productivity, they would today be as badly off as Tanzania. The world market demands a constant reassessment of comparative advantage; it is never unchanging but requires constant adjustment to competition and protectionism. Thus in the case of Korea, the composition of exports has varied continuously over the past twenty years.

The final lesson is continuity in economic policy. This presupposes, according to Kim, the stability of the state but also a certain degree of governmental immunity from political pressure. Comparing Latin America with the dragons of Asia, Kim believes that independence in economic decision making has been a decisive advantage, even though it has not been free of errors. In Korea, Taiwan, and Singapore, this autonomy is disappearing: the demands of democracy are interfering with economic rationality, and growth, it seems, is likely to be impaired. But besides the newly industrialized nations, no Third World country has successfully mediated between democracy and growth, and most have for the moment experienced neither.

If we believe Kim Man Je, the success of the newly industrialized nations is replicable and is not dependent on cultural factors unique to this part of Asia. This hypothesis contradicts an entire school of thought, which, following Max Weber, holds that economic behavior is nothing but the reflection of attitudes determined by each specific culture and civilization. By this cultural analysis of development, capitalism could not have sprung forth from anything other than the Protestant ethic. Similarly, many believe that Islam is inimical to economic development, that the African civilizations condemn the black continent to stasis, and that the explanation for the takeoff achieved by the four dragons and Japan is entirely due to Confucianism. It is to these propositions that I will now address myself, refuting them one by one starting with the last.

# FIFTEEN

# All the People Are Chosen

CHEN LI FOU DOES NOT INHABIT THE AUSTERE RETREAT THAT I EX-
pected of a Confucian master, but a glass and marble villa overlooking
Taipei, with an electric eye control for the main gate. The servant who
greets me asks for my card, as is the custom in China. Chen Li Fou does
not wear the long gray robe of the literati, but a charcoal three-piece
flannel suit, and evidently, I am disturbing this tall, erect, severe, elderly
gentleman pruning the bonsai on the terrace.

I was counting on him to reveal the secret of the Asian dragons' economic growth. Cruel deception! His first words were to complain about
his domestics, whose devotion to his service, he believes, is more a function of their level of remuneration than of their loyalty. Even without recourse to the golden age of Confucius who, destitution notwithstanding,
was never abandoned or betrayed by any of his disciples, social harmony
is not what it used to be!

The golden age referred to, which coincided with the Zhou Dynasty,
more than a millennium before the present era, is Chen Li Fou's point of
departure. Because humanity once attained such a state of perfection, it
is only fitting to refer back to it when seeking out criteria. Unlike Westerners, who idealize the future, Chen Li Fou exalts the glorious past.
This perfection of yesteryear, he claims, was based on a moral order in
which women respected their husbands, who, in turn, offered them protection and children obeyed their parents and received affection and
education. It was similarly so between the young and their elders and so

on, up to the end of a long chain where a good government[1] ensured the happiness of the people who, in turn, offered it their support. This society was perfect because, from top to bottom, every individual strived for perfection. Besides, asks Chen Li Fou, how could a dynasty have lasted for eight centuries unless it was founded on such harmony?

Thus for Chen Li Fou, Confucius, without church or priests, is a teacher, not a god or messiah, who points the way along a spiritual road where moral rectitude does not exclude the quest for material well-being. For Chinese philosophy it is important to balance opposites: positive and negative, idealism and materialism. The perfection of the universe, as that of the individual, depends on this constant search for balance.

In this lesson from the master, Confucianism leaves little room for social critique; its quest for the *perfect* order coincides with the justification of the *existing* order. With his simple answers to complex questions, does Chen Li Fou offer anything other than a bulwark for all forms of established authority, parental, patronal, or governmental?

To this ideological critique of Confucianism, which I recognize is not new, Chen Li Fou responds with a historical parable. In Confucius's lifetime, the Chinese emperors used his maxims to justify their power while denying him any role at the imperial court; was this not the worst injustice of that period—the Spring and Autumn Period—in Chinese history? For thus were the teachings of Confucius distorted from the start. But this philosophy and the betrayal of philosophy might be part of the interplay of complementary forces, of yin and yang.

This ambiguity in Confucianism is reflected in the personality of its latter-day master; Chen Li Fou, the sage, has also been a man of power. For 40 years he was personal secretary to Chang Kai-shek and then, as minister of education, he was responsible for incorporating the basic maxims of Confucius and Mencius into a required manual for Taiwanese students that teaches that *here* lies the real China and that the Beijing regime is an imposter. Chen Li Fou is also the author of a critique of materialism, which he considers fundamentally opposed to the "vitalist" tradition in China. Is not such a book made to order for Chang Kai-shek to do battle with communism on the moral and philosophical plane? The old master is well suited for the part.

I left Chen Li Fou to his dwarfed trees without knowing whether his wisdom was real or imagined, the road to perfection or a mere disguise for power.

# Let's Be Done with Confucius

Confucianism permeates the social organization, mentality, and behavior of Chinese and Koreans, resulting in internalized obedience to all forms of authority and a certain lack of critical spirit. The person who protests runs the major risk of being excluded from the community. In Taipei or Seoul, Confucianism certainly contributes to elevating good government above all suspicion and to guaranteeing the good boss both authority and social peace in the enterprise. But I cannot see how Confucianism could have contributed to development. Unchallenged authority tends to reduce initiative and motivation. After all, if Confucianism leads to prosperity, why did mainland China not develop when it was totally Confucian? Remember that Confucianism, today esteemed as a cause of development, had been an explanation for underdevelopment, particularly according to Max Weber.

It seems to me that there is a relationship between Confucianism and economic growth, but that it is negative. The death of Confucius liberated the four dragons from their traditional stasis. Thus Chen Li Fou would help us understand the development of Taiwan, not by his teachings but by his isolation. The old philosopher is the last of the Confucians; he belongs to the past and has no successor. My intuition would be confirmed sometime later in Seoul.

"At one time," explained Chong He Park, "the military was near the very bottom of the social hierarchy, just below the merchants. But in modern Korea, it is precisely the military and the merchants who run the nation. Harmony has been ruptured!"

Park is the same age as Chen Li Fou. He greets his guests and disciples in an ancient villa at Sung Kyun Kwan, Korea's first university. Founded in 1398, its painted wooden structures with their varnished tile roofs have changed little since they were built, although the students have been rehoused in nearby modern accommodations. An icy wind blows through the detached partitions and paper screens; the ginseng tea is hardly enough to combat the penetrating chill of the harsh Korean winter.

Of all the nations of Asia, according to this master of the order of Sung Kyun Kwan, Korea was the most Confucian, intransigent in the face of Buddhist and Christian "superstition." The Japanese colonizers banned the Confucian rites, in which they detected the foundations of national unity. After independence, however, Confucianism was not restored to the curriculum and is no longer taught except in the *Hyangkyo* voluntary study groups as a kind of literary and philosophical catechism. Because of this marginalization, according to Park, "morality is in a state of collapse, children no longer respect their parents, the generations are in conflict, and the students rebel." But this ancient order, mourned by Park, presided over a reign of poverty that no one in Korea would desire to restore. Certainly not the young!

While Park waxes nostalgic, shouts and explosions from the campus drown out our conversation. Is it another demonstration against the military government? It turns out that the students were eagerly applying themselves to military training and shooting practice. By coincidence the very same week, a survey by the large liberal daily *Dong A* found that 96 percent of the population considers itself Confucian, a surprising result in that one-third of all Koreans are Buddhist and one-fifth, Christian. In the same survey, however, the majority defined Confucianism as a "form of courtesy, particularly toward parents and old people."

Not only had Confucianism evaporated in Korea, but the whole of traditional society had collapsed. Colonization and the war scattered the feudal aristocracy, the big landlords, the capitalists, and the elites, thus disrupting the social structure. The only option left to this fragmented nation was to reconstitute itself. From that moment on, the great Korean passion for education and economic success truly manifested itself. Up until the 1960s, Koreans had been overwhelmingly Confucian and illiterate. Only in the new nation, born of a break with history, did the school and the workplace become the pathways to social role and individual identity. A new value system replaced the old. The past does not explain the present or culture development; it is not necessary to be Confucian to enter into the industrial society, and is better not to be.

But if religion is not a decisive determinant of development, does race play a role? Do certain people have a particular aptitude for development? For example, must one be Japanese? One might believe so on the basis of both Japanese and overseas Japanese success.

## Must One Be Japanese?

Tadashi Inouye, venerable president of the Cotia agricultural cooperative, works amidst woodblock prints depicting Mount Fuji and the temples of Kyoto. The studious atmosphere and the profusion of computers are typically Japanese, as is the attitude of the household. The members of the Cotia cooperative, says Inouye, share in a sense of belonging with their organization, a special and overarching affinity. Conversely, the cooperative offers its members total assistance in all life circumstances. Yet we are not in Japan; Cotia is located in a suburb of São Paulo. Tadashi

Inouye is not Japanese, but Brazilian, speaks only Portuguese, and has forgotten his ancestral tongue. His Brazilian name is Gervasio!

The Cotia cooperative was founded in 1927 by 83 Japanese peasants who brought with them to Brazil the art of intensive potato cultivation and the virtues of organization. By joining together to market their produce, they become masters of the São Paulo potato market. The depression of 1929, which hit Brazil hard, forced them to diversify their horticultural production in order to survive. During World War II, they responded to the fuel shortage by creating their own transportation network. Thus, through a series of collective responses to successive challenges, Cotia became the largest cooperative in the country, incorporating ten thousand individual producers, half of whom are now of other than Japanese origin. Top provider of fresh produce and potatoes to São Paulo for sixty years, Cotia today has begun to produce frozen french fries.

A century ago, Tadashi Inouye's ancestors, poor peasants from southern Japan, were attracted to São Paulo, along with several thousand of their compatriots, by the fraudulent advertising of coffee barons looking for a docile and exploitable work force. They thought that they would remain in Brazil for only two or three seasons, during which they would become wealthy, and then return home.[2] But most of them, exploited, poorly housed, and malnourished, succumbed to disease. The survivors settled, and today their descendants constitute the most prosperous collective in Brazil that has contributed decisively to making São Paulo an industrial metropolis.

This economic epic of the Japanese in Brazil, one of the most spectacular success stories of any transplanted Third World minority, became the topic of a considerable literature, which concluded that this people was of a superior stock. Nevertheless, this is not my analysis. When these Japanese emigrated, their country was miserable and poorer than Brazil; in the nineteenth century, Japan was considered the archetype of stasis. It is hard to see what in their cultural or genetic heritage predisposed them particularly to succeed, except that they chose to emigrate. Voluntary migration determined their destiny.

## The Virtues of the Migrant

Migration is to choose change over stability, innovation against routine; the migrant is always an economic adventurer. This is why, it seems to me, Tadashi Inouye has played such an important role in São Paulo, not because he is Japanese but because he is an immigrant.

Another condition that explains the Japanese success is the institutional framework of the receiving country. At the beginning of this century, Brazil was little regulated and economic initiative was largely open to all entrepreneurs. Also, the success of the Japanese community is not an isolated instance. Most of the large Brazilian enterprises are the work of immigrants, of Italians like Matarazzo and Arena, of Lebanese like Maksoud and Malouf, or of Germans like Odebrecht, not excluding a few descendants of the *bandeirantes* of yesteryear, who, faithful to their pioneering spirit, are now great captains of industry like the Mesquita family, which controls the two largest dailies in São Paulo, *O Estado* and *Journal da Trade*. All these names, which resonate with their origins, evoke success stories of the Brazilian economy.

On the basis of these impressions, it is tempting to sketch a theory of the migrant as a factor in development. The great nations that developed outside of Europe were built by migrants or refugees, and often, the ethnic communities that control much Third World economic activity came from elsewhere—Lebanese in West Africa, Arabs and Pakistanis in East Africa, Sikhs in Punjab, and overseas Chinese in Taiwan, Singapore, and all of Pacific Asia.

The history of Africa, as well as that of Asia and Brazil, underlines the economic virtues of migration. Certain countries in East Africa have made the case inadvertently; expelling the South Asian minority in Uganda or, to a lesser extent, Tanzania, demonstrate how effectively it had stimulated the local economy. Oppose this to xenophobic Africa, an Africa open to immigrants as exemplified by the Ivory Coast. The importance of the French community is only a partial testimonial to President Houphouet Boigny's Open Door policy; there are many others. Small-scale commerce is controlled by Mauretanians, trade by Lebanese, cotton cultivation and the hardest agricultural jobs are generally provided by Burkinabes. This immigration only seems to grow; on the road from Burkina Faso to Abidjan, there are Peul shepherds guiding their emaciated flocks after having trekked thousands of kilometers to start a new life. Driven by drought and socialism, Burkinabes, Nigerians, Ghanaians, and Senegalese flock toward the south. Each people brings with it particular talents, and this immigration is without a doubt one of the main causes of relative prosperity in the Ivory Coast.

All this migration makes it impossible to establish the economic superiority of any one culture over another. There is a lesson here on the benefits of the free movements of people: migrants, by bringing new values and modes of economic behavior to the host country, permit that country to break with its complacent traditionalism, a major cause of poverty. Taiwanese, Koreans, Japanese, and Ivory Coasters all embarked on a development process after their culture was shaken by some fundamental challenge. The critical shock and the crisis of traditional values appear in all cases at the origin of growth.

Perhaps this crisis even today is opening up new economic horizons in black Africa.


## The Three Cultures of Iba Der Thiam

Iba Der Thiam is Wolof by birth, Muslim by religion, and French by education. Three cultures might seem too many on a continent that it is sometimes said, is "acculturated," but Thiam, minister of education under President Abdou Diouf, has a diploma in history and changes with ease from a three-piece suit into a magnificent green embroidered boubou. Thiam nurses no grudge against his former colonizers; as he reminds us, the inhabitants of Dakar, Rufisque, Gorée, and Saint Louis have followed the Napoleonic Code since 1830 and voted since 1848.

Thiam does not escape African custom; late into the night his home is invaded by neighbors asking to use the telephone, and protocol makes it difficult for him to refuse. Thiam, however, is considering locking the phone up; he no longer has the means to carry out the obligations of traditional solidarity. Economic difficulties have introduced individualism and frugality to Senegal much more rapidly than a century of European influence. Property and work, concepts that did not heretofore have the same meaning as in the West, have acquired a new value. Everything has become quantified, and the old social networks are collapsing. Students, whose degrees no longer guarantee them a secure future, have become both more competitive and more oriented toward individual performance. Thiam, a person of culture imbued with tradition, bemoans the loss of the old ways, but admits that the new relationships being woven into the social fabric of Senegal constitute the warp and woof of development. In the traditional system of solidarity, he recognizes that it was virtually impossible to be entrepreneurial. How could one rationally invest in economic enterprises when customary obligations were entirely unforeseeable in both their number and their cost? Everything conspired to favor the short term, rapid gain, and conspicuous consumption because traditional solidarity excluded a priori the calculation of profit.[3]

The paradox inherent in the contemporary paroxysm of African society is that it gives rise to a new sense of development and organization surrounding the notion of enterprise, thereby contradicting the somber prognoses of the West vis-à-vis the continent. Through this crisis, Africans are constrained to enter into the dynamic of capitalism.

## Africans Are Entrepreneurial

The entrepreneur has become Africa's new popular hero as public sector employment has lost some of its prestige. After independence in Dakar, virtually all graduates in law and literature entered public administration. This is no longer the case. The reduction in the number of available slots, particularly at the National School of Administration and Law, stimulates the pursuit of other opportunities. The entrepreneurial graduate is fast becoming the substitute for the bureaucrat as the symbol of success in the new Senegal.

In the Ivory Coast, the traditionally commercial ethnic groups constitute the kernel of a new African capitalism. "If my people, the Malinke, dominate trade in the Ivory Coast, it is because we never lie," declared Lamine Fadiga, president of the Abidjan Chamber of Commerce, with aplomb. "Economic success, he added, "requires not money but principles." This tidy formula was addressed to the interminable audience accorded by Lamine to enterpreneurs in search of advice. "You see," adds Lamine, for the benefit of a young citizen intending to set himself up in transport, "your word is your capital; if you honor it, you will receive credit. And beware your freeloading cousins!"

Ageless, wearing a blue embroidered boubou, the eternal Davidoff cigar at his lips, Lamine sprawls on the back seat of his chauffer-driven, telephone-equipped Mercedes. When not giving audiences, Lamine shuttles between his shops, factories, and hotels, all which are the fruit of his savings. He has never borrowed and assures me of his incorruptibility. Of course he allied himself with the Old Man (President Houphouet Boigny), but, he says, name one bourgeoisie that has come into being without a special relationship with the powers that be. Lamine may not have advanced degrees, but on this point his knowledge of history is irrefutable.

Soon, he assures me, he will yield all of his presidential titles to his son, who comes by way of political science in Paris and business school in Washington. From primitive capitalism Abidjan will pass, without transition, into the managerial era. "But," concludes Lamine, "my son doesn't know everything yet; I still have to teach him about the ethics of business."

# The Shariᶜa Is No Obstacle to Business

There is no contradiction between Islam and capitalism, and capitalism is as neutral vis-à-vis Islam as it is toward any culture or religion. Unlike socialism, free enterprise does not pretend to substitute for traditional beliefs, and this, according to Maqbool Qureshi, is its principal virtue in the eyes of a Muslim.

Maqbool Qureshi, it is said in Karachi, is a holy man, which is not to say that he devotes himself to prayer. On the contrary, he works a fourteen-hour day despite frail health and a large family; one as much as the other is sacrificed to his career. For Qureshi, the bank is an ascetic calling that, by all appearances, consumes him; with his emaciated visage, dark, wide-set, almond-shaped eyes, and long white hair carefully brushed back, he resembles Mohammed Ali Jinnah, the founder of Pakistan, whose portrait hangs above his desk. The Banker's Equity, created by Qureshi, is not a regular bank, but an Islamic bank progressively modifying its financial methods to conform to the shariᶜa, or code of the faithful. The shariᶜa is uncompromising with regard to interest loans; it demands that the lender share the risks as well as the returns with the borrower. Qureshi does accordingly.

It is also Islamic solidarity that drives Qureshi to participate in the boards of directors of his clients' enterprises. Thanks to the shariᶜa, he has become one of the most powerful men in Karachi. But Islam, he assures me, is in favor of personal enrichment; according to the Koran, there is no contradiction between the individual who seeks to get rich and the well-being of the community. Islam does not make a fetish of destitution. The Koran also favors private property as "a mandate of God." Thus, according to Qureshi, the Muslim world has a special affinity to capitalism, and nothing is more Islamic than a joint stock company because it is based on the fair distribution of profits and losses. Furthermore, the shariᶜa discourages hoarding and promotes investment by requiring that the faithful each year redistribute to the poor 2.5 percent of their financial gains. This redistribution (*iakat*) maintains economic activity through mass consumption, Keynesianism before its time.

If Muslims, says Qureshi, seem more disposed toward trade than industry, it is not because of Islam, but because of the society in which they live. If Pakistan is capitalist and India socialist, it is not, as commonly believed, because of American influence, but because of Islam. It is the Hindu caste system that locked Muslims into trade; similarly, the economic behavior of the Muslims of the Arab world, or of Africa, is a product of colonization, not of Islam.

Three thousand miles from Karachi, in Cairo, Yahia Hakky, an Egyptian writer of great renown in the Arab world, felt bound, as if an echo of Qureshi, to invite me to "render to Mohammed what is Mohammed's and to repay to colonialism and socialism—the two modern plagues of Egypt—that which is their due." Hakky is a marvelous storyteller of the Cairo literary school, molded from French culture and old Arab texts, married to a Breton, but "100 percent Muslim," he insists. Egypt is poor not because it is Islamic, but because it was exploited by the Europeans; it is inefficient because it was bureaucratized by Nasser's socialism. Fundamentalism, Hakky assured me, is a betrayal of Islam, a religion of moderation and tolerance, and, to all true Muslims, distressing to be identified with fanatics and see the West confuse the dictatorship of a mullah in Iran with the rule of Islam.

Africans and Muslims thus appear ready to rally to capitalism. If the Third World converts to free enterprise, who will this capitalism profit? If the people of the Third World are good for capitalism, is it good for them? Is it not the vehicle of inequalities and injustices? According to Gatsha Buthelezi, capitalism is not only efficient and neutral with regard to faith, but also just. Of all the leaders I met in the Third World, Buthelezi is the most ardent defender of free enterprise. He sees it not only as a way out of poverty, but also as a tool for social justice, which is an even more provocative hypothesis in that we are now discussing South Africa.

## The Just Capitalism

Everything that happens in South Africa is important because South Africa is a microcosm of the relations between the industrialized world and the Third World. These worlds—black and white, mixed race and Indians, rich and poor, tribal era and nuclear age, subsistence agriculture and supermarkets—are intertwined here like nowhere else on our planet. This cohabitation between races, cultures, and the two worlds plays itself out here, and success or failure will broadly predict the outcome elsewhere.

In Buthelezi, two persons coexist. The first is affable, educated at Cambridge, with pride in his British humor. Democratically elected prime minister of the province of Kwazulu, he is the legitimate representative of seven million citizens of the Zulu nation. This Buthelezi is pure Commonwealth, with a passion for suits—provided they are from London—that he collects by the dozen. He is black, but of those with whom South African whites might one day get along.

The other Buthelezi dons a leopard skin robe and brandishes the staff of office, the insignia of royal power. This Buthelezi has nothing British and lives surrounded by servants and bodyguards. He is sharp and aggressive and reminds one that he is an authentic prince of royal blood descended from Chaka, the black Napoleon who united the Zulus at the beginning of the nineteenth century. He was also one of the founders of the African National Congress, the most radical antiapartheid movement, and remains faithful to his imprisoned friend Nelson Mandela.

Two men in one, two cultures, two legitimacies, historical and democratic, Chief Gatsha Buthelezi is the perfect incarnation of both the authenticity and the divisions of the Zulu. But because Buthelezi declares himself conservative and procapitalist, he is less popular among the conformist left in Europe and the United States and less spectacular for the media than the fighters of Soweto or committed clerics. Buthelezi is not a moderate, but in his own way an ideologue set against apartheid. Close to the U.S. economists, in particular Milton Friedman, he puts forward an analysis and solutions that are opposed to all the commonplace wisdom propagated onto South Africa. He believes that to get rid of apartheid, large-scale capitalists in South Africa are the blacks' best allies. Capitalism will free the blacks not out of the goodness of capitalist hearts, but because the development of their enterprises requires that blacks enter the labor force, receive proper training, and become consumers.

In any case, notes Buthelezi, it is the South African capitalists who are demanding the elimination of all geographic, professional, and educational barriers; higher wages for Blacks, along with schools and housing; and even freedom of access to property and ownership of enterprises. Conversely, Buthelezi says, and for material reasons that are equally self-evident, labor unions, small white property owners, and bureaucrats are the traditional supporters of apartheid.

Buthelezi defends himself against the charge that he is a pawn of the South African ruling class by saying that those who make this accusation believe that capitalism can only be white. Yet nothing in Zulu traditions prevents them from becoming capitalists in their own right. If up to now they have not manifested a particularly enterprising spirit, it is not because they are incapable, but that they have not had access to opportunity. It is apartheid, not some cultural incapacity, that explains the virtual absence of blacks from the ranks of business leadership and large agricultural producers. As proof of blacks' ability rapidly to climb the professional ladder, Buthelezi recalls World War II, when labor markets were deregulated and blacks quickly moved from the unskilled employment to which they had been relegated to semiskilled jobs previously held by whites. In any case, if the aptitude of Blacks was naturally inferior to that of Whites, the latter would not have to protect themselves from competition by a complex system of labor reserves. The real solution to apartheid, according to Buthelezi, thus consists in freeing up the initiative of both blacks and whites. In this way economic and political progress would proceed in tandem, not in mutual isolation as they have previously done in Africa. "I would render ill service to my people," says Buthelezi, "if I made them pay, like the rest of the continent, for their independence with poverty."

The great virtue of capitalism, he concludes, is that it does not require whites and blacks to like each other, but only to recognize their mutual need for one another. If the two communities understood their own interests, they could enter into peaceful coexistence, without violence, which is useless, and without love, which is improbable.

## The Arthur Lewis Model

The whole world can be developed, Arthur Lewis says with assurance. Of all the economists I met during this study, Lewis is the only one to enjoy unanimity of opinion on his work. No doubt this is because his entire life has been devoted to scientific research, far removed from political compromises and battles for influence. He is not an ideologue, but an observer; he is not easy to categorize for he does not identify with any system. Of Jamaican origin, Lewis was the first black professor at Princeton University. In 1979, the Nobel Prize for economics became his reward for a life devoted entirely to development.

The entire world can become developed, says Lewis, but relatively; history, culture, climate, traditions, natural resources, and geopolitics play a determinant role that it would be absurd to deny. The point of departure confers on each actor both trump cards and handicaps, but there is almost no room to maneuver around these fundamental factors. That is not the case, however, with policies, whose strategies may aggravate the handicaps or augment the trump cards. Each nation is thus relatively developable if its institutions lend themselves to the process.

Lewis adds that the problems of the Third World are not different than those of the industrialized countries, but they are more intense. In both places, that which we refer to as crises have been born out of a loss of confidence between private initiative and public power. If the entrepreneurs, large or small, are not assured of a stable and predictable institutional framework, they stop taking risks, favor their immediate needs, and create neither jobs nor wealth. The Third World, like the West, thus demands that a contract be signed between civil society and a state that is respectful of the fundamental economic rights: property, currency, reasonable taxation, and an honest government bureaucracy. This presupposes—and Arthur Lewis insists on this point—that there be a true state. In the industrial world, the contract was often broken by excesses on the part of the state; in the Third World, by the excesses of government and the lack of a legitimate state.

This legitimate state is not coterminous only with democracy, but with the concept of an open, plural society of which democracy is but one aspect. Only the open society in which political power is distinct from economic power permits risk and innovation. The closed or monistic society invites only conformity and repetition. According to Arthur Lewis, this idea of a contract between political power and economic power summarizes, in its most basic terms, the whole of his research.

This model presupposes the renouncing of political myths like revolution, but of technological myths such as the computer as shortcut to development and other fantasies of development experts. But if the whole world can be developed and if the path to follow is so clear, why isn't the whole world developed? Because, concludes Lewis, in the history of humanity, poverty and oppression are the norm, prosperity and freedom the exception. The real puzzle is therefore not underdevelopment, but development; the conjunction in Europe—an unforeseeable spark— of technical innovation and social mutation: the steam engine and the rise of the bourgeoisie.

In my search for the causes of mass poverty and its solutions, did I only pursue an illusion?

# SIXTEEN

# The Isle of Passion

WHAT COULD BE FARTHER AWAY THAN ZANZIBAR? OFF THE AFRICAN
coast, it faces Dar es Salaam, and the only way to get to there is to brave
the stormy seas for five hours in an ancient dhow with triangular sails.
Although the skiff smells of Asia and Africa put together, anything is
better than the erratic Air Tanzania flight schedules. But go to Zanzibar I
must, if for nothing else than to meditate on history's lost civilizations.

Governed for a long time by the sultans of Oman, Zanzibar was the
shining star of Swahili culture that dominated East Africa. All that is left
is a crumbling medina of incongruous Arab architecture. Of the century-
long British protectorate, only Africa House and Spice Inn, two jewels of
colonial hostelry, have survived, but both are musty and worm-eaten, unable to cope with the onslaught of the equitorial heat, and completely
wiped off the tourist map. In the golden days, Zanzibar owed its fabulous
wealth to its monopoly of the clove trade as well as to slave trafficking
between Africa and the Persian Gulf. Whiffs of clove still assail your
nostrils as you enter the port. But the island has ceased to enjoy its stranglehold, for the Javanese, who make cigarettes with a blend of tobacco
and cloves, discovered that they could produce cloves far more cheaply at
home. The slave trade vanished when the British officially put an end to
it in 1895. Now all that remains are the prison ruins on which merchants
display their fruit and vegetables. Lest you think Zanzibar a lost haven,
spared from tourist hordes and the upheavals of our mad world, dispel
your illusions. It is an isle of passion par excellence, reflecting all the tur-

moil and destructive madness of our troubled times. Of modest dimensions, with a mere six thousand inhabitants, it is here that I come to my
journey's end, on this island that has come to epitomize the many tempests that have wrecked the Third World and that has today become the
dumping ground for the ideological fantasies of the West and the frenzied
passions of decolonization.

These seemingly peaceful, slow-moving Zanzibaris—with their blue
eyes and strange looks, a cross between the slaves and their old masters—
had just after their independence in 1964, responded to the call of a
Ugandan dock worker and tried to exterminate the entire Arab population in a night of vengeance. Those few Arabs who managed to survive
fled by sea to Oman, the faraway land of their origin. Following close on
the heels of the first revolution came a second one, this time of Maoist
inspiration led by Mohamed Babu, a Cuba-trained intellectual. It did not
take long for him to be ousted by Abeid Karume, a populist politician,
who took advantage of a cyclical rise in clove prices to distribute stoves
and refrigerators to the people. From this period, Zanzibar retains a collective housing complex that would fit right in Eastern Europe; in fact,
the inhabitants call this concrete block—the last thing you would expect
to find under the scorching equatorial sun—East Berlin. In a final con-
vulsive movement, Zanzibar united with Tanzania, going in the direction
of African socialism. Julius Nyerere adopted the same policies here as he
did on the mainland: all intermediaries, Indian and Arab, were eliminated, trade became the monopoly of the state, and agricultural prices
were lowered. From there on clove cultivation never picked up, the
Zanzibaris stopped tending to their trees and, to survive, fell back on subsistence agriculture.

History's ultimate irony is that a few Oman Arab princes returned to
Zanzibar to build palatial villas wherein they ended their days. The local
population welcomed them back, as the sultanate was associated with the
affluence of the bygone era. Although the slave trade has been abolished, there is nothing to stop the inhabitants from handing their daughters in marriage to these prosperous Omanis. To complete the picture,
we must speak of the development expert. He is generally Scandinavian,
represents an international organization such as the Food and Agriculture Organization of the United Nations, and spends his time introduc-
ing the natives to activities completely alien to their ethos, such as irrigated rice cultivation. As soon as the expert leaves, the peasants go back
to their old ways.

With their economy, civilization, and society in shambles, what makes
the Zanzibaris tick? Perhaps the anticipation of the next revolution. In
the sleepy stalls of the medina, I see Ayatollah Khomeini's portrait plas-

tered everywhere. How has it come to pass that the Zanzibaris, after having been the slaves of the Arabs and then having completely exterminated them, identify with this somber icon, given the distance that separates them from Iran? Why does Islam, after slavery, colonization, and socialism, appear to be the ultimate recourse? The Swahili writer Abdul Rahman Batibo tells me in private that no one in Zanzibar believes in economic development any more, the corruption of the politicians being there for all to see. The Zanzibaris no longer trust their own mullahs. Iranian fanaticism is omnipresent because Islam is all they've got left. Islam stands for law, justice, and faith; it provides answers to ordinary day-to-day problems as well as hope in the other world.

My isle of passion is thus a symbol of the Third World, simmering with anger and religious ideologies. For entire populations who do not see any hope of a better life and who are stripped of their traditional culture, what other way can there be but utopia? Religious fundamentalism and revolutionary zeal, then, become substitutes for meaningless technical mumbo jumbo, discredited socialism, liberalism that has been misunderstood or badly implemented, and results so slow that they are barely perceptible.

I leave Zanzibar firmly convinced that the only realistic solutions to poverty are those that look beyond economics and technology, those that capture the imagination of human beings with all their follies, those that take into account the overwhelming need for justice as much as the desire for prosperity.

# Postscript

## Liberal Capitalism and the Third World

After having spent three years traveling in eighteen countries, I found
that people were the victims of bad policies based on fallacious reasoning. There is no country in the Third World whose people are irrevo-
cably doomed to poverty because of their culture, climate, or lack of
resources. By and large, those countries that opted for a path of development open to the outside world, for private initiative and decentralized
capitalism have won the day. Those that went in for autarchy, centralization, and state initiative lost out. The time has come to assess underdevelopment in economic rather than cultural or ideological terms; only
sound economic policies can pull the teeming masses of the Third World
out of the morass of poverty.

## Determinants

Underdevelopment cannot be attributed to natural factors. Taiwan has
no natural resources to speak of, and Singapore has to bear with equatorial heat. Africa's Ivory Coast has had a certain amount of success in
Africa even though she started out with the same or less as her neighbors

Ghana and Guinea, both of whom followed a catastrophic path. The relationship between culture and development is just as uncertain; for more than a century South Korea was looked upon as the archetypal static society. The impact of imperialism is equally difficult to gauge; both India and Pakistan were part of the same empire yet Pakistan's growth rate is twice that of India's. In Asia the four dragons, Korea, Taiwan, Singapore, and Hong Kong, all endured Japanese colonialism but with what seems to have been a beneficial economic influence. After the British withdrew from East Africa, Tanzania began to crumble whereas neighboring Kenya moved ahead. In all these cases the sole determining factor seems to have been the economic model that each country adopted after independence.

Are some people more enterprising than others? Are the economic policies of a given people nothing more than a reflection of the civilization to which they belong? Economically active minorities do exist in every nation, sometimes as immigrants like the Indians in Kenya, the Chinese in Thailand, the Japanese in Brazil, and the Burkinabes in the Ivory Coast, but more often as indigenous minorities, such as in Korea. The enterprising spirit can be seen, however, where it has not been crushed by violence or slowly sapped through taxation or expropriation.

When all is said and done, I believe that neither cultural nor natural factors are determinative. That is not to say that they do not exist; no two countries have the capacity to develop at the same pace, and there is no single solution that can be universally applied. The issue in the Third World is the choice between policies that aggravate a country's weaknesses or those that highlight its strengths.

## Liberal Capitalism Versus State Capitalism

Socialism—centralized decision making, planning, collectivism—has not brought progress to any Third World country for more than a generation. The controversy, then, centers around liberal capitalism versus state capitalism. State capitalism is based on the monopoly of bureaucratic initiative, restrictive trade practices, and centralized investment. This more or less corresponds to the model adopted by India and Brazil, which has created powerful industrial groups, a strong state, and an upper middle class with the same vested interests as the ruling class. Private initiative has been confined to the fringes; even worse, most Indians and Brazilians have been left out of the development process because it is based on capital, not labor. State capitalism has created a cleavage within these countries and given rise to extreme power as well as to extreme poverty.

The alternative is a more decentralized, outward-looking capitalism, of which Taiwan is a good example. By opting for a developmental strategy based on comparative advantage in a competitive world market, the working population has stood to gain and the entire nation has reaped the benefits of progress. Prosperity and social equity go hand in hand. Experience has shown that the liberal model is the most efficient and most just; although it exists nowhere in its pristine form, it makes sense to move toward it rather than away from it. Korea has gradually switched from state capitalism to liberal capitalism, India may well do so, and China is toying with the idea.

## An End to Starvation

Wherever land has been collectivized and the peasant ruined either by low prices or by corrupt intermediaries, famine raises its ugly head, as in Tanzania and the Sahel, or agricultural production does a nosedive, as in Argentina. Wherever the economic rationality of the peasant has been respected (India, Thailand, the Ivory Coast) or re-established (China), agricultural progress is assured.

Twenty years ago, Asia was a starving continent; today famines are a thing of the past thanks to appropriate technology and sound economic decisions. The Green Revolution combined a judicious selection of inputs and peasant mobilization to achieve spectacular results. At one time dependent on the monsoons, Asia now has rice surpluses; India's food reserves are equal to those of the European community's. In China, too, the redistribution of agricultural lands to peasant families along with the right to market their surplus, seems to have wiped famine off the map. If Africa is lagging behind, it is, for the most part, because of faulty policy decisions, namely, the failure to disseminate innovative techniques and low agricultural pricing. As Ethiopia, Sudan, and Mozambique illustrate, where there is war, famine cannot be far off.

## Overpopulation?

Mention the Third World and people's first thought is of teeming millions standing in the way of development; so they say that the birth rate must be brought down, by compulsion if necessary. I reject such ideas as the most fallacious and clichéd. Most Third World families opt for a large number of children because the economic cost is negligible and because children are the mainstay of parents in their old age. Birth control policies of the Indian and Chinese variety are at odds with deep-rooted popular convictions and run counter to the economic rationale of the people. In truth, only development will lead to voluntary birth control, look at Taiwan and Thailand. In any case, we have nothing to fear from the population explosion: in China and India the number of inhabitants per square kilometer is lower than in Holland and their people better fed than they were in 1965 when their populations were less than half of what they are today.

## Aid?

International aid cannot tear a Third World country from the grips of poverty. For example, Tanzania, a country that has received more aid than any other in black Africa, is also the most impoverished since its independence under the leadership of Julius Nyerere, the founder of African socialism. In most instances, public aid serves only to maintain the bureaucracy and support the policies of impoverishment. In contrast, government-to-government aid may be justified for diplomatic or military considerations that have little to do with development.

Humanitarian aid offered by private associations is just as dubious and above suspicion only when rendered in cases of emergency or at the grass roots level. It serves no purpose except to assuage our feelings of guilt. Aid, then, is neither good nor bad in itself, but it will never be able to replace good policies.

## Debts?

Third World debts, in particular Latin America's, are not the cause of impoverishment, but the consequence of bad management. The greatest part of the sums lent by Western banks were not invested in these countries, but immediately consumed or embezzled. For Argentina and Mexico, this misappropriation may have amounted to as much as 70 percent of their debts, which makes repayment difficult! Thus it is their own elites who are causing the poor of the Third World countries to starve, not Western bankers.

Although certain countries, such as Korea and Pakistan, are paying their debts without difficulty, many countries of Latin America cannot repay the loans they have received; these countries should follow the International Monetary Fund (IMF) recommendations: renegotiation of the debts, combined with fairer domestic policies. The so-called austerity measures proposed by the IMF are chiefly for Third World governments that are forced to reduce their civil and military expenditures. For the people, however, is that not a guarantee that in the future they will have a more stable currency and be able to keep the fruits of their labor and their thrift?

# Is Democracy Indispensable?

In India and Brazil the difference between the living conditions of the state bourgeoisie and those of the wretched masses is considerable, and universal suffrage has not brought about a just redistribution of wealth. Authoritarian Chile has developed more rapidly than democratic Argentina; Korea is repressive, but developing; China, too, is repressive, but not developing, all of which make the relationship between democracy and development difficult to ascertain.

Democracy and universal suffrage, then, should not be confused. The choice is between the authoritarian state and the totalitarian state, the state of law and the absence of law. Chinese and North Korean totalitarianism have hindered development because imagination, initiative, and compensation have been stifled. Authoritarian regimes, in contrast, monopolize political power, but often tolerate economic initiative.

For development to take root, private property, contractual obligations, savings, fair pricing, and security of goods and life must be respected. When individuals are threatened by their own governments, they try to shield themselves from exaction, violence, and corruption by falling back on their own meager resources for subsistence and do not make the slightest effort to produce for posterity. That both Korea and Taiwan are now moving toward greater political plurality illustrates how development leads to the creation of middle classes who aspire to a greater degree of participation in the political process. In the long run, democracy, law, and development intermingle, for all three are based on a universal system of moral values.

# Right Thinking Is the Need of the Hour

The Third World is veering between two alternatives. The first one, liberal capitalism, has been steadily gaining ground over the last few years not because leaders have had a sudden change of heart but because they no longer have a choice. Several factors—the failure of collectivist solutions, bankruptcy, lenders' refusals of further credit, pressure of international organizations, and mounting public opinion—have forced governments from Beijing to Buenos Aires, from Dar es Salaam to Cairo, to bow down to the dictates of economic wisdom.

The second alternative, fundamentalism, which is also on the rise, has assumed various forms. The Middle East has witnessed the upsurge of Khomeinism, and Castroism has taken over Latin America. These different forms of fundamentalism, which thrive on the failure of development strategies, are running neck and neck with sound policies that seek to reconcile growth with equity. Such policies can only be implemented by "good" governments. The West must therefore be more selective in choosing its friends and in handing out aid. It is time for those intellectuals who have been flooding the Third World with wrong ideas to reassess and become active in promoting realistic ideas within the Third World.

# Notes

## Chapter 1

1. The students, taking advantage of the Olympic Games being held in Mexico City, demonstrated, as did students everywhere else in the world that year. The name of the plaza derives from its proximity to a colonial cathedral, an Aztec pyramid, and a skyscraper.
2. In 1987 all of the candidates to the presidency of the republic were the sons of governors or ministers and in 1976 President Lopez Portillo made his son minister of the budget; his mistress, the minister of tourism; his sister, director of state television; his cousin, minister of health; and his wife, director of the Fund for Cultural Development.
3. On the Mexican side of the border, the government has authorized, since the beginning of the 1980s, the establishment of *maquiladoras,* factories under contract to multinational corporations in free trade or export zones producing for the export market in North America, Europe, and Japan. Mexican labor thus works in a Western context, with results comparable to the best enterprises in Taiwan. The maquiladoras have become, after oil, the second-largest source of foreign exchange for Mexico. Their success proves that it is not the temperament of the Mexican worker that is the cause of the poor economic condition of the country.
4. In Latin America, Argentina, Bolivia, Brazil, Chile, Cuba, Mexico. In Asia, China, Korea, Hong Kong, India, Pakistan, Singapore, Taiwan. In Africa, South Africa, Ivory Coast, Egypt, Senegal, Tanzania.

## Chapter 3

1. Indians and those of mixed blood have been pushed to the northern and southern extremities of this gigantic country, where they live on the fringes of society.
2. Peron ruled from 1943 to 1955 and from 1973 till his death in 1974. His second wife, Isabel, succeeded him until a March 1976 military coup.

3. Brazil is an exception; it is the only country in Latin America that has actually invested most of its borrowed capital. The country was unable to pay its debts because the government decided to give an impetus to domestic consumption on the eve of the 1986 elections.
4. "Finance and Development," March 1987, *IMF Review.*
5. Carlos Gardel, born in Toulouse, author of the greatest tango classics.

## Chapter 4

1. They are in fact Levantines who immigrated at the turn of the century with Turkish passports.
2. The origin of the word is unknown. It most probably refers to the palm leaves used by the Cariocas as a roof for their dwellings.
3. The definition of Brazilians as cordial gentlemen was first formulated in 1946 by the historian Sergio Buarque de Holanda.
4. In 1986 in Argentina, Raul Alfonsin decided to build a new capital in Patagonia.
5. In the case of Argentina, farmers' organizations such as the Aacrea (Association Argentina de consorcios regionales de experimentacion agricola), entrepreneurs' associations like Idea (Instituto para el Desarrollo de Empressarios en la Argentina), or student organizations such as the Union of Centrist students deserve to be mentioned. In Brazil, the Liberal Institute of Rio de Janeiro; in Chile, the liberal student organizations. The antiauthoritarian thinking of these new circles is reflected in major newspapers such as the *Journal da Tarde* and *Visão* in São Paulo; the *Nacion* in Buenos Aires; *El Norte* in Monterrey, Mexico; *El Mercurio* in Santiago, Chile; and the *ul Ultima Hora* in La Paz.
6. In 1986–1987 the Cruzado plan tried to bring down inflation and give an impetus to domestic consumption. However, the methods used—price control, for example—were illusory; such a policy was cast to the winds once the elections were over. The 1987 price rise is to the tune of about 100 percent per annum.

## Chapter 5

1. Rajiv Gandhi is Indira Gandhi's son and Nehru's grandson but, despite the homonym, is no relation to Mahatma Gandhi.
2. These anti-American sentiments don't preclude the elites from sending their offspring to the United States to complete their educations.
3. Lyndon Johnson tried to tie wheat deliveries during the famine in Bihar in 1965 to Indian support for his Vietnam policy.

4. This phrase was coined by Jean-Alphonse Bernard in *L'Inde: le pouvoir et la puissance* (India: Power and Strength), Fayard, 1985.

5. Forty percent of the rural and fifty percent of the urban population live below the poverty line defined in 1971 by a Ford Foundation study, *Poverty in India,* by V. M. Dandekar and N. Roth. The method consisted of determining the per capita income necessary to ensure the minimum for subsistence in both countryside and town based on food, clothing, and fuel norms.

6. This building is the work of the great English architect Edwin Luytens, who planned New Delhi beginning in 1912.

7. "Each village in India constitutes a small, complete society in which is found everything necessary to life, government, and even well-being for civilized men; the administrator, the tax collector, the school master, the priest, the husbandman." Alexis de Tocqueville, *Ecrits Politiques* (Political Works), 1843.

8. In Bengal and Karnataka, Chief ministers Basu and Hegde, the two most respected politicians in India, the former a communist, the latter a conservative, recently reinforced the panchayats in their respective states by effecting genuine financial decentralization.

9. Pilkana is the City of Joy described by novelist Dominique Lapierre. Since his inquiry, however, the shacks have been rebuilt of brick, and water, electricity, and drainage have considerably improved the daily lives of rural-urban migrants in Calcutta. Calcutta is no longer the hell on earth imagined by Westerners, and corpses are no longer plucked from the sidewalks.

10. One rupee was worth U.S. $0.08 in 1987.

## Chapter 6

1. Film by Sydney Pollack about the life and work of Isak Dinesen.

2. A pyramid in pink cement in Atujiji in Tanzania commemorates the place where the journalist John Routands Stanley met David Livingstone. This quest excited civilized Europe in 1871.

3. The cashew nut, a traditional export of Tanzania, offers a good illustration of the pricing system under the Nyerere regime. From 1,300 shillings per ton in 1970 on the international market, the price rose to 6,000 shillings in 1981, a 350 percent increase for the seller. During the same period, the price paid by the state monopoly to the peasants of the Tanzanian brushland went from 910 to 1,714 shillings, an increase of only 91 percent. The producer thus received in 1981 only one-third of the world price as against two-thirds ten years earlier. The state's share has increased by 1000 percent. It stands to reason, then, that the Tanzanian peasant will stop growing cashew nuts, that the Western buyers will look to other suppliers, and that the Tanzanian government will denounce "the deterioration in the terms of trade in the international market."

4. For example, Dodoma in Tanzania and Abuja in Nigeria.

## Chapter 7

1. Civilian aid is in the high price that the Soviets pay for sugar and oil in rubles that the Cubans resell on the international market on a dollar basis.
2. Sugar accounts for 75 to 80 percent of Cuba's exports.

## Chapter 8

1. Claude Martin, "Les hutongs de Pékin," no. 1 (1985) *Revue française de Chine*.
2. To overcome the extreme division of land and the rural exodus, the Sichuan government is experimenting with extreme caution, lest land become a negotiable commodity—with letting the farmer hire out his land and even workers.

## Chapter 9

1. It is claimed that since 1985 one-fourth of the trade sector is being privately run.
2. Maxim's in Beijing had a hundred-odd unqualified staff thrust on it, much to the surprise of its owner, Pierre Cardin.
3. In 1986, the average wage was between 80 and 140 yuan. The standard of living is not as bad as these figures would have us believe, as several services are almost free, for example, accommodation. The latter is linked to the job one does and further strengthens the bond between the wage earner and his place of work. Moreover, it is the noneconomic advantages, not the wages, that distinguish the elite, as is the case in all socialist countries.

## Chapter 10

1. Paz won a majority in parliament even though his two contenders were said to have a better chance. Apparently, $100,000 was the going rate for a member of Parliament (undoubtedly an Andean legend).

## Chapter 11

1. The Indian constitution expressly allows Sikhs to carry their daggers, even on Indian Airlines flights.
2. The irrigation network in Punjab was established by the British in the colo-

nial era: irrigated surface went from thirteen to twenty million hectares between 1900 and 1930, thereby invalidating the idea that the colonizers hampered India's development.

3. The "Song of Hope" (*Asa Di War*) is a religious song of the Sikhs. It is also the title of a wonderful book on the Green Revolution by Murray Leaf.

4. Undernourishment still exists in India because a vast majority of the population—urban in particular—is too poor to buy the food available on the market.

5. Chinese authorities recognized in July 1987 that despite all restrictions, 40 percent of rural women had at least three children.

6. The birth rate in Kerala is 25 percent as against 40 percent in Uttar Pradesh. Fifteen percent of the women are literate in Uttar Pradesh as against 65 percent in Kerala.

## Chapter 12

1. In 1987, Chung gave up his post of chairman of Hyundai in favor of his younger brother.

## Chapter 13

1. In Bihar, India, landlords purchased land in the names of their pets to get around land reform.

2. The Korean language belongs to the Finn-Ugrian family of languages.

## Chapter 14

1. One-quarter of all Koreans are named Kim; together with Park, Lee, and Choi, these four names represent half the population, testimony to the extraordinary homogeneity of this nation.

2. Notwithstanding Kim's solid arguments, Korean planning has numerous admirers outside of Korea, especially in the United States because many economists favorable to planning have projected onto the Korean experience the hopes dashed by other nations. If these economists can prove that planning played an important role in Korea's destiny, planning remains a viable enterprise. Korean planning thus plays the same part in the development literature as does the Ministry of Industry and Trade (MITI) in Japan. The same school of thought that explains Japanese development via the prescience of MITI bureaucrats explains that of Korea via the plan. One egregious error of Korean planning was the proposal in the early 1970s to construct a petro-

chemical industry, even though Korea imported its entire oil supply. The increase in oil prices was of course unforeseeable, even by the world's best planners!

## Chapter 15

1. Confucianism exercised a considerable influence on eighteenth century Europe, particularly among French philosophers. Voltaire kept a portrait of Confucius in his study, and enlightened despotism is not unrelated to Confucius's concept of good government.
2. This story has been brought to the screen by Japanese-Brazilian director Tizuja Yamazaki in the remarkable *Gaijin*.
3. Iba Der Thiam abetted this profound transformation of Senegalese society by creating the *Groupement de Recherche et d'Etude sur le Senegal Nouveau* (GRESEN, Study and Research Group on the New Senegal). GRESEN has more than a thousand member-intellectuals, all holders of key state positions and all graduates of higher education. Through its publication and by the solidarity between its members, GRESEN popularizes the new ideas: the spirit of enterprise, individual initiative, and government disengagement.

# Bibliography

The following works have been used as references in the course of my inquiry.

## Chapter 1

Bauer, Peter. *Reality and Rhetoric.* London: Weidenfeld & Nicholson, 1984.

Paz, Octavio. *Une planete et quatre ou cinq mondes.* Paris: Folio, 1985.

Paz, Octavio. *Le labyrinthe de la solitude.* Paris: Gallimard, 1972.

Pazos, Luis. *Futuro Economico de Mexico.* Mexico City: Diana, 1977.

Reynolds, Lloyd. *Economic Growth in the Third World, 1850–1980.* New Haven, Conn.: Yale University Press, 1985.

Riding, Alan. *Distant Neighbors.* New York: A. Knopf, 1985.

Smith, Adam. *An Inquiry into the Nature and Causes of the Wealth of Nations.* New York: Edwin Cannan, 1937 (reedition).

## Chapter 2

Cardoso, Fernado. *Dependence Development in Latin America.* Berkeley: University of California Press, 1979.

Hirschman, Albert. *A Bias for Hope: Essays on Development in Latin America.* New Haven, Conn.: Yale University Press, 1971.

Jagdish, N. Bhagwati. *Wealth and Poverty.* Oxford, Eng.: Blackwell, 1985.

Lal, Deepak. *The Poverty of Development Economics.* London: Institute of Economic Affairs, 1983.

Little, Ian. *Economic Development.* New York: Basic Books, 1985.

Myrdal, Gunnar. *The Political Element in the Development of Economic Theory.* New York: Simon and Schuster, 1954.

*Pioneers in Development.* London: Oxford University Press, 1984.

Prebich, Raul. *El Desarollo economico de America Latina y algunos de sus principales problemas.* Santiago de Chile: Economic Commission for Latin America, 1950.

Staniland, Martin. *What Is Political Economy? A Study of Social Study and Under-development.* New Haven, Conn.: Yale University Press, 1986.

## Chapter 3

De La Blacha, Guibal. *Historia de la Agricultura Argentina.* Buenos Aires: Editorial Belgrano, n.d.

Borges, Jorge Luis. *Essai d'autobiographie.* Paris: Gallimard, n.d.

Bourguinat, Henri, and Mistral, Jacques. *La Crise de Pendettement international.* Paris: Economica, 1986.

Coscia, Adolfo. *Segunda revolucion agricola de la region Pampeana.* Buenos Aires: Orientacion Grafica, 1983.

Ferrari, Osvaldo. *Borges en Dialogo.* Buenos Aires: Grijalbo, 1985.

Luder, Italo. *Ideas y propuestas.* Buenos Aires: Corregidor, 1986.

Lynch, Alberto Benegas. *Liberalismo para liberales.* Buenos Aires: Emece, 1986.

O'Donnel, Guillermo. *El Estado burocratico autoritario.* Buenos Aires: Editorial Belgrano, 1982.

Quesada, Maria Saenz. *Los Estancieros.* Buenos Aires: Editorial Belgrano, 1985.

Schwab, Martin. *El Estado Eficaz.* Buenos Aires: Editorial Fraterna, 1985.

## Chapter 4

Botana, Natalio. *La Tradicion republicana.* Buenos Aires: Sudamericana, 1985.

Evans, Peter. *Dependent Development: The Alliance of Multinational State and Local Development.* Princeton, N.J.: Princeton University Press, 1979.

Freyre, Gilberrto. *Maitres et Esclaves.* Paris: Tel, 1974.

Furtado, Celso. *Le Bresil apres le miracle.* Paris: Maison des Sciences de l'Homme, 1987.

Jaguaribe, Helio. *Brasi 2000.* Rio de Janeiro: Paz e Terra, 1986.

de Macedo, Gilberto. *Casagrande y senzala; obra didactica.* Rio de Janeiro: Catedra, 1979.

Maksoud, Henry. *O poderes de governo.* São Paulo: Visao, 1984.

Paim, Antonio. *Pensamento filosofico brasiliero.* São Paulo: Carvivio, 1985.

Ravello de Bastro, Paulo. *Baroes y boias frias.* Rio de Janeiro: Cedes, 1982.

# Chapter 5

Akbar, M. J. *India: The Siege Within*. London: Penguin Books, 1985.

Bernard, J. A. *L'Inde: le pouvoir et la puissance*. Paris: Fayard, 1985.

Brata, Shasti. *India*. New York: Norton, 1985.

Chambard, Jean-Luc. *Atlas d'un village indien*. Paris: Ecole des Hautes Etudes en Sciences Sociales, 1985.

Chaudhuri, Nirad. *The Continent of Circe*. Bombay: Chatto & Windus, 1965.

Dumont, Louis. *Homo Hierarchicus*. Paris: Gallimard, 1967.

Gupte, Pranay. *Vengeance: India after the Assassination of Indira Gandhi*. New York: Norton, 1985.

Lapierre, Dominique. *City of Joy*. New York: Warner Books, 1986.

Myrdal, Gunnar. *Le Drame de l'Asie*. Paris: Le Seuil, 1974.

Nandy, Ashis. *The Intimate Enemy*. London: Oxford University Press, 1983.

# Chapter 6

Amin, Samir. *Le Development du capitalisme en Cote-d'Ivoire*. Paris: Editions de Minuit, 1967.

Berg, Robert. *Strategies for African Development*. Berkeley: University of California, 1986.

Brunel, Sylvie. *Greniers vides, greniers pleins*. Paris: Economica, 1986.

Diakite, Tidiane. *L'Afrique malade d'elle-meme*. Paris: Karthala, 1986.

Dumont, Rene. *Pour L'Afrique? J'accuse*. Paris: Plon, 1986.

Faure, Y. A., and Medard, J. F. *Etat et Bourgeoisie en Cote-d'Ivoire*. Paris: Kathala, 1982.

Lamb, David. *The Africans*. New York: Random House, 1985.

Lele, Uma. *The Design of Rural Development: Lessons for Africa*. Baltimore, Md.: Johns Hopkins University Press, 1975.

Michailof, Serge. *Les Apprentis Sorciers du developement*. Paris: Economica, 1986.

Naipaul, Shave. *North of South*. London: Penguin Books, 1978.

Rydenfelt, Sven. *A Pattern of Failure*. New York: Harcourt, Brace, Jovanovich, 1984.

Toure, Abdou. *Les Petits Metiers d'Abidjan*. Karthala, 1986.

Toure, Abdou. *La Civilisation quotidienne en Cote-d'Ivoire*. Paris: Karthala, 1981.

## Chapter 7

Cambassedes, Oliver, ed. *Atlaseco de Poche*. Paris: Editions S.G.B., 1986.

Castro, Fidel. *Entretien sur la religion avec Frei Betto*. Paris: Cerf, 1986.

Eberstadt, Nick. *Fertility Decline in the Less Developed Countries*. New York: Praeger-C.B.S., 1981.

Gereffi, Gary. *The Pharmaceutical Industry in the Third World*. Princeton, N.J.: Princeton University Press, 1983.

## Chapter 8

Aubert, C.; Chevrier, Y.; and Domenach, J. L. *La Societe Chinoise apres Mao*. Paris: Fayard, 1986.

*Pekin*. Paris: Editions Autrement, 1985.

Fairbank, J. K. *The Great Chinese Revolution*. New York: Harper & Row, 1985.

Heng, Liang. *After the Nightmare*. New York: A. Knopf, 1986.

Pr Ma Hong, *New Strategy for China's Economy*. Beijing: New World Press, 1983.

Martin, Claude. "Les Hutongs de Pékin." *Revue francaise de Pékin,* no. 1 (1985).

## Chapter 9

*Almanach of Chinese Economy*. Hong Kong: Modern Cultural Co., Ltd., 1981.

Domenach, Jean-Luc. *Le Mariage en Chine*. Paris: Fondation nationale des Sciences Politiques, 1987.

Rhee, Sang Who. *China's Reform Politics*. Seoul: Sogang University Press, 1986.

## Chapter 10

Abdalla, Ismail Sabri. *Images of the Arab Future*. Cairo: United Nations University, 1983.

Brisset, Claire. *La Santé dans le Tiers Monde*. Paris: La Découverte, 1984.

Naqvi, Syed N. H. *Economy Through the Seventies*. Islamabad: Pakistan Institute for Pakistan's Development, 1985.

Weise, Agustin Saavedra. *Bolivia en el contexto international*. La Paz: Editorial Los Amigos, 1985.

# Chapter 11

Dalrymple, Dana. *High Yielding Varieties of Wheat and Rice*. Washington, D.C.: U.S. Aid, 1978.

Escher, Carl. *Agricultural Development in the Third World*. Baltimore, Md.: Johns Hopkins University Press, 1985.

Etienne, Gilbert. *Dévelopment rural en Asie*. Paris: P.U.F., 1982.

Gourou, Pierre. *Riz et civilisation*. Paris: Fayard, 1984.

Gupte, Pranay. *The Crowded Earth*. New York: Norton, 1984.

Kuo, Shirley. *The Taiwan Economy in Transition*. Boulder, Colo.: Westview Press, 1983.

Leaf, Murray. *Song of Hope*. New York: Rutgers, 1984.

Mellor, John, and Desal, Gurvant. *Agricultural Change and Rural Poverty*. Baltimore, Md.: Johns Hopkins University Press, 1985.

Ruttan, Vernon. *Agricultural Research Policy*. Saint Paul: University of Minnesota Press, 1984.

Simon, Julius. *The Ultimate Resource*. Princeton, N.J.: Princeton University Press, 1981.

Singh, Khushwant. *A History of the Sikhs*. London: Oxford University Press, 1963.


# Chapter 12

Bauer, Peter. *Dissent on Development*. Cambridge, Mass.: Harvard University Press, 1972.

Esman, Milton. *Local Organization, Intermediaries in Rural Development*. Cornell University Press, 1984.

Max, Sol. *Penny Capitalism*. Chicago, Ill.: University of Chicago Press, 1963.

Nair, Kusum. *In Defense of the Irrational Peasant*. Chicago, Ill.: University of Chicago Press, 1979.

Rangel, Carlos. *Le Tiers Monde et l'Occident*. Paris: Robert Laffont, 1985.

Schultz, Theodore. *Il n'est de richesse que d'hommes*. Paris: Bonnel, 1983.

Schultz, Theodore. *Transforming Traditional Agriculture*. New Haven, Conn.: Yale University Press, 1983.

Scott, James. *Weapons of the Weak*. New Haven, Conn.: Yale University Press, 1985.

Sothworth, Herman. *Agricultural Development and Economic Growth*. Ithaca, N.Y.: Cornell University Press, 1967.

World Bank. "Report on Development." Washington, D.C.: World Bank, 1986.

## Chapter 13

Chen, Philip. *Prospect for the Pacific Century*. Taipei: Asia and the World Institute, 1986.

Dumont, René. *Taiwan, le prix de la réussite*. Paris: La Découverte, 1986.

Joe, L. Wanne. *Traditional Korea, A Cultural History*. Seoul: Chung'Ang University Press, 1972.

Kuo, Shirley. *The Taiwan Success Story*. Boulder, Colo.: Westview, 1981.

Li, Kwoh Ting. *Experiences and Lessons of Economic Development in Taiwan*. Taipei: Academia Sinica, 1982.


## Chapter 14

Adelman, Irma, and Morris, Cynthia Taft. *Society, Politics and Economic Development: A Quantitative Approach*. Baltimore, Md.: Johns Hopkins University, 1967.

Balassa, Bela. *Chance and Challenge in the World Economy*. New York: St. Martin's Press, 1985.

Balassa, Bela. *Les Nouveaux Pays industrialises dans l'économie mondiale*. Paris: Economica, 1986.

Berger, Peter L. *The Capitalist Revolution*. New York: Basic Books, 1986.

Jones, Leroy. *Public Enterprise and Economic Development: The Korean Case*. Seoul: K.D.I., 1975.

Jones, Leroy, and Sakung, Il. *Government, Business and Entrepreneurship: The Korean Case*. Cambridge, Mass.: Harvard University Press, 1980.

Kerr, Clark. *The Future of Industrial Society*. Cambridge, Mass.: Harvard University Press, 1983.

Kuznets, Simon. *Modern Economic Growth*. New Haven, Conn.: Yale University Press, 1966.

Park. *Social Security in Korea*. Seoul: K.D.I., 1975.

*The Singapore Economy: New Directions*. Singapore: Ministry of Trade and Industry, 1985.

Woronoff, Ian. *Korea's Economy: Man-Made Miracle*. Seoul: Si Sa Yong O-Sa, 1983.


## Chapter 15

Abdul-Rauf, Muhammad. *A Muslim's Reflection on Democratic Capitalism*. Washington, D.C.: American Enterprise Institute, 1984.

Kolm, Serge Christophe. *L'Homme pluridimensionnel*. Paris: Albin Michel, 1986.

Lamb, David. *The Arabs.* New York: Random House, 1987.

Lewis, Arthur. *The Evolution of International Economic Order.* Princeton, N.J.: Princeton University, 1978.

Louw, Leon, and Kendali, Frances. *South Africa, The Solution.* Ciskei: Amgi, 1986.

Moodley, Adam S. *South Africa without Apartheid.* Berkeley: University of California Press, 1986.

Morishima, Michio. *Capitalisme et confucianisme.* Paris: Flammarion, 1987.

Mottahedesh, Roy. *The Mantle of the Prophet.* London: Chatto and Windus, 1985.

Naipaul, V. S. *Crépuscule sur l'Islam.* Paris: Albin Michel, 1981.

Naqvi, S. H. *Principle of Islamic Economic Reform.* Islamabad: P.I.D.F., 1984.

Rosenberg, Nathan. *How the West Grew Rich.* New York: Basic Books, 1986.

Servan-Schreiber, Jean-Jacques. *Le Défi mondial.* Paris: Fayard, 1980.

Sowell, Thomas. *The Economics of Race.* New York: Basic Books, 1984.

# Index

# About the Author

*Guy Sorman* has been a Professor of Economics at L'Institut d'Etudes Politiques de Paris for seventeen years; a journalist whose columns often appear in *Le Figaro*, the *European Wall Street Journal*, and other popular international newspapers and magazines; the director of his own publishing company, Les Editions Sorman; and the author of *The American Conservative Revolution* (1984), *La Solution libérale* (1984), *L'Etat minimum* (1985), and *Freedom on Bail: The Real Thinkers of Our Time* (1990). Professor Sorman is also the founder and current president of Action Internationale contre la Faim, a humanitarian association active in Third World countries.